BEST BABY NAMES FOR GIRLS

THE **nameberry** GUIDE

BEST BABY NAMES FOR GIRLS

Linda Rosenkrantz & Pamela Redmond Satran

INTRODUCTION

Why, you may be wondering, buy a baby name book in this era of more and better and free name information online?

Indeed, every name in this book, along with our trademark information about it, is available on **Nameberry**, the website that incorporates everything we've written about names in our ten bestselling books.

But what you get with this book, what you can't find on our site or anywhere else, is our personal curation of the best choices for girls from the massive universe of names. There are nearly 20,000 girls' names on Nameberry. In this book we've winnowed that number down to the 650 most appealing, most usable, all-around best girls' names.

By selecting the best names for you, we make it easier for you to pick the best name for your baby. This is the book that you'll curl up in bed with at night, which you'll discuss over dinner with your partner, which is most likely to be the source of the name you'll ultimately choose for your daughter.

These 650 best names are drawn from a wide range of styles and choices, from simple and strong, to more dainty and frilly

- **Classic Girls' Names**—Here you will find the most enduring girls' classics, ranging from the timeless Elizabeth, Katherine and Jane and the biblical Sarah, Abigail and Hannah, to ancient names like Alexandra and Penelope, and floral perennials Rose, Lily and Daisy, all with detailed information on their history and current standing and appeal.
- **Stylish Name for Girls**—Which popular and trending names will transcend the moment and prove to be lasting choices? We include picks from the top of the pops, such as Isabella and Sophia, and also highlight cool choices that fit in with current styles but stand further from the spotlight: Coraline and Luna, for example.
- **Adventurous Names**—What are the most usable unusual names? You'll find hundreds of unique choices here for your baby girl, from revived classics like

Theodora and Ottoline, to names with foreign flair, such as Lilou and Cosima, to nontraditional first names including Ever and Madrigal, Vienna and Plum.

All the names here link back to Nameberry, making it easier for you to discover more about your favorites: You can track down which lists include the names you like best (or create your own lists around them), read blog posts about them, see what people say about them on the forums and what related names they like, and maybe use them as jumping off points to find other choices you like even better, beyond the 650 here.

We believe this book will be the centerpiece for your conversations and the process of choosing a name for your baby girl. It's the perfect place to start, the central point from which to explore, and the place you'll likely end your journey, with your choice of the very best of the best.

A

Abigail

Hebrew, "my father is joyful"

Abigail, an Old Testament name—she was the wife of David, renowned for her beauty, wisdom, and prophetic powers—that became a term for a maid in the early nineteenth century, leading to a fall from favor. Now, Abigail's back in a big way—it is Number 7 on the 2012 list—liked for its slightly proper vintage charm.

Abigail has been the name of two of our First Ladies—three, if you count the character on *The West Wing*—and Abby has been the name of a host of television and movie characters—she has been seen on screen in everything from *Mad Men* to *The Lovely Bones*.

Abigail's biblical roots and her sensible image combined with cute, accessible nickname Abby make her popularity understandable. But whatever style currency Abigail had over the past decade is beginning to flag. There may be a lot of reasons you still might want to choose Abigail for your baby girl, but fashion shouldn't be one of them.

If you like Abigail but want something fresher, you may consider such other biblical choices as Lydia and Priscilla or names popular in Revolutionary Era America that have been neglected in recent years, such as Susannah and Eliza.

Abilene

English from Hebrew, "grass"; American place name

Abilene is a rarely used place name, mentioned as such in the New Testament, that combines the cowboy spunk of the Texas city with the midwestern morality of the Kansas town where Dwight D. Eisenhower spent his boyhood. Abilene is a much more untrodden path to the nickname Abbie/Abby than the Top 10 Abigail.

In 1857, Eliza Hersey named the frontier village of Abilene, Kansas after a vast plain described in Luke's gospel.

"Abilene" is the title of a Sheryl Crow song, and the book *The Miraculous Journey of Edward Tulane* by Kate DiCamillo features a sweet character named Abilene.

Abra

Hebrew feminine variation of Abraham, "father of multitudes"

Abra is a soft, sensitive feminine form of Abraham that was the name of a soft, sensitive character in the John Steinbeck book and movie, *East of Eden*. In the Bible, Abra was a favorite of King Solomon, and it was a popular name in seventeenth century England. Abra is also a West African name used for girls born on Tuesday. The magical "abracadabra" is thought to have originated in the Aramaic language.

Acacia

Greek, "thorny"

Acacia is an attractive, rarely used Greek nature name, enhanced by its popular beginning-and-ending-with-'a'-construct, and is gradually beginning to catch on with baby namers.

The acacia is a shrub of the mimosa family, with clusters of showy white or yellow blossoms, which symbolizes resurrection and immortality—making the name especially appropriate for an Easter-season baby.

Named by an early Greek botanist, the acacia is known for its fine wood and medicinal properties. It also has biblical ties, since the Ark of the Covenant was made out of Acacia wood.

As a given name, Acacia has had some popularity in Australia, where the acacia (sometimes known there as the wattle) is a common plant and sometime national symbol.

Ada

German, "noble, nobility"

Ada was a favorite at the end of the nineteenth century that has started to come back in the past few years. Some may seek it out as an alternative to the over popular Ava, and it's also part of the trend toward simple, old-fashioned names beginning with a vowel, like Ivy and Ella.

A worthy namesake is Ada Lovelace, mathematician daughter of the poet Lord Byron, who worked with Charles Babbage on the forerunners to the calculator and the computer. In his poem "Childe Harold's Pilgrimage," Byron addresses her as "Ada! sole daughter of my house and heart."

Ada has a number of fictional references as well, appearing in Dickens's *Bleak House* and Nabokov's 1969 novel *Ada*, in addition to which characters with the name were portrayed by Holly Hunter in *The Piano* and Nicole Kidman in *Cold Mountain*.

Adah, pronounced AH-da, is a biblical name, one of the first female names mentioned in the Book of Genesis.

Ada returned to the Top 1000 in 2004 after being off since the 1980s; by contrast, Ada was a Top 100 name in the 1880s.

Adair

English and Scottish, "shallow place in a river near oaks"
This undiscovered unisex name has lots of flair. It was first noticed as a girl's name, starting in the 1980s, on the long-running daytime drama *Search for Tomorrow*, with the character Adair McCleary, who had ahead-of-their-time-named brothers Hogan, Cagney and Quinn. But since Adair has yet to find many takers, it would make a fresh and appealing choice.

Adela

German, "noble"
This variation of Adele sounds somewhat more feminine than the original by virtue of the a- ending. It could join the army of popular 'A' girls' names, especially with its tie to the recent celebrity-related success of Adele.

Adela, which came to England with the Normans in the eleventh century, has a royal pedigree via William the Conqueror's youngest daughter.

Adela Quested is a character in E. M. Foster's novel *A Passage to India*, and the name also appears in an Agatha Christie story. Journalist/novelist/screenwriter Adela Rogers St. Johns was a colorful character in Golden Age Hollywood.

Adelia is another appealing variation, an alternative to the rising Amelia.

Adelaide

German, variant of Adelheid, "noble, nobility"
Adelaide is now heading straight uphill on the coattails of such newly-popular sisters as Ava, Ada, and Audrey, and in the company of Adeline and Amelia. It was chosen by actress Katherine Heigl for the name of her second daughter.

Adelaide will have to share the nickname Addy with all the Addisons, Adelines and Adeles out there.

Adelaide gained fame as the noble German princess who married the British King William IV in 1830 and became known as 'Good Queen Adelaide,' inspiring the name of the Australian city and a craze for her name. Earlier, St. Adelaide was married to Otto the Great and became Empress of the Holy Roman Empire, described as "a marvel of beauty and goodness."

When Aussie actress Rachel Griffiths (also mother of son Banjo) chose Adelaide for her daughter, she said she'd been inspired by the city, Miss Adelaide in *Guys and Dolls,* and the Disney character in *The Aristocats.* Adelaide can also be found in works by Thomas Hardy and Agatha Christie.

Adele

French form of Adela, "noble, nobility"
Credit the award-winning, single-named British singer for taking Adele from a quiet semi-retirement to a red-hot success. This year she made it back to the Top 1000 but is surely slated to move much higher.

Adele is both a saint's and a royal name, having originated as the French version of the German Adela.

Molly Ringwald chose Adele for one of her twins, and Fred Astaire's first dancing partner was his older sister Adele.

Historically, Adele was the name of the youngest daughter of William the Conqueror. Music lovers might associate the name with a character in Johann Strauss's operetta *Die Fledermaus*, while a prime literary reference is Jane Eyre's young charge.

Adele's more elaborate sisters, Adeline and Adelaide, are also gaining in popularity.

Adeline

French diminutive of Adele, "noble, nobility"
Adeline has a lovely, old-fashioned "Sweet Adeline" charm and is a less-used cousin of the trendy Madeline.

Adeline was introduced to England by the Normans in the eleventh century, was very common during the Middle Ages, then vanished until the Victorian Gothic revival.

The song "Sweet Adeline" is an old barbershop quartet favorite. JFK's grandfather John F. Fitzgerald, mayor of Boston, made it his theme song, and Mickey Mouse serenaded Minnie with it in a 1929 cartoon.

Pronounced ad-a-line in America, it's usually ad-a-LEEN in France.

Adriana

Latin feminine variation of Adrian, "from the Adriatic"

This a-ending feminine form of Adrian, from the northern Italian city of Adria, is a soft and lovely Italian choice. It appears as a character in Shakespeare's *The Comedy of Errors*.

The name had quite a different image in *The Sopranos*, where it was pronounced with a hard initial 'A'.

Adriana Lima is a Brazilian model and actress, best known as Victoria's Secret Angel.

Africa

Place name, various meanings

Most Africas today would be named for the continent, but the name actually existed in Scotland in medieval times, where there was a Celtic queen named Affrica. Africa has also been a Spanish name for girls since 1421. The church of the Virgin "Nuestra Senora de Africa" is in Ceuta, the Spanish city she is Patron of, in North Africa.

There have been several other theories as to the origin of the name. Some believe it refers to the name of the ancient Berber people who inhabited North Africa, others believe Africa means "greyish" in reference to the color of sand, and yet another theory is that it is a Phoenician word meaning "colony," as Africa was once a colony of the Roman Empire. To complicate matters further, spelled Affrica, it is also used in Spanish-speaking countries, meaning "pleasant."

Africa has been a recorded name in the U.S. since the eighteenth century.

Agatha

Greek, "good woman"

Agatha until recently summoned up visions of martyred saints, mauve silk dresses, and high lace collars, but now that some dauntless excavators have begun to resurrect it, we're sure more will follow their lead. Actor Thomas Gibson used it for his daughter in 2004.

Popular in the Middle Ages, Agatha was brought to England at the time of the Norman Conquest by a daughter of William the Conqueror. Agatha is the name of the patron saint of firefighters and nurses and, in more modern times, has been closely tied to the period mysteries of Agatha Christie. P.G. Wodehouse created the vivid character of Bertie Wooster's daunting Aunt Agatha.

Also boasts the cute nickname Aggie.

Agnes

Greek, "pure, virginal"

Agnes, though it was the third most common English girls' name for four hundred years, has long been stuck in the attic. But now it looks like Agnes was so far out it's just about ready to come back in. It did look cute on the little girl in *Despicable Me*, and nickname Aggie has lots of retro appeal.

And Agnes has been making inroads in the celebrisphere—first actress Elisabeth Shue chose Agnes for her third child, and more recently Jennifer Connelly and Paul Bettany named their daughter Agnes Lark.

In medieval times, St. Agnes was a very popular saint, leading to its popularity as a girl's name. *Agnes Grey* is the title of one of the two novels written by Anne, the third Bronte sister. French pronunciation—ahn-YEZ—makes it more attractive, but few Americans would comply. Other interesting variations: the Welsh Nesta, the Latin/Scandinavian Agneta, the Spanish Inez/Ines/Ynez, and the Scottish Segna—which happens to be Agnes spelled backwards.

Aida

Arabic, "returning visitor"; Italian, "happy"

Aida is a melodic name largely associated with the title character of the 1871 Verdi opera, an enslaved Ethiopian princess who dies to save her people. In the past, her name was rarely heard outside the Latino community, but in the current time of love for all A-starting girls' names, this could very well change.

Aida did have a period of some U.S. popularity; in 1954, it reached as high as Number 663 but fell off the list in 1976.

Arabic families often pronounce it with two syllables—as EYE-dah—rather than three.

Aida Turturro played Tony Soprano's sister in *The Sopranos*.

Ailsa

Scottish, "elf victory"

Ailsa is a traditional Scottish name related to a rocky island in the Firth of Clyde called Ailsa Craig. It might make an interesting alternative to the outdated Ashley or overly popular Ella and could also be thought of as a relative of Elizabeth or Elsa.

Some other Ailsa relations: Ailis, Ailse, Ailsha, Allasa, Elsha, Elshe.

Aisling

Irish, "dream, vision"

Aisling is currently a very popular name in Ireland. Pronounced variously as ASH-ling, ASH-lin, or ash-LEEN, it was part of the revival of authentic Irish names in the twentieth century and is now being used sparingly by U.S. parents in place of the dated Ashley—though often spelled phonetically as Ashlyn or Ashlynn.

An aisling is a poetic genre that developed in late seventeenth-century Ireland, a type of patriotic-romantic poetry in which Ireland is addressed as a beautiful woman.

Alabama

Choctaw, "vegetation gatherers"; place name

Alabama is a hot southern place name, picking up from Georgia and Savannah. This is not a geographical name come lately, though—there have been girls named Alabama dating back well over a century.

Hip couple Drea de Matteo and Shooter Jennings named their daughter Alabama Gypsy Rose, and rocker Travis Barker has an Alabama Luella.

Alexa

Diminutive of Greek Alexandra, "defending men"

Alexa—the simple and most feminine form of the Alexandra-Alexis group—has retained its staying power. It entered the popularity list in 1973 and had been in the Top 50 for the last five years until it slipped to Number 55 in 2011. It now rests at Number 57.

Alexa stands at the happy midpoint between the bare-bones simplicity of nicknamey Alex and the elaborate Alexandra.

Alexandra

Greek feminine form of Alexander, "defending men"

Alexandra, the feminine form of Alexander, has been in the Top 100 for over twenty years and shows no signs of fading. Strong, tasteful, and elegant, Alexandra maintains a chic aura despite its popularity, has a solid historic pedigree, and offers an array of softer nicknames, from the boyish Alex to the bouncy Lexi to the more dramatic Alexa and Xandra.

Alessandra and Alejandra are attractive, more exotic variations.

Alexis

English variation of Alexios, "defending men"

Alexis, a one-time Russian boys' name, has surpassed sister Alexandra in popularity—it's just inside the Top 40, with more than five thousand babies named Alexis last year.

Alexis zoomed to popularity following the introduction of the *Dynasty* character Alexis Carrington in the 1980s—which gave it a sexy, sleek image—and has had remarkable staying power.

One of the few notable female pre-Carrington Alexises was 1940s actress Alexis Smith, who had some minimal impact on the name, which entered the list in 1943. A current bearer is Alexis Bledel, who played Rory on *Gilmore Girls*.

Alice

German, "noble"

Alice is a classic name that's both strong and sweet, which got a big bounce via Tina Fey's choice of the name for her daughter. In the past three years alone, Alice has jumped from Number 258 to 127!

Alice is quite unique among traditional girls' names—more feminine and dainty than Mary and Helen, more substantive than Ann or Jane, yet with more lightness and innocent charm than Margaret or Katharine.

Alice is a darling of literature, from the immortal heroine in *Alice in Wonderland* to an unusual number of fine modern writers like Alices Munro, Walker, Sebold, Hoffman, McDermott, Adams, and Elliott Dark. In other fields there were First Daughter Alice Roosevelt, painter Alice Neel, food innovator Alice Waters, and literary figure Alice B. Toklas, to name a few.

Alice is also a British royal, as Queen Victoria's second daughter, the princess who shocked her Victorian mother by breastfeeding her baby.

At the moment, Alice is being revived all across the Western world: she's the top name in Sweden, a surprising Number 9 in Italy, and in the Top 50 in England and Wales, France, Belgium, and Australia.

Alicia

Spanish variation of Alice, "noble"

Alicia was more popular than its mother name for several years, adding a lacy, more balletic feel to the original. Taken for its sound alone, Alicia is a lovely, feminine name, but parents should be aware that its innumerable phonetic versions, such as Alisha and Alysha, have robbed it of some of its character.

Two high-profile Alicias are actress Silverstone and soul singer Keys; in the past there were ballerina Alicia Markova and the great Spanish classical pianist de Larrocha. Alicia is the birth name of Jodie Foster, and the singer known as Pink was originally Alecia.

Allegra

Italian, "joyous"

In music, the term allegro means "quickly, lively tempo," which makes this still-unusual and quintessential ballet dancer's name all the more appealing.

One of the most creative sounding of names, Allegra has been associated with the American prima ballerina Allegra Kent, and has been chosen as a first or middle name for their daughters by poets George Gordon, Lord Byron, and Henry Wadsworth Longfellow, as well as by R. Buckminster Fuller and Donatella Versace. Caveat: There is that current connection to the allergy medication.

Alma

Latin, "nurturing, soul"

Alma is a somewhat solemn, soulful name that had a burst of popularity a century ago, and then faded into the flowered wallpaper—though we can see it beginning to find its way back.

In addition to being familiar via the term alma mater, Alma has many cultural ties, one of the most recent being the character Alma Del Mar played by Michelle Williams in the 2005 film *Brokeback Mountain*. Other characters named Alma have appeared in *Deadwood, The Hunger Games,* and *The History of Love* by Nicole Krauss. In the Tennessee Williams play *Summer and Smoke*, a character named Alma explains that her name is "Spanish for soul."

The name became fashionable in England following the Battle of Alma—named for the Russian river—during the Crimean War.

Always well used in Hispanic families, Alma seems to be on the brink of making a comeback, à la Ella and Ada, appreciated for its simplicity, integrity, and—yes—soul.

Althea

Greek, "with healing power"

Althea is a poetic, almost ethereal name found in Greek myth and pastoral poetry, associated in modern times with the great tennis player Althea Gibson, the first African-American to win at Wimbledon.

Althea appears in Greek mythology as the mother of the hero Meleager and was revived by the seventeenth-century poet Richard Lovelace as a poetic pseudonym for his beloved.

These days, parents would also appreciate the short form Thea.

Amabel

Latin, "lovable"

Amabel is an older name than Annabel and a lot more distinctive. Amabel was a very common name in the twelfth and thirteen centuries, then was revived during the nineteenth century British fad for medieval names.

In a short story by H.H. Munro, about Amabel, the vicar's daughter, it is said, "Her name was the vicar's one extravagance."

Amabel's shortened form Mabel overtook the mama name early on.

Amalia

Latin form of German Amala, "work"

Amalia is a widely cross-cultural name, heard from Italy to Romania to Germany to Spain to Scandinavia, and recently chosen for the Dutch royal baby. It can be pronounced ah-MAH-lee-a or ah-mah-LEE-a.

Amalia's popularity was spread in eighteenth-century Europe due to the fame of Anna Amalia, a Duchess who was a great patron of the arts.

Amalia would make a lovely and more distinctive alternative to Amelia; a spelling variation is Amalya.

Amanda

Latin, "much loved"

After a long run as the prettiest senior in class, this romantic name has lost some of its glossy sheen, though it's still quite lovely and well used. Amanda was one of the romantic-sounding names that rocketed to stardom in the 1980s, along with Samantha, Vanessa, et al.

Despite its somewhat trendy feel, Amanda is a certifiable classic—it appears in a play as early as 1694, was prominent among saints, eighteenth-century literary heroines, and in plays by Noel Coward and Tennessee Williams. But if you're looking for a fresher alternative, you might consider the French Amandine or Shakespearean Miranda.

Amandine

French diminutive of Amanda, "much loved"

This fragrant, almond-scented name has hardly been heard in this country, which is a pity—we've loved it since John Malkovich used it for his now grown daughter.

A French diminutive of Amanda, it was the birth name of novelist George Sand—born Amandine Aurore Lucile— and currently ranks at Number 87 in France.

Of course, amandine is also a French culinary term for a garnish of almonds.

Amaryllis

Greek, "to sparkle"

If you're looking for a showier flower name than Lily, but in the same botanical family, you might consider Amaryllis, which is not as outré as it might at first sound. It was used in Greek poetry as the appellation of pure pastoral beauties; Amaryllis is the heroine of Virgil's epic poem *Ecologues*, after whom the flower was named. Other references are characters in the George Bernard Shaw play *Back to Methuselah* and *The Music Man*. James Bond-creator Ian Fleming had a half-sister named Amaryllis Maris-Louise Fleming, who was a noted British cellist.

Amelia

English variation of Amalia, "work"

Amelia, a lovely Victorian name, with a heroic connection to aviatrix Amelia Earhart, is one of the fastest-rising girls' names as an alternative to the overused Emily and Amanda, jumping 169 places in ten years. Amelia emerged as the top British name in 2011 and retained the Number 1 spot in 2012, is in the Top 10 in Australia and Poland, and has now risen to Number 23 in the U.S. So while Emilia and Emelia are sound-alike names closer to the mega-popular Emma and Emily, it's the Amelia version that's on the fast track.

Kids might associate Amelia with the wacky children's book character Amelia Bedelia, while adults could appreciate its Shakespearean cred as a character in *A Comedy of Errors*—spelled Aemilia—as well as the eponymous heroine of the Henry Fielding novel, characters in novels by Trollope and Thackeray, as a *Harry Potter* name, and as detective Amelia Peabody in the Elizabeth Peters series. Angelina Jolie played patrol cop Amelia Donaghy in *The Bone Collector*.

Amelia became a British royal name via the daughters of Kings George II and III. An American hero is feminist Amelia Bloomer.

Trivia tidbit: Amelia is the birth name of Minnie Driver.

Amelie

French variation of Amelia, "work"

This French favorite has been gaining notice here thanks to the charming 2001 French film *Amélie*; it entered the American popularity list in 2002 and has been rising ever since. Also spelled Amalie, the pronunciation is like Emily but with a short 'a' sound at the beginning.

There's definitely a lot of confusion over the roots of, and differences among, all these related names, but Emily, Emma, and Amelia all derive from different roots and have different meanings, and Amelie is a descendant of the Amelia branch.

Amelie is currently enjoying great popularity in the U.K. (it's Number 54 in England and Wales), Scotland (Number 22), Australia, and Belgium, as well as in France.

Probably inspired by the name of French King Louis Philippe's consort Marie-Amelie, Balzac used the name for two of his prominent characters.

Amethyst

Gem and color name

As flower names become more exotic, so can gem names move beyond Ruby and Pearl to names like Topaz, Sapphire and Peridot. Amethyst, the purple birthstone for February, has never been in the Top 1000, but could have some appeal, joining similarly-hued Violet and Lilac.

In the M.M. Kaye children's novel *The Ordinary Princess*, the protagonist is Princess Amethyst Alexandra Augusta Araminta Adelaide Aurelia Anne of Phantasmorania—Amy for short—who has been given the "gift" of ordinariness.

Amity

Latin, "friendship"

Amity—what nicer gift to give your little girl than a name that signifies friendship and harmony? This virtue name is also more rhythmic and feminine than the single-syllable Hope, Faith, and Grace.

Amity is a neglected gem that could make a distinctive namesake for an Aunt Amy.

Amy

Latin; French, "beloved; friend"

Amy was second only to Jennifer for the whole decade of the 1970s and, though far less used for babies today, remains a short, sweet *Little Women*-style classic. When asked which seventies name might make a comeback, several Berries placed their bets on Amy.

Amy rocketed to popularity in the late nineteenth century along with the other Louisa May Alcott *Little Women* names (Amy was the artistic one), fell from favor, then burst onto the scene again in the 1960s when parents were turning back to basic names like Jessie, Maggie, and Molly.

The many notable Amys on the scene today include actors Amy Adams, Amy Ryan and Amy Poehler, singer Amy Grant, director Amy Heckerling, and author Amy Tan.

Amy was the name of Little Dorrit in the Dickens novel.

Anais

French Provençal and Catalan version of Anne, "gracious"

Anais is an unusual, exotic name forever attached to the daring French-born American novelist and diarist Anaïs Nin (born Angela, with middle name Anaïs), who was the inspiration for the naming of the daughter of musician Noel Gallagher. It is also familiar as the name of a popular perfume.

Anais has some interesting literary references as a character in the Balzac novel *Lost Illusions* and in Colette's *Claudine* books.

Anais would make an attractive, creative choice.

Anastasia

Greek feminine variation of Anastasios, "resurrection"

Anastasia is no longer a forbidding, regal Russian name, but is now seen as a viable—and increasingly popular—American option… elegantly beautiful.

Anastasia's greatest claim to fame is via the "lost" daughter of the last czar of Russia, whose story has been told and retold in books and movies.

An old Greek name and also that of an ancient saint—the patron saint of weavers— Anastasia was well used in ancient Britain and in Ireland, as well as Russia.

Anastasia's meaning relates to resurrection, making it an apt choice for an Easter or spring baby.

Andrea

Italian feminine variation of Andreas, "strong and manly"

Andrea—a feminine form of Andrew (and a male name in several European cultures) comes with a good selection of pronunciations—ANN-dree-a, AHN-dree-a, or ahn-DRAY-a— each with a slightly different image: girl next door/slightly affected/downright exotic.

Andrea's popularity, while never huge, has remained surprisingly steady—it has never been off the Top 100 since 1962! There have been countless featured on-screen characters named Andrea, on vehicles from the original *Beverly Hills 90210* to *The West Wing* to *The Devil Wears Prada*.

Originally the Italian male form of Andrew, Andrea is found across many European cultures—for one gender or the other.

Andromeda

Greek mythology name, "advising like a man"

The beautiful daughter of Cassiopeia who, like her mother, literally became a star—the constellation that bears her name. Andromeda makes a dramatic and adventurous choice in a time when four-syllable mythological names are gradually making their way into the mainstream.

Andromeda Tonks (née Black) is a *Harry Potter* character

Cousin name Andromache belonged to the tragic wife of the Trojan Hector, appeared in Shakespeare's *Troilus and Cressida,* and was the subject of plays by Euripedes and Racine.

Anemone

Greek, "wind"; flower name

Anemone is a floral name that relates to the ancient Greek myth of the famous love story of Aphrodite and Adonis, in which Aphrodite transforms her wounded lover's blood into a flower, the crimson anemone, whose blossoms are opened by the wind—accounting for its other name, windflower.

This makes an interesting, if challenging, choice for someone seeing an exotic flower name.

Angelica

Italian, Polish and Russian diminutive of Angela, "divine messenger"

Angelica is by far the choicest form of the angelic names, more delicate than Angelina, more feminine than Angel, more modern than Angela. But though Angelica is so lacy and poetic, it lags behind the bolder Angelina—probably for obvious reasons.

Angelica was introduced to England from Italy in the seventeenth century and is heard in early poetry and plays, including *Romeo and Juliet.*

Anjelica is a variant spelling, as in Anjelica Huston.

Angelina

Greek, Italian, Spanish, and Russian diminutive of Angela, "angelic"

The gorgeous Angelina Jolie has promoted the star power of her name and changed Angelina's image from delicate to intense, from older Italian mama to stylish multicultural child. Kids might relate to the dancing mouse in the series of charming children's books, *Angelina Ballerina*, or to the *Harry Potter* character, Angelina Johnson Weasley, a member of Dumbledore's army.

A notable namesake is Angelina Grimké, an important American abolitionist and suffragist.

Anna

Latinate version of English Ann and Hebrew Hannah, "grace"

Anna has become the dominant form of the Ann family, having been firmly in the Top 25 for years and only slipping in the past couple of years. Anna offers a touch of the exotic and a bit more style than the oversimplified Ann, used for generations throughout Europe, from Russia to Italy, Spain to Romania—it is still Number 2 in Hungary and Austria, Number 4 in the Netherlands, and Number 8 in Norway.

Classic and simple, Anna would be an excellent choice for parents in search of a name that will bridge two different cultures, say Jewish and Italian.

In literature, Anna is associated with Tolstoy's *Anna Karenina*. Three current bearers are actresses Anna Kendrick, Anna Friel, and Anna Paquin.

Anya takes it more into the territory of the exotic.

Annabelle

Variant of Amabel, "lovable"

This is a charming name on the rise along with other -belle names, especially in this form, but also appealing in the more streamlined Annabel spelling, made famous by the Edgar Allen Poe poem *"Annabel Lee."* Annabelle is saucy and stylish, a tad upscale, has a sense of humor, and is melodious and lively.

Annabelle was well used in the early twentieth century, took a long rest, then resurfaced in 1995. Now, at Number 100, it's at its highest point ever.

Variations Annabel and Annabella, are also rising in popularity.

Annalise

Combination of Anna and Lise

Variously spelled Annalise and Annaliese, this is not a modern smoosh but a traditional German combo name, the liese part coming from a short form of Elizabeth, with a definite Heidi-esque feel. But though it may be seen as old style in Germany, it's a recent success in this country: Annalise jumped onto the popularity list for the first time in 1997 and is now at Number 510.

Anne

French variation of English Ann and Hebrew Hannah, "grace"

The name of the sainted mother of the Virgin Mary was among the top girls' baby names for centuries in both the original English Ann spelling and the French Anne. Both left the Top 100 around 1970, but Anne is still Number 561 on the list of U.S. most popular baby names, appreciated by some parents for its classic simplicity, although others are more likely to choose the original Hannah, the Anna variation, or even Annabel or Annabella.

Anne was the name of six queens of England, two of them wives of Henry VIII, as well as the name of the present Queen Elizabeth's only daughter plus French and Russian royalty.

Anne has too many distinguished namesakes to enumerate—but among them are Anne Hathaway, (both Shakespeare's wife and the contemporary actress), Anne of Green Gables, Anne Brontë, Anne Frank, and Anne Morrow Lindbergh.

Anouk

Dutch and French variation of Anna, "grace"

Anouk, made famous by French actress Anouk Aimée, is a singular name with a lovely sound. Anouk Aimée was born as Françoise, but adopted the first name of the character she played in her debut film.

Anouk, which is currently Number 52 in The Netherlands, was the name of the young daughter in the French film *Chocolat*. (some other interesting character names in that movie are Vianne, Roux, and Dedou.) The Belgian supermodel spells her name Anouck Lepère.

Anouk is one of the most appealing of the An-starting names.

Anthea

Greek, "flowery"

This unjustly neglected floral name has a BBC accent and a Greek mythological heritage; Anthea is an epithet of Hera, the Greek queen of the gods, and her name has been used as a poetic symbol of spring.

Anthea Disney is a high-powered business executive and distant relative of Walt.

So if you want to go even beyond Azalea and Anemone, you might consider Anthea.

Antonia

Latin, "priceless one"

Antonia is stronger than most feminized boys' names, reflecting the pioneer spirit of Willa Cather's classic novel *My Antonia*. Antonia has recently fallen off the Top 1000, which is an excellent reason for you to use it.

Antonia was borne by several prominent women in ancient Rome, including the mother of the Emperor Claudius.

A recent distinguished namesake is British historian/biographer Lady Antonia Fraser. It is also the full name of actress Nia Vardalos.

Antonella is a pretty feminization—Antoinette, not so much.

Anya

Russian diminutive of Anna, "grace"

Anya is an exotic Russian version that succeeds in making Ann dynamic. It is climbing the U.S. baby names popularity list, now at Number 395; it reentered the list in 1998.

Anya is the form found most frequently in Russia, Poland, and other Eastern European countries, while Anja is the spelling usually preferred in Germany, Norway, Denmark, Germany, Sweden, and The Netherlands.

Anya is often used as a character name with a bit of foreign flair. Aside from its authentic use in Chekhov's *The Cherry Orchard*, it has appeared as Audrey Hepburn's name in *Roman Holiday*, on *Buffy, the Vampire Slayer*, and as the latest Spider-Girl, who is also known as Arana. In literature, Anya Seton is the pen name of Ann Seton, author of such best-selling mid-century historical novels as *Dragonwyck*.

Aphra

Possible variation of Aphrah, biblical place name

Aphra would make an interesting choice—especially since it's the name of the first professional female writer in English, the seventeenth century's Aphra Behn. Born in 1640, she was a prolific dramatist of the English Restoration.

Aphra was originally a name for a woman from Africa that eventually became a given name, and was borne by several Roman saints. It can also be spelled Afra.

Apollonia

Greek feminine variation of Apollo, the Greek sun god.

This name of a third century Christian martyr has an exotic, appealing feel in the modern world. It first came to American attention via Prince's love interest in the film *Purple Rain*.

St. Apollonia of Alexandria propelled her name into great popularity in the Middle Ages; her name is invoked against toothaches.

Apolonia, one 'l,' is the name of a character in John Steinbeck's novel, *The Pearl*.

Arabella

Latin, "yielding to prayer"

Arabella, lovely and elegant, has long been well used in Britain and finally made it onto the American list in 2005; it is now nearing the Top 200, as more and more parents see it as a distinctive alternative to the mega-popular Isabella. Its meaning may also be interpreted as "beautiful," thanks to -bella.

Arabella has been a great favorite in English novels, dating as far back as Samuel Richardson's *Clarissa* and Henry Fielding's *Tom Jones*, and also appeared in *The Vicar of Wakefield*, Dickens's *Pickwick Papers*, George Eliot's *Felix Holt*, Thomas Hardy's *Jude the Obscure*, and, more recently, in *Harry Potter*.

Arabella is the title of a lyric comic opera by Richard Strauss and was chosen by Ivanka Trump for her daughter.

Arabella is a recommended, sophisticated choice.

Araminta

Invented hybrid name from Arabella and Aminta

Araminta is an enchanting eighteenth-century playwright's invention that's familiar in Britain and just beginning to be discovered here. It was created by the versatile Sir John

Vanbrugh—playwright, as well as the architect of Blenheim Palace—for his comedy *The Confederacy*.

In the Enid Bagnold novel *National Velvet*, Araminta is the name of the central character's mother.

Arden

English, "valley of the eagle"

Arden, the name of the magical forest in Shakespeare's *As You Like It*, is poised to join the other 'A' names on the popularity list, with its strong, straightforward image. Another reason to love Arden: its similarity to "ardent." Arden is a name with a unisex feel that also embodies the best feminine qualities—a winner.

Arden is more familiar as a surname, as in cosmetics entrepreneur Elizabeth and actress Eve, and in the narrative poem by Tennyson, *Enoch Arden*. And Shakespeare's mother was Mary Arden.

Aria

Italian, "air"; Hebrew, "lioness"

The light and airy Aria is an operatic choice moving quickly up the charts and also a current favorite on Nameberry. Aria entered the list in 2000 and has risen 800 places since then, 66 just in the past year.

Television is definitely helping to popularize the name with a character on *Pretty Little Liars* named Aria and *Game of Thrones* featuring a young heroine named Arya.

Aria is also a saint's name.

Arianna

Italian variation of Greek Ariadne, "most holy"

A smooth, exotic choice, Arianna's on the rise with both single and double 'r's and 'n's. Single 'r' Arianna is these days associated with Greek-born blog queen Arianna Huffington.

Arianna has been steadily climbing in popularity for twenty years; it's also a Top 25 name in Italy.

There are no less than four Arianna-titled operas, including Handel's *Arianna in Creta*.

Cousin name Ariane is represented by a young Dutch princess, sister of Amalia and Alexia.

Ariel

Hebrew, "lion of God"
Ariel is a biblical name, seen there as the messenger of Ezra, and also used as a symbolic name for the city of Jerusalem, while Shakespeare used it for a (male) sprite in *The Tempest*.

For girls, Ariel enjoyed a considerable burst of popularity with the 1989 release of Disney's *The Little Mermaid*: by 1991 it had reached Number 66.

Although its wave has crested, Ariel is still a name any little girl would love. It is also associated with the poetry of Sylvia Plath and with the Chilean-American writer Ariel Dorfman. The popular historian Ariel Durant was born Ida Ariel Ethel.

In Israel, Ariel is used as much—or more—for boys.

Artemis

Greek mythology name
Artemis, one of the key figures of the female Greek pantheon, is the ancient virgin goddess of the hunt, wilderness, animals, childbirth, and a protector of young girls. It was later associated with the moon. Artemis is the equivalent to the Roman Diana, but is a fresher and more distinctive, if offbeat, choice.

Artemis was the twin sister of Apollo, one of the twelve deities who lived on Mount Olympus. She features in three of the fifth-century plays of Euripides.

Artemas, on the other hand, is a male name, though some gender confusion could arise from the *Artemis Fowl* novels.

Arwen

Welsh, "noble maiden"
Arwen is well known as princess of the Elves in Tolkien's *Lord of the Rings*—a lovely name with an authentic Welsh ring. She was played in the film by Liv Tyler.

If you love Arwen, you might also want to consider Anwen, Bronwen, and Rhonwen.

Trivia tidbit: The International Astronomical Union names all colles (small hills) on Saturn's moon, Titan, after characters in Tolkien's work; in 2012, they named a hilly area "Arwen Colles" after Arwen.

Arya

Sanskrit, "noble"

Arya is an unusual and exotic name on the rise thanks to a popular book and television series. She entered the popularity charts in 2010 and then jumped 529 places the following two years.

The prime impetus is the fiercely independent young character Arya Stark in the TV series *Game of Thrones*, based on the George R. R. Martin books *A Song of Fire and Ice*. Another influence is the Elven princess in Christopher Paolini's *Inheritance Cycle* trilogy, basis of the movie *Eragon*.

The name resembles the musical Aria, which is also growing in popularity.

Asia

Place name

This still attractive and exotic place name was one of the first to gain popularity, though it now probably owes some of its favor to its similarity to Aisha. Asia ranked as high as Number 195 on the U.S. baby names popularity list in 1997.

In Greek myth, Asia is the daughter of Oceanus and Tethys and mother of, among others, Atlas and Prometheus.

The best-known modern bearer of the name is Italian actress, singer, and director Asia Argento, who is probably responsible for its popularity in Italy.

Aspen

Nature and place name

Aspen is the name of a graceful tree in the poplar family with heart-shaped leaves so delicate they quiver in the gentlest breeze, as well as that of a trendy Colorado ski resort. Aspen started as a unisex name possibility but now is much more often worn by girls.

It entered the popularity list in 1993, now ranks at Number 504, and is a good bet to start climbing higher as more and more parents respond to the appealing place and nature image it evokes.

Aster

English, "star"

This is a fresh new addition to the botanical list; comedian Gilbert Gottfried made it a real bouquet when he named his daughter Lily Aster. And the name of the little girl on television's *Dexter* sounds like Aster but is actually spelled Astor, which invokes a more high-society image. Aster also relates to the Greek word for star.

Astrid

Norse, "divinely beautiful"

Astrid has been a Scandinavian royal name since the tenth century—and more recently in Belgium—but has never really assimilated into our culture the way Ingrid did. Many people associated it with the Swedish author of the *Pippi Longstocking* stories, Astrid Lindgren.

With the renewed interest in ethnic names, Astrid might be worth consideration by parents with Norse roots, or who even have enjoyed a holiday among the fjords.

Astrid is the name of the teenaged heroine of the novel *White Oleander* and has appeared as a character in *How to Train Your Dragon* and the TV shows *Fringe* and *Once*.

Astrid is currently a Top 25 name in her native Sweden.

Athena

Greek mythology name

Athena is the name of the daughter of Zeus who was the goddess of wisdom, warfare, handicrafts, mathematics, and courage (and that's just a partial listing), and the great patroness-goddess of the city of Athens. In the *Odyssey*, Homer describes her as "sparkling-eyed Athena."

Athena is a distinctive name that could appeal to enlightened parents who particularly prize intelligence. At Number 247, it is now at its highest U.S. ranking ever.

Athene is another version, and Athena's Roman counterpart is Minerva.

In the Disney movie *The Little Mermaid*, Athena is the mother of Ariel.

Tina Fey turned to her Greek heritage for both of her second daughter's names—Penelope Athena—and this has spurred interest in Athena, even though it's in middle place.

Aubrey

English from French version of German Alberic, "elf ruler"

The unisex name Aubrey is scooting up the girls' popularity charts, along with the revived Audrey; it has been in the Top 50 for the past four years and is now at an all-time high Number 15. After being a 100% male name, it tipped to female in 1974 and is now 98% girls.

Aubrey was a relatively popular male name in England in the Middle Ages, then fell from favor. One possible factor in its popularity for girls is the song about a girl named Aubrey by the group Bread in the 1970s. Most prominent bearer now is deadpan comic actress Aubrey Plaza, breakout star of *Parks and Recreation*. Terrence Howard is the father of a grown daughter named Aubrey.

Auden

English, "old friend"

A softly poetic surname name, associated with poet W.H., Auden is enjoying quiet but marked fashion status. It was chosen for his daughter by Noah Wyle and is definitely one to watch.

Audrey

English, "noble strength"

Audrey is one of the girls' names that have been rising due to their connection to Old Hollywood glamour—in this case the eternally chic and radiant Audrey Hepburn. Audrey has been in and around the Top 50 for the past six years. Celebs who have chosen Audrey include Greg Kinnear, Steve Zahn, and Faith Hill and Tim McGraw.

St. Audrey was a sixth-century saint who was particularly revered in the Middle Ages. Shakespeare bestowed her name on a rustic character in *As You Like It*.

A current representative is the French actress Audrey Tatou—who made her mark in *Amélie*, *The Da Vinci Code*, and as Coco Chanel—and who shares some of the charm of Audrey Hepburn.

Augusta

Feminine variation of Augustus, "great, magnificent"

Augusta is a dignified name reminiscent of wealthy great-aunts, but with the fashion for both August and Gus for boys, Augusta could get some fresh energy.

Augusta was the title of honor given to the wives and daughters of Roman emperors, which then morphed into a given name, brought to England by the German princess who became the mother of George III.

Augusta is also a saint's name and a place name. Her literary Great-Aunt image was formed via the characters Lady Augusta Bracknell in Oscar Wilde's *The Importance of Being Earnest*, an elderly relative in the *Harry Potter* books, and Aunts Augusta in both Graham Greene's *Travels with My Aunt* and P.G Wodehouse's *Jeeves and Wooster* novels.

Augusta has a choice of two friendlier nicknames—Aggie and Gussie.

Aura

Greek, "soft breeze"

Aura has an otherworldly, slightly New Age-y glow but is beginning to sound more and more like a legitimate name. In Greek mythology, Aura was the Titan of the breeze and the fresh, cool air of early morning. But at odds with her peaceful—well—aura, the mythological Aura is a tragic figure, ultimately transformed into a fountain by Zeus.

At the end of the nineteenth century, Aura was not that unusual: she reached Number 511 on the Social Security list in 1882. Princess Aura was a character in the old comic strip *Flash Gordon.*

Aura is currently popular in some areas of Central America.

Aura alternatives for those who like the name's sound but want to temper the spiritual feel: Auria, Aurora, Aurelia.

Aurelia

Latin, "the golden one"

Aurelia is the shimmering female form of the Roman classic Aurelius, very common in the Roman Empire but rarely heard in modern America. The name of several minor early saints, Aurelia has the right sound, feel, and meaning to rise again. Aurora and Oriana are Aurelia cousins you might also want to consider.

Aurelia was the name of the mothers of Julius Caesar, the writer Sylvia Plath, and Arnold Schwarzenegger, who, in her honor, made it one of his daughter's middle names.

Aurora

Latin, "dawn"

Aurora, the poetic name of the Roman goddess of sunrise whose tears turned into the morning dew and of (Disney's) Sleeping Beauty would be sure to make any little girl feel like a princess.

The radiant Aurora, also associated with the scientific term for the Northern Lights, has consistently been on the popularity list since the nineteenth century, but is now at its highest point ever—and looks to climb even further. Aurora came in at Number 17 on the recent list of most popular girls' names among Nameberries.

Aurora Leigh is the name of an epic poem by Elizabeth Barrett Browning, and Aurora Greenway was the moving Shirley Maclaine character in *Terms of Endearment.*

An Aurora nickname possibility with a totally different feel: Rory.

Ava

Latin variation of Eve, "life"

Ava was given a huge popularity boost—she's currently at Number 5—when dozens of high-profile stars such as Reese Witherspoon and Hugh Jackman chose Ava for their daughters. This Glamour Girl name via Hollywood beauty Ava Gardner is attractive but epidemically popular!

Some parents who love Ava's simplicity and style have looked on to other choices that might take her place: Eva, Avery, Ada, Aveline, and so on. The result, as with other popular names such as Hailey and Aiden that have spawned a raft of imitators, is that Ava is beginning to feel even more ubiquitous than it might based on its Top 5 standing.

Ava seemed to be headed towards Number 1—it's no accident we titled our most recent book on baby name style *Beyond Ava & Aiden*—but, though it seems to have been somewhat side-swiped by the Olivia-Isabella-Sophia group, it will still certainly stay in the Top 10 for years to come. It's a lovely name on many levels, but if you want something that will stand out, keep looking.

One of the most fascinating things about Ava is that it's a much more ancient name than its modern-feeling sleekness would suggest. St. Ava was the daughter of King Pepin who was cured of blindness and became a nun.

Avalon

Celtic, "island of apples"

Avalon, an island paradise of Celtic myth and Arthurian legend—it was where King Arthur was taken to recover from his wounds— and also the colorful capital of the California island of Catalina—makes a heavenly first name. Actress Rena Sofer and British musician Julian Cope used it for their daughters.

Avalon manages to blend the appeal of Ava and Evelyn, while sounding more interesting and unique.

Avery

English, "ruler of the elves"

Though this unisex name has been around for a few decades, Avery has now definitely heated up for girls, partly as an alternative to the epidemic Ava. The female Avery has had a meteoric rise, moving up from Number 802 in 1990 to 13 in 2012. Angie Harmon and Jason Sehorn may have started it all when they chose it for their daughter in 2005, just as they did with daughters Finley and Emery. Amy Locane used the name in 2009, and now Dr. Phil has a granddaughter named Avery.

On *30 Rock*, Elizabeth Banks had an extended cameo playing Alec Baldwin's glamorous fiancée, Avery Jessup.

Aviva

Hebrew, "springlike, fresh, dewy"

Aviva is vivacious and memorable, a fresh spin on the Vivian and Vivienne names that have been getting more popular since Angelina and Brad chose one for their twin daughter.

Another A-beginning palindrome name: Aziza.

Azalea

English, "azalea, a flower"

Azalea is one of the fresher flower names, along with Zinnia and Lilac, that is new to the name bouquet—in fact she just entered the Social Security list for the first time in 2012. So if Lily and Rose are too tame for you, consider this brilliant pink springtime blossom with a touch of the exotic that has been growing in popularity.

Azalea is the name of the princess heroine of the novel *Entwined*, and, with the addition of another vowel, is the name of singer/rapper Azealia Banks.

Aziza

Hebrew, "strong"; Arabic and Swahili, "precious"

Aziza is a zippy palindromic choice that also means "precious" in Swahili and Arabic. All in all, an attractive and interesting option—a Turkish variation is Azize.

In African mythology, the Azizi are a supernatural race of forest dwellers who give practical and spiritual advice.

Aziz is the male version, as represented by rising comedian Aziz Ansari, one of the stars of *Parks and Recreation*.

Azure

Color name

Azure is a colorful choice for a blue-eyed child. Among other blue-toned color name possibilities: Indigo, Cerulean, and Blue itself.

In the Middle Ages, azure was another name for lapis lazuli, the gemstone used to make the brilliant pigment seen in much medieval art.

B

Bay

Latin, "berry"

One of the most usable of the pleasant, newly adopted nature/water names (like Lake and Ocean), especially in middle position.

There was a character named Bay Kennish on the show *Switched at Birth*; conservative political commentator Bay Buchanan was born Angela Marie.

Other associations with bay are the bay laurel tree—prized since ancient times for its medicinal and culinary (bay leaves!) properties—and the reddish-brown color usually applied to horses.

Beatrice

Latin, "blessed; she who brings happiness"

Beatrice is back. Stored in the attic for almost a century, the lovely Beatrice with its long literary (Shakespeare, Dante) and royal history is being looked at with fresh eyes by parents (such as Paul McCartney, Bryce Dallas Howard) seeking a classic name with character and lots of upbeat nicknames, like Bea and Bee.

Nickname Bea actually stood alone on the popularity lists for four years at the beginning of the twentieth century—and it could happen again. Bea is sleek and modern, while Trixie sounds vintage and sassy—though if you favor Trixie, you may want to consider the Beatrix version of the name. What's the difference between the two? Beatrix is reminiscent of watercolorist and children's author Beatrix Potter and has that surprising 'x' ending, while Beatrice feels gentler and more classic.

The Duke and Duchess of York, aka Fergie and Prince Andrew, thrust Beatrice back into the public eye when they chose it for their older daughter in 1988. The name can be pronounced with two syllables, as bee-tris; with three, as in bee- or bay-ah-tris; or, as the Italians say it, with a magisterial four: bay-ah-TREE-chay.

Beatrice was the name of Queen Victoria's youngest child. And in Dante's great poem *The Divine Comedy*, Beatrice is his guide through Paradise and is idealized as the embodiment of the spirit of love. In Shakespeare's *Much Ado About Nothing*, Beatrice is the witty, high-spirited heroine.

Other names that mean happiness: Felicity and Hilary, either of which would make a good twin or sister name for Beatrice.

Beatrix

Latin, "blessed; she who brings happiness"

Beatrix, has a solid history of its own apart from Beatrice, with that final 'x' adding a playful, animated note to the name's imposing history. It has been largely associated with Beatrix (born Helen) Potter, creator of Peter Rabbit, and Beatrix has been Queen of The Netherlands since 1980.

The main character in Quentin Tarantino's movie *Kill Bill* was Beatrix Kiddo, played by Uma Thurman.

Actress Jodie Sweetin has a daughter called Beatrix, and designer Kate Spade chose it for her daughter Frances's middle name.

Both Bea and Trixie are adorable nicknames, and Beatriz is the Spanish form.

Bella

Diminutive of Isabella, Italian, "beautiful"

Everything ella, from Ella to Bella to Arabella, is red hot right now. Bella was one of the less overused examples, with the hint of a nice Old World grandmotherly veneer until it became attached to *Twilight*'s Bella Swan. Bella shot up the charts in 2009, jumping 64 spots to number 58. It's now holding steady in that general vicinity, though if you're thinking of naming your daughter Bella, be aware that there are a lot of little girls whose proper names are Isabella, Arabella, etc. who are called Bella.

In pre-*Twilight* literature, Bella Wilfer is the central character in Charles Dickens's *Our Mutual Friend*.

Mark Ruffalo, Billy Bob Thornton, and Eddie Murphy are all dads to Bellas. A strong feminist namesake is Bella Abzug.

Bella was in use as far back as the thirteenth century, then disappeared until the eighteenth when it became fashionable.

Belle

French, "beautiful"

Belle has nothing but positive associations, from "belle of the ball" to "Southern belle" to the heroine of Disney's *Beauty and the Beast*. Though the Twilight-influenced Bella and longer forms like Isabella and Annabella have overshadowed it, Belle has its own Southern charm and would make a pretty choice as a first or middle name.

Belle was a Top 100 name in the 1880s but left the list in 1934. Its most famous bearer was the legendary Western outlaw, Belle Starr (born Myra); Belle Watling is a character in *Gone with the Wind*.

Bernadette

French feminine diminutive of Bernard, "brave as a bear"

Although feminizations ending in -ette are not particularly popular now, Bernadette is a pleasant, feminine, but strong name that doesn't feel prohibitively dated. And though closely associated with the saint who saw visions of the Virgin Mary—Saint Bernadette of Lourdes—it is now no longer strictly inhabiting the Catholic diocese.

Bernadette was much more widely used at one time than it is now. The year after Saint Bernadette was canonized, her name reached Number 252, and not long after the successful film *The Song of Bernadette* was released, it hit Number 188 in 1946.

Bernadette Peters is a contemporary bearer, and Minnie Driver's breakthrough film role was as Bernadette 'Benny' Hogan in *Circle of Friends*.

Bessie

Diminutive of Elizabeth, "pledged to God"

After a century of association with horses and cows, this name could just be ready for revival by a fearless baby namer—after all, it did happen to Jessie and Becky.

Bessie has been in use since the seventeenth century and is found as characters in *Jane Eyre* and in Sean O'Casey's play *The Plough and the Stars*. More recently, she was an animated automotive character in the movie *Cars*.

On the popularity lists until 1975, Bessie was a Top 25 name from 1880 to 1906, reaching Number 9 in 1889. Notable namesakes include the great blues singer Bessie Smith and Bessie Coleman, the first African-American female aviator.

And if you want to go more refined, you could simplify to Bess.

Betty

Diminutive of Elizabeth, "pledged to God"
Combine the popularity of Betty White and *Mad Men*'s glamorous Betty Draper Francis, with the residual sweetness of *Ugly Betty*'s Betty Suarez, and the result is an impending return of the name. It's got presidential cred via Betty Ford and feminist history through Betty Friedan.

Betty's image is still very World War II, when Betty Grable was a hot pin-up girl and Betty was the all-American girls' name blanketing the country, second only to Mary from 1928 to 1934.

So, yes, Betty has been out for so long now that we are starting to imagine a new generation of adorable baby Bettys.

Bette Davis pronounced her name "Betty," while Bette Midler is "Bet."

Bianca

Italian, "white"
Bianca, the livelier Italian and Shakespearean version of Blanche, has been chosen by many American parents since the 1990s, just as Blanca is a favorite in the Spanish-speaking community.

Miss Bianca was an elegant mouse (voiced by Eva Gabor) in Disney's 1977 *The Rescuers*, and Bianca features as a character in two Shakespeare plays, *Othello* and *The Taming of the Shrew*—and its musical offshoot, *Kiss Me Kate*.

Bianca was brought to prominence here by the first Mrs Mick Jagger. Her name entered the U.S. popularity ranks in 1973, reaching a high of Number 84 in 1990. Bianca was chosen for her daughter by actress Tia Carrere.

Billie

Diminutive of Wilhelmina or Wilma, "resolute protection"
Billie is a tomboy nickname name, part of the growing trend for using boyish nicknames for girls.

To track its path from blue to pink, Billie was 100% male in 1880, was 55% female just a decade later, in the girls' Top 100 by 1928, and is now 88% female.

Billie is a possible retro choice for fans of jazz great Billie Holiday, born Eleanora. Other conceivable namesakes are *The Wizard of Oz*'s Glinda—Billie Burke (born Mary William), silent screen star Billie Dove (born Bertha), actresses Billie Whitelaw and Billie Piper (born Lianne) and tennis legend Billie Jean King (born Billie). Another cultural reference is the Michael Jackson hit song 'Billie Jean.'

Billie was picked for their daughters by Carrie Fisher, *My Name is Earl* actor Ethan Suplee, and Rebecca Gayheart and Eric Dane.

Birdie

English, "bird"

Birdie was until recently a middle-aged Ladies' Club member wearing a bird-decorated hat—but now it's just the kind of vintage nickname (think Hattie, Josie, Mamie, Millie) that's coming back into style in a big way. Actress Busy Philipps named her baby Birdie (inspired by First Lady Lady Bird Johnson), as did soap star Maura West.

In an earlier heyday of nickname names—the 1880s—Birdie was a Top 200 name.

Blanche

French, "white"

Blanche, which originated as a nickname for a pale blonde, was in style a century ago, ranking in the double digits until 1920. She then had to fight the stereotype of faded Southern belle, a la Blanche DuBois in Tennessee Williams's *A Streetcar Named Desire* and Blanche Devereaux in TV's *Golden Girls*. Now all three of the Golden Girls— Blanche, Rose, and Dorothy—could be ready for revival, with Blanche sounding like a stronger, simpler alternative to Bianca.

One possible powerful namesake is Blanche Scott, one of the original daredevil aviatrixes.

Blue

Color name

Blue suddenly came into the spotlight as the unusual color name chosen by Beyoncé and Jay-Z for their baby girl Blue Ivy. Blue is also a starbaby middle name du jour, used for both sexes in different spellings and forms, from John Travolta and Kelly Preston's Ella Bleu to Alicia Silverstone's Bear Blu. Dave 'The Edge' Evans named his daughter Blue Angel back in 1989.

Blue is the heroine of the trendy Marisha Pessl novel *Special Topics in Calamity Physics*.

Blythe

English, "happy, carefree"

Blythe embodies a cheerful, carefree spirit and could be the next Blair/Blaine/Blake/ Brett/Britt with the advantage that it's clearly pink. It joins other light-hearted names for girls like Felicity and Hilary.

Blythe is the middle name of Drew Barrymore—in her case a surname from her rich theatrical history.

The title of the memorable Noel Coward play *Blithe Spirit* is taken from Shelley's poetic line, "Hail to thee, blithe Spirit"—a nice tribute to a baby Blythe.

Bree

Anglicized variation of Irish Brigh, "strength"

A short, breezy name with a sophisticated yet upbeat image, that doesn't betray its Irish roots. Bree first came to notice here in 1971 via the complex prostitute character in the movie *Klute*, which earned Jane Fonda an Oscar. More recently, it was tied to the character of Bree Van de Kamp on *Desperate Housewives*.

Other recent references include Stephenie Meyer's novella *The Short Second Life of Bree Turner* in the *Twilight* franchise. And in the popular *Fancy Nancy* children's book series, Bree is Nancy's BFF.

The Bree spelling is much preferable to the cheese-related Brie.

Bridget

Anglicized variation of Irish Brighid, "exalted one"

An early Irish immigrant to the U. S., Bridget, the most familiar form of the name of the Celtic goddess of wisdom, is still used by traditionalists but also carries some modern spark and a great meaning.

Bridget is the name of the most famous female saint of Ireland, who became the patroness of her country, as well as patron saint of scholars, poets, and healers. Because of her sanctity, the name did not come into common use in Ireland until the seventeenth century, after which it became wildly popular, eventually used as a generic name for an Irishwoman.

According to Irish myth, there were three sister goddesses named Brigid: the goddess of poetry, the goddess of healing, and the goddess of agriculture.

Most prominent Bridgets today are actresses Fonda and Moynahan, op artist Bridget Riley, and the fictional hapless Bridget Jones—she and her diary the protagonist of three books and two movies.

Irish variants include Brighid, Brigid (as in the devious character in *The Maltese Falcon*), Bridie, Biddy, and Bedelia.

Briony

Spelling variation of Bryony, "to swell"; plant name

Briony may be the variation and Bryony the original, but many parents will see this as the more authentic-feeling version of this attractive botanical name. Still unusual in the U.S., Briony is in the British Top 100 and may appeal to parents as a fresh spin on Briana or Brittany.

Briony Tallis is the young girl who sets the plot in motion in Ian McEwan's novel *Atonement*—played on screen by Saoirse Ronan, for which she received a Best Supporting Actress Oscar nomination.

Briony is a variant spelling of Bryony, coming from the Greek meaning "to swell, to grow luxuriantly." Bryony/Briony is an unusually strong plant name—the bryony being a wild climbing vine with green flowers.

Pronunciation is like Brian with an -ee at the end.

Bronte

Irish, "bestower"

This lovely surname of the three novel-writing sisters, now used as a baby name, makes a fitting tribute for lovers of *Jane Eyre* and *Wuthering Heights*. While the original name took an umlaut over the 'e,' modern English speakers may find that more trouble than it's worth. Trivia note: The Anglo-Irish clergyman who was the father of Charlotte, Emily and Anne changed his name from the original Brunty.

Many people first noticed the name in the film *Green Card* as the name of the Andie MacDowell character.

Bronwen

Welsh, "white breast"

Bronwen is widespread in Wales, but still rare enough here to sound somewhat exotic—we think Bronwen is a real winner. (Note: the Bronwyn spelling is strictly for males in its native land.)

Bronwen Morgan is the lovely heroine of the classic novel and movie *How Green Was My Valley*. In Welsh mythology, Bronwen was the daughter of Llyr, the god of the sea.

Close cousin Branwen appears in Welsh medieval literature as a tragic figure who was turned into a bird. The ancient Welsh worshipped her as goddess of the moon and love.

Brooke

English, "small stream"

Brooke has long projected an aura of sleek sophistication and can also be seen as a stylish water name.

It was Brooke Shields (born Christa) who took it from quietly fashionable to ultra trendy when she was just a young girl; socialite Brooke (born Roberta Brooke) Astor gave it social status. Although Brooke peaked in popularity a decade ago, she's well liked enough to still sit just outside the Top 100.

Brookes have appeared on soaps like *The Bold and the Beautiful* and *All My Children*, and on *Melrose Place* and *One Tree Hill*.

Chynna Phillips and Billy Baldwin have a daughter named Brooke.

C

Cadence

Latin, "rhythm, beat"

The musical word name Cadence, barely heard a few years ago, seemed to come out of nowhere to zoom up the charts. Some might see it as a trendy feminine relative of the popular Caden. Kadence and Kaydence are also rising.

An early Cadence sighting was in the 1992 Armistead Maupin novel *Maybe the Moon*, in which the narrator heroine was a small actress called Cadence Roth, nicknamed Cady. January Jones played a Cadence in *American Wedding*.

Calista

Greek, "most beautiful"

Spelled with either one 'l' or two, Calista came to the fore in 1997 when Calista Flockhart hit it big as Ally McBeal. Flockhart, who bears her mother's middle name, didn't just introduce a name, she introduced a whole sensibility. Pretty and delicate, Calista is definitely worthy of consideration, especially for parents with Greek roots.

In ancient myth, Calista (or Calisto) was a nymph loved by Zeus, whose jealous wife Hera turned her into a bear.

Calla

Greek, "beautiful"

Calla is a lily name that is much more distinctive and delicate than Lily. Rarely heard today, it did appear in the popularity lists in the last decades of the nineteenth century.

Calla is the eponymous heroine of the Rebecca Wells novel *The Crowning Glory of Calla Lily Ponder*, and there's an English rock band called Her Name is Calla.

Actress Mare Winningham named her daughter Calla way back in 1987.

Camellia

Flower name

Camellia is an exotic flower name with distinct roots related to the Camille/Camila group and has varied associations to the moon, water, wealth, and perfection. It could be thought of as a floral replacement for Amelia.

The attractive flowering tree was named by Linnaeus for the Moravian Jesuit botanist Georg Joseph Kamel and has been used, if sparingly, as a first name since the 1930s.

In the language of flowers, the camellia denotes admiration and perfection, and it's the state flower of Alabama. The Dumas novel *The Lady of the Camellias* is the basis of the opera *La Traviata* and the Garbo film *Camille*.

Cameo

Word name

This evocative term for a stone or shell carved in relief could make a striking first name for a girl, though she would have a starring role in her story, rather than a cameo.

Cameron

Scottish, "crooked nose"

Cameron Diaz almost single-handedly transported this sophisticated Scottish male surname into the girls' camp, where it has had a rapid rise to popularity—though it's never caught up with the boys. Another actress, Camryn Manheim (born Debra), did the same thing for the phonetic, more feminine spelling.

Cameron entered the girls' list in 1980, reaching as high as Number 176 in 1990, though it is now slightly slipping.

Camilla

Latin, "young ceremonial attendant"

The Spanish Camila, pronounced ka-MEE-la, is the fastest rising version of this ancient Roman name, now in the Top 50. In Roman myth, Camilla was a swift-footed huntress so fast she could run over a field without bending a blade of grass.

Camilla has been in English-speaking use since the sixteenth century and appeared in Virgil's *Aeneid* as a virgin queen. It was later popularized by an eponymous Fanny Burney novel, and, in modern times, Camilla Macaulay is the protagonist of Donna Tartt's *The Secret History*. Today, the name is connected to the former Camilla Parker Bowles, now the Duchess of Cornwall.

The floral name Camellia has also begun to bloom.

Camille

French variation of Camilla, "young ceremonial attendant"

At one time just the sound of the name Camille could start people coughing, recalling the tragic *Lady of the Camellias*, the heroine played by Greta Garbo in the vintage film based on a Dumas story, but that image has faded, replaced by a sleek, chic, highly attractive one.

Among its namesakes are Camille Claudel, a French sculptor, and Camille Paglia, a feminist writer and critic. Princess Stéphanie of Monaco is the mother of a Camille, and it is the middle name of both Nicole Richie and Willow Smith.

Camille is a unisex name in France, where distinguished male bearers include the composer Saint-Saëns and the painter Pissarro.

Campbell

Scottish, "crooked mouth"

This unisex name, the seventh most popular surname in Scotland, can make a more unusual Cameron alternative. It is represented on the girls' side by TV news correspondent Campbell Brown, for whom it was a family name; Brown was born Alma Dale Campbell—Alma Dale being her grandmother's name and Campbell her mother's maiden name.

Authors Nicholas Sparks and Jodi Picoult have both created female characters named Campbell.

As a surname, Campbell is connected to philosopher-writer Joseph, singer Glen, actress Neve, model Naomi, GB Shaw muse Mrs Patrick, and Andy Warhol's soup cans.

Carlotta

Italian variation of Charlotte, feminine form of Charles, "free man"

Carlotta has a large measure of finger-snapping exotic charm and substance—despite being a not too pleasant character in *The Little Mermaid*. Carlotta is also the diva/prima donna in *The Phantom of the Opera*, and there was an Empress Carlotta of Mexico.

Carlotta (spelled with one 't' in Spanish) has not been heard much since the 1960s—which might add to its appeal to someone looking for a more exotic spin on Charlotte.

Carmen

Spanish variation of Carmel, "garden"

Carmen has long been associated with the sensuous, tragic heroine of Bizet's opera, based on a novel by Prosper Merimee, and then by two other bombshells: Carmen Miranda (born Maria) and Carmen Electra (born Tara), as well as the great jazz singer Carmen McRae.

She has plenty of childhood references as well: Carmen Elizabeth Juanita Echo Sky Brava Cortez is a character from the *Spy Kids* trilogy, Carmen Lowell appears in the *Sisterhood of the Traveling Pants* series, Carmen de la Pica Morales was a character on *The L Word*, and Carmen Sandiego is the clever anti-hero in the *Where in the World is Carmen Sandiego?* computer-game franchise—she was named for Carmen Miranda and the city of San Diego.

In the Latin community, Carmen is also used as a male name.

Carolina

Latinate feminine variation of Carolus, "free man"; also place name

Languid, romantic, and classy, this variation heats up Caroline and modernizes Carol, adding a southern accent.

Pronounced Caro-LINE-a in English-speaking countries, it is heard as Caro-LEEN-a in Italian, Spanish, and Portuguese. Nicknames can include Caro and Lina, as well as Carrie.

A prominent bearer is Venezuelan fashion designer Carolina Herrera (born Maria Carolina), who has designed clothes for First Ladies from Jacqueline Kennedy to Michele Obama. A hauntingly melodic theme song is James Taylor's "Carolina on My Mind."

Carolina now ranks at Number 430, while Caroline stands at 80.

Caroline

French feminine variation of Carolus, "free man"

Caroline is a perennial classic, in the Top 100 since 1994. It is now at Number 80—roughly the same position it held in 1885. Caroline has an elegant patina, calling to mind the Kennedy Camelot years and Princess Caroline of Monaco.

Caroline came to England with George II's wife, the German Queen Caroline of Ansbach in 1705, and then George IV married another German Caroline in 1795. In the U.S., Caroline has been a First Lady name via President Benjamin Harrison. Jane Austen named one of her less pleasant characters in *Pride and Prejudice* Caroline, and the name was also borne by Lady Caroline Lamb, the mistress of the poet Lord Byron, as well as the mother of the *Little House on the Prairie* brood.

The song "Sweet Caroline" was a huge soft-rock hit for Neil Diamond, released in 1969, and inspired by the then eleven-year-old Caroline Kennedy (for whom he sang it at her fiftieth birthday party).

Carolina is the more feminine (and place name) version; the Carolyn spelling takes it a bit down-market.

Carys
Welsh, "love"
Common in Wales, this name was introduced to America when Welsh-born Catherine Zeta-Jones and husband Michael Douglas chose it for their daughter in 2003. It didn't come into use in Wales until the late nineteenth century. It's currently Number 239 in England and Wales.

Carys is one of that sweet group of girls' names with a loving meaning, and this also has a subliminal link to the word 'caress.'

Cerys is also heard in Wales.

Cassandra
Greek, "prophetess"
The name of the tragic mythological Trojan princess who was given the gift of prophecy by Apollo but was condemned never to be believed, Cassandra has been used for exotic characters in movies and soap operas. Ethereal and delicate, Cassandra was in the Top 70 throughout the 1990s but is now descending in popularity.

Cassandra was the name of Jane Austen's mother, sister, and two cousins. Cassandra Wilkins is a character in John Dos Passos's novel *Manhattan Transfer*, but in the 2007 Woody Allen thriller, *Cassandra's Dream*, Cassandra was not the name of a person, but a sailboat.

Currently, Cassandra Wilson is a noted jazz singer; Charlie Sheen has a daughter Cassandra born in the 1980s.

Cassia
Greek, "cinnamon"
Cassia is one of the rare names that's truly unusual yet has a stylish feel. Cassia has the added attraction of the sweet smell of cinnamon; a cassia tree or bush, which has yellow

flowers, produces a spice that can be a substitute for cinnamon. We predict Cassia will become much more popular along with her brother names Cassian and Cassius.

Keziah, the Biblical equivalent, is also due for rediscovery, while Kassia is another, Kardashian-style spelling.

Catalina

Spanish variation of Catherine, "pure"

This name of an island in sight of Los Angeles makes an attractive and newly stylish variation on the classic Catherine or overused Caitlin.

Santa Catalina of Siena is, along with Saint Francis, one of the two patron saints of Italy and was a respected spiritual writer of the Church. Catalina de Aragón y Castilla is the original Spanish name of the first wife of Henry VIII, known to history as Catherine of Aragon. In a completely different vein, Catalina Aruca was a sexy Bolivian character on the sitcom *My Name is Earl*.

Catherine

Greek, "pure"

Catherine is one of the oldest and most consistently well-used female names with endless variations and nicknames. The Catherine form feels more gently old-fashioned and feminine than the more popular 'K' versions. Most stylish nickname for Catherine right now: Kate…or Cate, à la Blanchett.

While the popularity of the Catherine form has been waning in favor of Katherine with a K, we think that might turn around now that Catherine Middleton, who reportedly hates the name Kate and never uses it, married Prince William and put a modern, stylish gloss on her already classy name.

The Catherine spelling was a Top 100 name until the millennium; it reached as high as Number 18 in the 1910s.

Catherine has been well used throughout history for saints (one of whom, Catherine of Alexandria, is the patron saint of philosophers, students, craftsmen, nurses, and librarians), queens, and commoners alike.

Catherine has also been associated with some of the great romantic heroines of literature, including Heathcliff's love in *Wuthering Heights* and the passionate nurse Catherine Barkley in Hemingway's *A Farewell to Arms*.

And if you're wondering about all of those interchangeable 'C's and 'K's, it's because when the name was introduced into Anglo-Saxon Britain, Catherine was spelled with a 'C' since the letter K did not yet exist in the English alphabet.

Parents may also want to consider one of the attractive foreign variations, such as Caterina.

Cecilia

Latin feminine form of Cecil, "blind"

Cecilia, a delicate and lacy feminine form of Cecil, which derives from a Roman clan name, has definitely been rediscovered. The martyred Saint Cecilia was designated the patron of musicians, either because she supposedly sang directly to God while the musicians played at her wedding, or because as she was dying, she sang to God—in either case making it a fitting name for opera star Cecilia Bartoli.

On TV, the Cecelia spelling variation was the name chosen for Pam and Jim's baby on *The Office*; in real life, it's the name of the daughters of Vera Wang and Soledad O'Brien.

Cecilia is also a Dickens character name in *Hard Times* and appears in the novels *Atonement*, *The Virgin Suicides*, and *The Hunger Games* series, as well as being the subject of a memorable Simon & Garfunkel song.

Cecilia, Celia, and Cecily are all Nameberry faves. Cecelia is an accepted spelling variation you may want to consider if you plan to shorten the name to Celia or Cece.

Cecily

Feminine form of Cecil, "blind"

Cecily is as dainty as a lace handkerchief and she has a wide assortment of namesakes. One Cecily was the mother of King Richard III whose beauty gained her the title "the Rose of Raby," Cecily Parsley is a Beatrix Potter bunny, Cecily Cardew is a character in *The Importance of Being Earnest*, and Cecily von Ziegesar is the author of the *Gossip Girl* books.

Sisters of Cecily that may also interest you: Cecilia, Cicely, and Celestia. Cicely has a distinguished bearer in actress Cicely Tyson and was used by Sandra Bernhard for her now grown daughter.

Celeste

Latin, "heavenly"

Celeste is a softly pretty and somewhat quaint name with heavenly overtones, which kids might associate with Queen Celeste of Babar's elephant kingdom. She's a light and lovely choice that's finally getting noticed.

Celeste has been in the Top 1000 every year since 1880 and now ranks at Number 470. Best-known modern Celeste is Oscar-winning actress Celeste Holm.

If you want a more unusual variation, consider Celestine, Celestia—or even Celestial.

Celestia

Latin variation of Celeste, "heavenly"

Celestia is a heavenly name that sounds more ethereal than Celeste. Celestia might make a distinctive, feminine choice if your taste runs toward names like Angelina and Seraphina.

Celestia was more popular than you might think in the late nineteenth century—it made the popularity list six times in the 1880s. Celestia was the middle name of Caroline (Carrie) Ingalls in *Little House on the Prairie*.

Celestine

Latin, "heavenly"

Celestine is a pretty, crystalline extension (actually a diminutive) of Celeste that would make a choice that is both delicate and strong. It is commonly heard in France, where it currently ranks at Number 421.

Celestine was the name of painter Edgar Degas's Creole mother. Some people might associate it with the 1993 spiritual novel *The Celestine Prophecy*.

Celestina is another attractive version.

Celia

Latin, "heavenly"

Celia, splendidly sleek and feminine, is a name that was scattered throughout Shakespeare and other Elizabethan literature but still manages to feel totally modern.

Shakespeare has been credited with introducing Celia in *As You Like It*, and it was to Celia that the poet Ben Jonson penned the immortal line: "Drink to me only with thine eyes." Other literary Celias have appeared in works ranging from George Eliot's *Middlemarch* to T. S. Eliot's *The Cocktail Party* to Lionel Shriver's *We Need to Talk About Kevin*.

Celia Cruz was a superstar of Latin music.

Celia is not a short form of Cecilia, which has a completely different meaning and developed independently. But some contemporary parents are naming their babies Cecelia, especially with that spelling, and calling them Celia—which gives you two beautiful names in one.

Charity

English word name

Charity is one of the Big Three abstract virtue names, along with Hope and Faith, though far less widely used than the others. But as Faith, Grace and Hope grow more common, some parents are beginning to look at the more unusual three-syllable choices like Verity, Amity, Clarity, and Charity, which sound much fresher and also have that pleasingly rhythmic y-ending sound.

In the Dickens novel *Martin Chuzzlewit*, there are two sisters named Charity and Mercy, who are known as Cherry and Merry.

In the musical *Sweet Charity* the title character, Charity Hope Valentine, is an all too charitable girl with a heart of gold. In the novel *Harry Potter and the Deathly Hallows*, Charity Burbage is a Muggle Studies teacher at Hogwarts School of Witchcraft and Wizardry, and in *Two Broke Girls*, there's an Aunt Charity who's not very charitable.

Charity was in the Top 500 in the 1880s and 1890s, remained in the Top 1000 until 1927 when it dropped from sight, then reappeared in 1968. For a period in the 1970s and 80s, Charity was a Top 300 name.

Charlie

Diminutive of Charles or Charlotte, "free man"

Charlie is one of the friendly, tomboyish male nickname names—another is Sam—now used almost as frequently for girls: in 2012, it was Number 305 for girls, 233 for boys. The name Charlie, for females, has been jumping up the charts since it reappeared, after a fifty-year hibernation, in 2005.

Charlie has been a favorite for starbaby girls, including the twin daughter of Rebecca Romijn and Jerry O'Connell and the daughter of Julie Chen and Les Moonves. Jeremy Sisto has a hyphenated Charlie-Ballerina.

Charlotte

French feminine diminutive of Charles, "free man"

Charlotte is an elegant royal name, with a host of widely varied role models, from Charlotte Brontë to the spidery Charlotte of E. B. White's *Web* to the more recent Charlotte York, aka the prissy one, of *Sex and the City*. Charlotte is appealing to a wide range of parents because it sounds feminine yet grownup, sophisticated yet lush.

The name was popularized by England's Queen Charlotte Sophia, wife of King George III who ruled in the late eighteenth and early nineteenth century, was the mother of fifteen children, and a patron of Mozart and Bach; Charlotte and George ruled England during the French and American revolutions.

Charlotte is now a pop culture staple—it was Scarlett Johansson's character in *Lost in Translation* and has been featured on TV shows like *Lost* and *Revenge*. The band Good Charlotte was named for a children's book with that title. An all-around winner of a name, Charlotte has been chosen by Dylan McDermott, Colin Hanks, and Sarah Michelle Gellar and Freddie Prinze Jr. Nameberry favorite Charlotte, number one on this site in recent years, is climbing in popularity on the overall charts here and abroad.

In addition to Charlie, Lottie makes a cute nickname.

Chiara

Italian, "light, clear"

Chiara is a lovely and romantic Italian name that's familiar but not widely used here: a real winner. You might consider Chiara instead of Claire, Clara, Cara, or even Keira.

Santa Chiara, Anglicized as St. Clara, was a follower of Saint Francis of Assisi.

Two members of European cinema royalty, Catherine Deneuve and Marcello Mastroianni, named their now grown daughter Chiara.

Chiara currently ranks Number 8 in Italy and is also well used in Switzerland, Germany, and Austria.

Chloe

Greek, "young green shoot"

Much more dynamic than most of the other Greek-based romantic literary names of the seventeenth century, Chloe is a pretty springtime name symbolizing new growth, though by no means is as fresh as it once was. It has been shooting up the charts for several years, now sitting at Number 11, and is also mega-popular throughout Great Britain, Australia, and Canada. The creative spelling Khloe has been moving up as well, thanks solely to the Kardashian klan.

While Chloe has not been used for any recent celebrity babies, it is the name of the now-adult daughters of Olivia Newton-John and of Candice Bergen and the late French film director Louis Malle. Actress and style leader Chloë Sevigny is another high-profile bearer, as is rising young star Chloë Grace Moretz.

Chloe appeared in Greek mythology as an alternative name for the goddess of agriculture and fertility, Demeter, and in the Greek pastoral romance *Daphnis and Chloe*. It is also mentioned in the New Testament, appears in *Uncle Tom's Cabin*, and is the real name of Nobel prize-winning writer Toni Morrison.

Christina

Greek, "anointed"

Christina, a pretty and feminine, crystal clear classic, may be trending downward, but it's never out of style. Christina's short forms Chris, Christie, and Tina all seem dated—making the royal Christina best used in its full glory.

Christina became a royal name in Spain and Sweden (Greta Garbo played Queen Christina in one of her classic films) and is more usable today than the French Christine.

Christina is now well represented by actresses Applegate, Ricci and *Mad Men*'s Hendricks, and singer Aguilera. Previous bearers include British poet Christina Rossetti and Australian novelist Christina Stead.

Christiana is a more distinctive variation.

Cicely

Variation of Cecily, "blind"

This frilly Victorian name is a variant of Cecilia and Cecily, with which it might well be confused. Cicely was a surprise choice for comedienne Sandra Bernhard's daughter.

Literary Cicelys can be found in Sir Walter Scott's *Kenilworth* and the 1925 Dos Passos novel *Manhattan Transfer*.

A distinguished bearer is actress Cicely Tyson. Cicely, or Sweet Cicely is also a herbaceous plant with a strong taste reminiscent of anise and is sometimes used for medicinal purposes.

Claire

French form of Clara, "bright, clear"

Claire, luminous, simple, and strong, with a barely distinguishable French accent, is one of those special names that is familiar yet distinctive, feminine but not frilly, combining historical depth with a modern edge. And though Claire is enjoying revived popularity—it now ranks at Number 45—its highest ever—it will never be seen as trendy. Claire is also a great middle name choice.

Claire is usually seen as the French spelling of the name, while the equally appropriate Clare is English and Clair is, well…that's French too. Clara, once seen as a stuffier version, has lately gained some fashion edge, primarily because it has more vintage charm and is somewhat more unusual. The Italian Chiara is another recommended choice.

Famous women named Claire include the medieval Saint Clare of Assisi (who was made the patron saint of television in 1958 because of her reputed power to see events at a distance), writer Clare Booth Luce, silent screen siren Clara Bow, and actresses Claire Bloom and Claire Danes.

There have been countless fictional Claires as well, including ideal mom Clair Huxtable, Molly Ringwald in *The Breakfast Club*, and characters in *Heroes*, *Lost*, *Six Feet Under*, *Modern Family*, and the *Outlander* series.

Clara

Latin, "bright, clear"

Long relegated to an Olde World backwater, the European-flavored Clara has been speeding up the charts on sleeker sister Claire's coattails for the past few decades. Now, many would say the vintage chic Clara is the more stylish of the two names. Actor Ewan McGregor was an early celebrity adopter of the name for one of his daughters.

Clara has been a popularity list stalwart; now at Number 136, its highest point since 1947; it was a Top 10 name in the 1880s, at one time associated with the silent screen 'It girl,' Clara Bow, and before that with German musician and composer Clara Schumann and Red Cross founder Clara Barton, who was born Clarissa.

Clara is beloved for her leading role in *The Nutcracker* ballet and as Heidi's invalid friend.

Other Clara variations you might want to consider include Clarissa and Clarina, though Clarabelle seems still fit mainly for cows.

Clarissa

Latinized form of Clarice, "bright, clear"

Clarissa, the daintier elaboration of Claire, has a long literary history of its own, having been featured in the novels of Samuel Richardson, Charles Dickens, and Virginia Woolf—Clarissa was the title character of *Mrs Dalloway*—not to mention the 1990s TV teen show, *Clarissa Explains it All*.

Clarissa is a name definitely worth considering as an alternative to the overused Vanessa and dated Melissa. Appealing diminutives are Clarry and Claris.

Red Cross founder Clara Barton was born Clarissa.

ROSENKRANTZ & SATRAN • 53

Clarity

Virtue name

Clarity is one of the lightest of the newly rediscovered virtue names, with a bit of three-syllable sparkle, old-fashioned charm, and a clear vision for the future. Clarity is a very desirable quality in this confusing world, and it also, unlike some other newly-coined word names, has real meaning and history as a name.

Clarity is preferable to Charity and definitely to Chastity, with the possibility of Clare as a short form.

Claude

Latin, "lame"

Yes, we tend to think of Claude as a male name and Claudia and Claudette as the female, but this ancient clan name is used in France for girls as well as boys and could make a distinctively chic choice here, too. You may be surprised to know that Claude was in fairly regular use for American girls in the 1880s and 90s, reaching as high as 553 in 1880.

In her native country, there have been some famous female Claudes, including Queen Claude of France (1499 to 1524), daughter of Louis XII, and another sixteenth-century Claude de France, daughter of Henri II.

Later Claudes include the daughter of Claude Debussy, Claude-Emma (called Chouchou), the leading female character in Tracy Chevalier's novel *Lady and the Unicorn*, French actress Claude Jade and photographer Claude Cahun, and the widow of French Prime Minister Georges Pompidou.

Claudia

Feminine variation of Claude, "lame"

A classic name with a hint of ancient Roman splendor that has never been truly in or truly out, Claudia still feels like a strong, modern choice—one of our "sweet spot" names.

Claudia was a common female name in ancient Rome, borne by the wives of both Nero and Pontius Pilate. The name is mentioned in the New Testament in one of St. Paul's letters to Timothy as one of the Christian women in Rome, as a result of which it was taken up in the sixteenth century and has been in moderate use ever since.

There was a popular mid-century series of novels by Rose Franken, beginning with *Claudia: The Story of a Marriage*, and the name was also used by Agatha Christie and Penelope Lively, as well as being a main character in Anne Rice's *Interview With the Vampire*.

Model Claudia Schiffer gave it an infusion of glamour, as had earlier Italian actress Claudia Cardinale. Michelle Pfeiffer has a daughter named Claudia.

Clea

Literary name

An attractive and unusual name that may be a variation of Cleo—Clea was possibly invented by Lawrence Durrell for a character in his *Alexandria Quartet.*

Actress Clea DuVall is one noted bearer of the name, another is Paul Newman and Joanne Woodward's youngest daughter, who was named Claire Olivia but always called Clea.

Clemency

English, "mild, merciful"

One of the rarest of virtue names, Clemency could come back as an alternative to the more familiar Puritan virtue names such as Hope and Faith. It has a rhythmic three-syllable sound and offers a more virtuous alternative to the more popular Clementine.

Clemence is the medieval French form, also heard occasionally in the U.K. Writer Clemence Dane was born Winifred Ashton.

Clemmie makes a cute nickname.

Clementine

Feminine version of Clement, "mild, merciful"

Clementine is a Nameberry favorite even though it hasn't appeared on the U.S. Top 1000 for more than half a century. Still, its style value may mean there are more Clementines than you might guess in your neighborhood—it may be a name that raises Mom's eyebrows, but it won't surprise your friends.

If "Oh, My Darlin'" still rings too loudly in your ears, consider pronouncing Clementine as Clementeen—or even using Clementina, which rhymes with Christina. Stylish Claudia Schiffer chose Clementine for her daughter, as did Ethan Hawke and Rachel Griffiths, and Kate Winslet played one in *Eternal Sunshine of the Spotless Mind.* And for a kid reference—there's a Muppet named Clementine.

A female variation is the even-more-unusual Clement. Clementine's meaning suggests peace and happiness—a lovely image. Other girls' names with similar meanings: Beatrice, Felicity, Hilary, Arcadia, Irina, and Mercy.

Clementine is currently just outside the Top 100 in France.

Cleo

Greek, "glory"

Cleo, one of the few girls' names to boast the cool-yet-lively o-ending, is, of course, short for Cleopatra, the name of one of the most powerful women in history.

Cleo was most popular in the early decades of the twentieth century—when it was also used for boys. The opening of the Egyptian tombs along with the 1917 silent film starring Theda Bara popularized a range of now-obscure Cleopatra diminutives, including Cleora and Cleola.

A distinguished bearer is the British jazz singer Cleo Laine, and there have been Cleos on two TV dramas: *ER* and *Law & Order: Special Victims Unit*.

Maybe the fact that Cleo was recently chosen by *Friends'* David Schwimmer will ignite a welcome revival.

Sound-alike Clio is the name of the ancient Greek mythological muse of history and heroic poetry, one that is rich with modern charm and would also make an intriguing choice.

Clover

Flower name

Clover is a charming, perky choice if you want to move beyond hothouse blooms like Rose and Lily, and it's recently become a new celeb favorite, chosen by both Neal McDonough and Natasha Gregson Wagner, who used it to honor her mother, Natalie Wood, one of whose most iconic films was *Inside Daisy Clover*.

Clover also has a long association with good luck via the four-leaf clover and through the shamrock symbol of Ireland. It first came to wide notice by way of a couple of soap opera characters.

In the movie *The Good Shepherd*, Angelina Jolie's character is called Clover—but her birth name was actually Margaret.

Colette

French diminutive of Nicole, "victory of the people"

Modern parents might be attracted to this name because of the French novelist—though pen name Colette was actually her last name, Sidonie-Gabrielle her first.

Colette was one of a group of Gallic 'ette' names popular in the 1950s and 60s, including Nanette, Annette, Jeanette, and Paulette, but by 1986, Colette had dropped off the list completely—though it could be ready for reappraisal. Dylan McDermott used it for his daughter, as did actress Constance Zimmer.

There was an appealing animated Colette featured in the film *Ratatouille*.

Constance

English version of Latin Constantia, "steadfastness"

Constance is one of the subtler of the virtue baby names, but still has quite a prim and proper image. One impediment to its revival has been the decidedly dated nickname Connie, though modern parents might well opt for using the strong and dignified name in full.

One of William the Conqueror's daughters was named Constance, and in Shakespeare's *King John*, Constance is the devoted mother of King Arthur. Constance was widely used in the seventeenth century by Puritans: Constance Hopkins was a young passenger on the Mayflower.

The fictional Constance Billard School appears in TV's *Gossip Girl*, and Constance was the first name of the decidedly non-prim and proper Lady Chatterley.

Oscar Wilde's wife was Constance, and Mozart's spouse was the German form Constanze, nicknamed Stanzi.

Though Constance has been neglected here for a number of years, it still ranks at Number 120 in France.

Trivia tidbit: Constance was the birth name of the 1940s peekaboo-hairdo star Veronica Lake and also, not surprisingly, Connie Britton.

Consuelo

Spanish, "she who brings consolation"

Consuelo is a chic, highly sophisticated Spanish name that works well with Anglo surnames. It was regularly on the U.S. popularity list through 1983, reaching as high as Number 339 in 1930.

The name is a reference to the Virgin Mary, as Nuestra Senora del Consuelo—our lady of consolation.

Its most noted namesake in this country is Consuelo Vanderbilt, the beautiful only daughter of railroad millionaire William K. Vanderbilt. She was given the Spanish name in honor of her half-Cuban godmother. Another fashionable Consuelo was the American-born Italian countess Consuelo Crespi, the editor of Italian *Vogue*. In literature, Consuelo was used by George Sand for the title character of a novel about a beautiful Venetian singer. There have also been Consuelos in *West Side Story* and *Precious*.

Consuelo is still well used in Spanish-speaking countries and is especially popular in Chile. The unusual o-ending for a girl's baby name adds to her appeal.

Cora

Greek, "maiden"

Cora is a lovely, old-fashioned name—Cora was a daughter of Zeus, and Cora Munro is the heroine of *The Last of the Mohicans* (in fact, James Fenimore Cooper probably invented it for his 1826 novel)—that has been recently rejuvenated and strengthened by its contemporary-feeling simplicity.

Though she has never been completely out of favor, Cora has had her ups and downs. A Top 20 name in the 1880s, she had sunk to Number 876 in 1988, but then has gradually risen to its current ranking of 155, with every indication of climbing higher. A current inspiration is the appealing American-born Cora Crawley, Countess of Grantham on *Downton Abbey*.

In classical mythology, Cora—or Kore—was a euphemistic name of Persephone, goddess of fertility and the underworld.

While a complete name unto itself, some parents who love Cora may want to use it as a short form for such names as Cordelia or Coraline. Cora's fashionable sisters include Clara, Nora, Corinne, Corinna, and Coralie.

The soft and gentle Cora is definitely a recommended choice.

Coralie

French from Latin, "coral"

Coralie is a sweet French name not often heard here, though she's gaining some recognition via Neil Gaiman's similar sounding spooky and lovely children's book, *Coraline*. Other literary appearances: Coralie is the stage name of an actress in Balzac's *Lost Illusions* and a French girl in an 1850 Thackeray novel.

Coralie is currently very popular in French-speaking Quebec, and there is a contemporary French singer named Coralie Clement.

Cordelia

Possibly Celtic, meaning unknown

Cordelia, the name of King Lear's one sympathetic daughter, has style and substance, and is exactly the kind of old-fashioned, grown-up name that many parents are seeking today. If you're torn between Cordelia and the equally lovely Cora, you can always choose Cordelia for long and then call her Cora for short—or Delia, Lia, Del, or even the extremely different Cory.

Cordelia also appeared in Evelyn Waugh's *Brideshead Revisited*, Margaret Atwood's *Cat's Eye*, as detective Cordelia Gray in P.D. James's mystery novels, and was promoted by a character on both *Buffy the Vampire Slayer* and its spin-off *Angel*.

And then there's that quote from the heroine of *Anne of Green Gables*: "I would love to be called Cordelia. It's such a perfectly elegant name."

Corisande

Greek, "chorus singer"

Corisande is a very unusual, haunting choice with the aura of medieval romance—it is found in early Spanish romantic tales, arriving in the English-speaking world in the nineteenth century.

"La belle Corisande" was the poetic name applied to Diane de Poitiers, the beautiful and powerful mistress of King Henry II—Henri of Navarre—of France.

Lady Corisande is the leading character in Benjamin Disraeli's 1870 novel *Lothair*, and, more recently, was heard in Annabel Davis-Goff's novel *This Cold Country*.

Cornelia

Feminine variation of Cornelius, "horn"

In ancient Rome, Cornelia was considered the paragon of womanly virtue, making it a handsome name with an excellent pedigree. It's rare today, so if you want a name no one else is using, somewhat reminiscent of Amelia and the Shakespearean Cordelia, Cornelia should be on your list. Cornelia's short forms might include Cora, Nelia, or Nell—anything but Corny.

The name of the mother of famous second-century Roman reformers, Cornelia emerged in England in the seventeenth century, probably brought in by Dutch immigrants. The painter Jan Vermeer had a daughter named Cornelia.

Cornelia has not made a mark on the U.S. popularity list since 1965—so she's more than due for reconsideration. In the meantime, it's been associated with contemporary socialite Cornelia Guest, giving the name an elite image.

Cosette

French nickname, "little thing"

Cosette is best known as the heroine of *Les Misérables*. In the Victor Hugo novel, Cosette was the nickname given to the girl named Euphrasie by her mother.

Despite the popularity of *Les Mis* the musical and movie, the name was given to only eighty-five girls in 2012. Cosette would make a sweet, if coquettish, French choice.

Cosima

Feminine variation of Cosmo, "universe"

Cosima, the kind of elegant and exotic name the British upper classes love to use for their daughters, will almost certainly come into wider use here after being chosen by two high-profile celebs in the same month—cool couple Sofia Coppola and Thomas Mars, plus supermodel Claudia Schiffer. It was used earlier by celebrity chef Nigella Lawson, while the male form, Cosimo, was given to the son of Marissa Ribisi and Beck.

The most famous Cosima in history had strong musical ties—Cosima Wagner was the daughter of composer Franz Liszt and the wife of composer Richard Wagner. Cosima is well used in Germany, Italy, and Greece.

Cressida

Greek, "gold"

Cressida is a pretty mythological and Shakespearean heroine name much better known in Britain than it is here—an imbalance the adventurous baby namer might want to correct. For although the Trojan heroine of that name in the tale told by Boccaccio, then Chaucer, then Shakespeare, didn't have the greatest reputation—she was faithless to Troilus and broke his heart—the name today sounds fresh, crisp, and creative.

In Suzanne Collins's *The Hunger Games: Mockingjay*, Cressida is a film director character; Cressida Cowell is the author of the popular novel series *How to Train Your Dragon*.

Cynthia

Greek, "woman from Kynthos"

Cynthia is an attractive name—in classical mythology an epithet for Artemis or Diana—that was so overexposed in the middle of the twentieth century, along with its nickname Cindy, that it fell into a period of benign neglect, but now is ripe for reconsideration in its full form.

A favorite of Elizabethan poets, Cynthia was first used in the English-speaking world during the Classical period, from the late sixteenth to the eighteenth century. Some

English writers used the name to denote Queen Elizabeth I as a virgin moon goddess; Ben Jonson's allegorical comedy *Cynthia's Revels* features her as the main character.

One of Elizabeth Taylor's first grownup roles was as the young lead of the 1947 film *Cynthia*, and Cynthias have popped up in a number of movies since, including *Magnolia*, *Secrets & Lies*, and *First Wives Club*—and there is a mortal named Cynthia in the *Twilight* series.

Notable namesakes include ballerina Cynthia Gregory, writer Cynthia Ozick, actress Cynthia Nixon, and designer Cynthia Rowley. Both Cyndi Lauper and Cindy Crawford were born Cynthia.

A more modern, Cindy-avoiding nickname is Thea, and an attractive Italian form is Cinzia (CHIN-zia).

D

Dagny

Scandinavian, "new day"

If you're looking for a name with Scandinavian roots, this would make a stronger and more appealing import than Dagmar. With its meaning of "new day," it could make an ideal choice for a girl born around New Year's.

Dagny Taggart is the powerful railroad executive and steel mogul heroine of the Ayn Rand novel *Atlas Shrugged*.

Dagny is also a French place name.

Dahlia

Flower name

One of the rarer flower names, used occasionally in Britain (where it's pronounced DAY-lee-a), Dahlia seems to have recovered from what was perceived as a slightly affected la-di-dah air—it has risen 466 places since 2006! The flower was named in honor of the pioneering Swedish botanist Anders Dahl, which means dale.

In the Victorian language of flowers, Dahlia denotes elegance and dignity.

In P.G. Wodehouse's "Jeeves" stories, Dahlia is Bertie Wooster's more sympathetic aunt, described as being constructed along the lines of Mae West. Reporter Dahlia Lithwick covers legal matters for the online magazine *Slate*.

Daisy

Diminutive of Margaret, "pearl"; flower name

Daisy—fresh, wholesome, and energetic—is one of the flower names that burst back into bloom after a century's hibernation. Originally a nickname for Margaret (the flower was the symbol of Santa Margherita), Daisy comes from the phrase "day's eye," because it opens its petals at daybreak.

Daisy has a colorful literary and pop culture history—as the innocent Daisy Miller in the Henry James novella, as Daisy Buchanan, the hero's object of desire in *The Great Gatsby*, and as many movie and TV characters, including the sexy barefoot blondes in *Li'l Abner* and *The Dukes of Hazzard*, as the older Daisy in *Driving Miss...*, as well as Julia Roberts's character in her breakthrough movie, *Mystic Pizza*.

Meg Ryan has a daughter named Daisy True, chef Jamie Oliver has Daisy Boo.

Damaris

Greek, "dominant woman"
In the New Testament, Damaris was an Athenian woman converted to Christianity by St. Paul. Known for her charitable work, her name was a favorite among the Puritans. Having just slid off the bottom of the Top 1000, Damaris might be deserving of more attention by parents in search of a New Testament name that is unusual but accessible, especially since girls' names ending in 's' are coming back into fashion.

Damaris is a supermodel name via Damaris Lewis; it's currently a Top 100 name in Chile.

Danica

Slavic, "morning star"
Danica is a delicate, unique, and accessible European spin on the no longer fresh Danielle and Daniela; it's another name for the planet Venus.

Danica has two noted namesakes: Danica McKellar, who played Winnie Cooper on *The Wonder Years*, and Danica Patrick, the first woman to win an Indy car race. It has been used in this country since 1977, picking up speed and peaking in 2007.

Daphne

Greek, "laurel tree"
Daphne's origins may be Greek, but it's seen by Americans as quintessentially British—as in the Daphne Moon character on *Frasier*. In the past four years, it jumped from Number 538 to 476 and on up to 420, the highest it has ever been in this country. Though we don't see it becoming a Top 100 name, Daphne is obviously finding more widespread acceptance—and for a distinctive, deeply-rooted, attractive girls' name, that's a positive thing.

In Greek mythology, Daphne was a nymph who was saved from an over-amorous Apollo by her father, a river god, who transformed her into a laurel tree. Her name was taken from that of the shrub and became part of the British vogue for plant names at the end of the nineteenth century.

Its most famous bearer is Daphne du Maurier, author of such suspense novels as *Rebecca*. Fictional Daphnes have appeared in *Some Like It Hot* (Jack Lemmon as a woman), *The Jewel in the Crown*, *Scooby-Doo*, *Harry Potter*, *Heroes*, and *Frasier*.

Deborah

Hebrew, "bee"

Deborah has suffered from the fact that, in the mid-twentieth century, there were so many Debbies on the block that the beauty and meaning of the original name got lost. Now this lovely name of an Old Testament prophetess suddenly sounds fresher than overused Sarah, Rachel, and Rebecca.

The biblical Deborah was a poet, judge, and heroic prophet who first predicted that the Israelites would win their freedom from the tyrannical Canaanites, then led a successful revolt that helped accomplish it, celebrating the victory in a famous song of triumph.

Deborah was the second most popular name in the U.S. in 1955, remaining in the Top 10 from 1950 to 1962. The streamlined version, Debra, was hot on its tail, replacing it at Number 2 a year later.

Some notable bearers have been Revolutionary War heroine Deborah Sampson Gannett, actress Deborah Kerr, modern operatic soprano Deborah Voigt, Deborah (Blondie) Harry, and Debbie (born Mary Frances) Reynolds.

The original form Devorah is another possibility.

Decima

Latin, "tenth"

In the days of huge families, this name of the Roman goddess of prophecy and childbirth—and one of the Fates—would be saved for bambina number ten. Now it might be used for a girl born in October, the tenth month.

Some other Latin numerical names you might consider: Octavia, Tertia, Una, and Prima.

Delia

Greek, "born on the island of Delos"

Delia is a somewhat neglected, seductive southern charmer that stands on its own but also might be short for Adelia or Cordelia.

Delia's name is based on that of the Greek island of Delos, which in Greek myth was the home of Apollo and Artemis, was an epithet of the moon goddess Artemis, and was later taken up by the seventeenth-century pastoral poets.

In Britain, it has been associated with the cookbook writer and broadcaster Delia Smith—in the US with novelist/screenwriter Delia Ephron, who often collaborated with her sister Nora. There have been characters named Delia on *Everwood* and *Ghost Whisperer*.

Delilah

Hebrew, "delight,"; Arabic, "to flirt"

Delilah has shed the stigma of its biblical beguiling-temptress image and is now appreciated for its haunting, melodic, feminine qualities. Checking out Delilah's popularity graph shows that Delilah's use is heading straight for the top.

There is a Camille Saint-Saens opera *Samson and Delilah*, and Welsh singer Tom Jones has been singing the praises of Delilah for decades; other musicians who have sung about her include Chuck Berry and Queen. Delilah was Whoopi Goldberg's character's name in *When Stella Got Her Groove Back*, and Lisa Rinna and Harry Hamlin have a daughter named Delilah Belle. Kimberly Stewart and Benicio del Toro also named their baby girl Delilah.

Delphine

French from Latin, "woman from Delphi"

Delphine is a sleek, chic French name with two nature associations—the dolphin and the delphinium, a bluebell-like flower, as well as to the ancient city of Delphi, which the Greeks believed to be the womb of the earth. It is definitely a fresher choice than over-the-hill Danielle.

Balzac used the name in two of his novels, and Madame de Stael wrote the 1802 epistolary *Delphine*, which helped bring the name into fashion in France. Delphine Seyrig was a renowned French movie actress.

The attractive Spanish version is Delfina.

Demetria

Variation of Demeter, goddess of fertility

Demetria is a dramatic ancient Greek earth goddess possibility with the star-studded nickname Demi. Young actress/singer/songwriter Demi Lovato was born Demetria, but contrary to common hearsay, Demi Moore was born Demi.

An even more unusual cousin name is the Cornish Demelza, made somewhat familiar via the TV series *Poldark*.

You may be surprised to know that Demetria was on the Top 1000 list from 1964 to 1993, reaching as high as 479 in 1974.

Desdemona

Greek, "ill-starred"

Desdemona is as Shakespearean as a name can be, but because the beautiful and innocent wife of Othello came to such a tragic end, her name has been avoided for centuries. At this point in time, though, there might be some adventurous parents willing to overlook that.

Jeffrey Eugenides used the name for a character in his novel *Middlesex*.

And for those seeking some celestial cred, Desdemona belongs to the Shakespearean Portia Group of satellites, which also includes Bianca, Cressida, Juliet, Portia, Rosalind, Cupid, Belinda, and Perdita.

Destry

English variation of French surname, "warhorse"

This was the male hero's last name in the classic film *Destry Rides Again*, starring James Stewart and Marlene Dietrich, but in today's anything-goes naming climate, nobody blinked when the Steven Spielbergs picked it for their daughter. We think it's a real winner.

Destry also became a short-lived 1960s TV western series, starring John Gavin, and is a French place name.

Devon

English place name

This spelling of Devon, as opposed to Devin or Devan, makes it a pretty and popular British place name, evoking the beautiful county of farmlands and dramatic seascapes and moors in southwest England. A stylish ambigender name, particularly well used in the early nineties, Devon remains an attractive option—though be aware that, at this point in time, it is used more frequently for boys.

Dharma

Sanskrit, "truth"

In Buddhism, Dharma embodies the basic principles of cosmic existence—making it a fitting name for the hippyish character on the sitcom *Dharma and Greg*, whose middle name was Freedom.

Students of Beat literature will be familiar with the name via part of the title of a Jack Kerouac novel, *Dharma Bums*.

Dharma tends to evoke the feeling of good karma.

Diana

Latin, "divine"

Diana, the tragic British princess, inspired many fashions but, strangely, not one for her name. The classic and lovely moon-goddess name Diana hovered for years around Number 100, though now it's dipped below Number 200—its lowest point since the late 1930s—but for us, Diana is a gorgeous and still-underused choice.

Diana is the Latin name for the Roman goddess associated with the moon, virginity, hunting, and protection of wild animals; she is represented in myth as both beautiful and chaste.

Two of the name's most prominent bearers today are singers Diana (born Diane) Ross and Krall. Fictional Dianas appear in *All's Well That Ends Well*, *Jane Eyre*, and *Anne of Green Gables*.

Diantha

Greek, "divine flower"

Diantha, a mythological flower of the supreme Greek god Zeus, is a melodious and more unusual cousin of Diana, heard most often in The Netherlands.

Some similar choices: Diandra and Dianthe.

Dinah

Hebrew, "God will judge"

As the song says, "Dinah, is there anyone finer?" Dinah is a charming, underused Old Testament name, long shunned for its old slave-name stereotype—Dinah was the family cook in *Uncle Tom's Cabin*-- but has a rich literary and musical resume and would make a vivid, southern-accented name for a contemporary girl.

In the Old Testament, Dinah was the beautiful daughter of Jacob and Leah; she was the heroine of the best-selling Anita Diamant novel *The Red Tent*. In the George Eliot novel *Adam Bede*, Dinah Morris is a lovely young preacher who marries the hero, and in the classic film *The Philadelphia Story*, Dinah is the heroine's sassy kid sister.

The name Dinah was adopted by two great singers: Dinah Washington (born Ruth) and Dinah Shore (born Frances).

Dixie

Latin, "I have spoken"; French, "tenth"

A saucy showgirl, wisecracking waitress kind of name, Dixie can also be considered a place name, although it won't be found on any map, being a generic term for the whole American South (coming from either the ten—dix—dollar bills used in French-speaking

New Orleans, which came to be called dixies, or else from the Mason-Dixon line). Dixie, which had been as high as Number 167 in the late 1930s, jumped back onto the popularity list in 2007.

Dixie Carter was a TV actress best known for playing Julia Sugarbaker in the sitcom *Designing Women*, and the name is also associated with the country music band Dixie Chicks.

Kings of Leon frontman Caleb Followill and wife Lily Aldridge named their daughter Dixie Pearl in 2012.

Djuna

Invented name

Novelist Djuna Barnes introduced this interesting and unusual name with an arty, Bohemian feel to the mix. She explained that it was invented by her father, saying it came about as a combination of her infant brother's pronunciation of the word moon as 'nuna' and a character in a book her father was reading, *Prince Djalma*, and so he "put the Dj onto the 'una'." Result: the silent-D pronunciation (as in Django) of JOON-a.

Fellow writer Anais Nin adopted the name for a character in her 1950 novel *The Four Chambered Heart*, and Woody Allen had a young girl called Djuna in his 1996 film *Everyone Says I Love You*—nicknamed DJ.

All in an, an exotic and intriguing possibility.

Doe

English, "a female deer"

Doe is a soft and gentle-eyed middle name possibility and, like Fawn, one of the few animal names open to girls.

The Ballad of Baby Doe is a modern American opera based on the story of Elizabeth McCourt Tabor, known as Baby Doe.

So yes, use the sweet Doe as a middle name for your daughter—just not if her first name will be Jane.

Dolly

Diminutive of Dorothy, "gift of God"

Hello, Dolly! Okay, we couldn't resist, but be warned: Most people who meet your little Dolly won't be able to either. This nickname name, rarely heard since whatever decade Dolly Parton was born, is singing a fashionable note again along with sisters Dottie and Dixie; Dolly was chosen for one of their twin girls by Rebecca Romijn and Jerry O'Connell.

Dolly was a Top 300 name around the turn of the last century. The fourth First Lady of the United States spelled her name variously as Dolly and Dolley Madison.

Dominica

Italian feminine variation of Dominic, "belonging to the Lord"

Fashionably continental and much fresher than Dominique, though it's been used since the Middle Ages. Dominica can be spelled any number of ways, from Dominika to Domenica, but we prefer this version.

Hipper cousin Domino was a Bond Girl, a character played by Keira Knightley, and the name chosen for her daughter by British designer India Hicks. Dominy is an interesting unisex spin.

Domino

Latin, "lord, master"

One of those ultimate cool-girl names, played by Keira Knightley in a movie about a supermodel-turned-bounty hunter, but kids might associate it with the game. High-profile British designer India Hicks used it for her daughter.

Dominoes date back to twelfth century China; they appeared in Italy in the eighteenth century and then spread throughout Europe. The word came from their resemblance to a kind of hood worn during the Venice carnival.

Dora

Diminutive of Theodora and Isidora, etc., "gift"

Dora is poised for a comeback, right behind Laura, Nora, Cora, and Flora. First-time parents who haven't watched cartoons in a couple of decades should be aware of the *Dora the Explorer* connection, which has its pluses and minuses.

Dora became popular during the Victorian era, largely via Dora Spenlow, the child-wife of Dickens's *David Copperfield*. Two noted real-life bearers were Dora Maar (born Henriette), a Picasso model and muse, and Dora Carrington, a British painter who was a member of the Bloomsbury Group. The name suffered a bit of a setback from being the title of the long-running comic strip, *Dumb Dora*.

While Dora can stand on its own, it can also be short for Dorothea, Dorothy, Isidora, or Theodora. Dory is a cute diminutive.

Dorothea

Greek, "gift of God"

Dorothea is a flowing and romantic Victorian-sounding name that was popular in the early decades of the twentieth century but has been off the charts since 1970. Definitely due for a revival!

Dorothea has had a long literary tradition, including as a clever, beautiful character in *Don Quixote* and the idealistic heroine of George Eliot's *Middlemarch*.

Worthy namesakes include Dorothea Dix, a Civil War nurse and nineteenth-century activist for the mentally ill, and the influential documentary photographer Dorothea Lange, known for her moving portraits taken during the Great Depression.

Appealing nickname possibilities include Dorrie, Doro, Dodie, Dot, Dottie, and Thea,

Dorothy

English variation of Greek Dorothea, "gift of God"

In the 1930s, Dorothy left Kansas and landed in the Land of Oz; by the 80s, she had become a Golden Girl, living in Miami with roommates Blanche and Rose, giving her a decidedly older image. But parents today seeking a quiet classic are bringing Dorothy back—she reentered the Top 1000 in 2011 after almost completely disappearing.

Dorothy was once one of the most popular names in the U.S.; she was in the Top 10 from 1904 to 1939, and held the Number 2 spot for eight years.

Dorothy has been used in Britain since the sixteenth century and was so common there that nickname Dolly led to the word 'doll.' Nowadays some Brits are reviving the cute nickname Dot.

There are numerous worthy Dorothy namesakes, including writers Dorothy Parker and Dorothy L. Sayers, journalist Dorothy Thomson, social activist Dorothy Day, actresses

Dorothy Gish, Dandridge, McGuire and Lamour, and figure skater/haircut icon Dorothy Hamill. Actress Faye Dunaway was born Dorothy.

Some parents now are favoring the more flowing, romantic original, Dorothea.

Dottie

Diminutive of Dorothy, "gift of God"

Dottie and Dot are old Dorothy nicknames that some cutting-edge Brits are bringing back into fashion. It's been half a century since Dottie ranked on its own in this country, one of those nickname names that flourished in the 1890s.

Probably the most prominent bearer of the name was the seminal country music singer Dottie West—born Dorothy, of course. In the movie *A League of Their Own*, Geena Davis's leading character Dottie Hinson was based on real life women's pro baseball player Dottie Kamenshek.

Dot can make an adorable middle name—if your last name isn't Com.

Dove

Nature name, "dove, a bird"
One of the new bird names, like Lark and Wren, this one's associated with the billing and cooing sounds of love. Soft and gentle, Dove also has the admirable association with peace.

Dove was actually an early bird, used as a first name in the seventeenth century and included in the U.S. Top 1000 through the 1890s.

One admirable surname association is with Rita Dove, the Pulitzer Prize winning poet and former United States Poet Laureate.

Dree

Diminutive of Andrea, feminine form of Andrew, "strong and manly"
This unique one-syllable name was added to the mix by Mariel Hemingway for her now grown model/actress daughter; it could make a distinctive middle name or Bree substitute.

Drew

Diminutive of Andrew, "strong and manly"
Drew is an elegant formerly male-only alternative to Andy that joined the stylishly upscale Paige-Brooke-Blair sorority, thanks largely to Drew Barrymore. Barrymore comes by her first name legitimately: it was the maiden name of her paternal great-grandmother, Georgiana 'Georgie' Drew Barrymore, one of many esteemed actors in her family history.

Jessica Simpson used Drew as the middle name of her daughter Maxwell.

Drusilla

Latin, "strong"
Drusilla is an ancient Roman name, (probably) borne by descendants of Antony and Cleopatra, and is one of the 'illa' names that are ready for revival, especially with its cute short form Dru.

Drusilla appears in the New Testament as the wife of Felix (twin alert?), and later made appearances in Thomas Hardy's *Jude the Obscure*, Wilkie Collins's *The Moonstone* and Faulkner's *The Unvanquished*. Drusilla is a vampire in *Buffy the Vampire Slayer* and *Angel* and was a long-running character on the soap *The Young and the Restless*.

An alternate spelling is Drucilla.

Dulcie

Diminutive of Dulcibella, "sweet"

A sweet-meaning and sounding name dating back to the Roman Empire and later found in the antebellum South, Dulcie has, in the modern era, been heard most often in Australia.

In Agatha Christie's mystery *Murder on the Links*, there are twin sisters named Dulcie and Bella, who were a vaudeville duo known as "The Dulcibella Kids." In *Don Quixote*, the hero's love is Dulcinea.

Dune

English word name

Dune is a haunting and evocative sandy-beach name, which also has sci-fi connections. *Dune* is a science fiction franchise that was launched by Frank Herbert's 1965 novel. Some interesting *Dune* character names include Alia, Leto, Siona, Bellonda, and Tamalane.

An alternate spelling is Doon, created by photographer Diane Arbus for her daughter; it came to her as she walked along the beach.

E

Easter

English from German goddess name Eostre

Easter has been used as a name for several hundred years as part of the day-naming tradition; now, this rarely heard holiday celebration name would make a novel choice for a springtime baby. Backstory: The early Anglo-Saxon monk and scholar Bede took the name of a goddess—Eostre—whose feast was celebrated at the vernal equinox and gave it to the Christian festival of the resurrection of Christ.

Easter appeared on the Top 1000 list during the first few decades of the twentieth century. It was heard for the character played by Jasmine Guy in the TV miniseries *Queen*.

International versions include Pascal, Pasqua, and Pascua.

Easton

English, "east-facing place"

Easton is a stylish, Waspy-sounding surname that's climbing up the popularity charts. TV actress Elisabeth Rohm named her daughter Easton August Anthony, which seemed like a real gender bender, and now Rachel Leigh Cook has made it the middle name of her baby Charlotte. Note that Easton is just outside the Top 100 for boys—for whom directional names are a real trend—but we won't be surprised to see more and more little lady Eastons arriving.

Echo

Greek mythology name

Echo, the pretty, resonant name of a legendary nymph, was the heroine of Joss Whedon's sci-fi series *Dollhouse*. Nick Hexum, of the band 311, named his daughter Echo Love.

In the Greek myth, Echo was a nymph whose unrequited love for Narcissus caused her to fade away until all that was left was the sound of her voice. Obviously, a name with a lot of reverberations.

Eden

Hebrew, "place of pleasure, delight"

Eden is an attractive, serene name with obvious intimations of Paradise, one of several place names drawn from the Bible by the Puritans in the seventeenth century.

Eden entered the Top 1000 in 1989 and got a real bump in visibility when *Desperate Housewives'* Marcia Cross used it for one of her twin girls. It is now at Number 164 and even higher in France and Australia.

There have been Edens on the old soap opera *Santa Barbara* and the shows *Heroes* and *Extras*.

Pronounced ED-en, Eden is also a Hebrew name for boys.

Edie

Diminutive of Edith, "prosperous in war"

Edie is part of the Evie-Ellie et al family of cute and friendly short forms that sometimes stand on its own. Briefly popular in the 1960s, it could well be due for rediscovery.

Several Ediths have chosen to be known by this pet form, including socialite and Andy Warhol superstar Edie Sedgwick, actress Edie Falco, singer Edie Brickell and the Jacqueline Bouvier Kennedy relatives called Big and Little Edie in the iconic documentary *Grey Gardens*. Edie Britt was the character portrayed by Nicolette Sheridan in *Desperate Housewives*.

British actress Samantha Morton chose Edie for her daughter.

Edith

English, "prosperous in war"

Edith was a hugely popular name a hundred years ago that's being revived among stylish parents in London—and is beginning to gain traction here among those with a taste for old-fashioned names with a soft but strong image.

The name of two American First Ladies, Mrs Theodore Roosevelt and Mrs Woodrow Wilson, as well as that of the wife of William the Conqueror, Edith is one of the oldest surviving Anglo-Saxon names. Widely used in nineteenth-century novels, Edith was chosen by Louisa May Alcott for the heroine of her first novel, *The Inheritance*, written when she was seventeen.

Edith Wharton makes a fine literary namesake, with other noted bearers including poet Edith Sitwell, iconic Hollywood movie designer Edith Head and, for francophiles, there is the reference to Edith Piaf. With the rise of so many other E-starting names from Ella to Evelyn and the adorable short form Edie, we predict that Edith will soon sound more like a cute toddler than a dated granny, especially with the emergence of one of the most interesting characters on *Downton Abbey*, Lady Edith Crawley.

Edwina

Feminine variation of Edwin, "wealthy friend"
Edwina may still be taking tea in the parlor, but we can see her joining friends like Matilda and Josephine for a comeback, especially if pronounced like Edwin rather than Edween.

She had a very non-vintage-mauve image in the Coen brothers' cult favorite, *Raising Arizona*, in which Holly Hunter played a police officer named Edwina who was usually called Ed.

Edwina was on the Social Security list every year through 1969, reaching a high of 378 in 1943.

Eleanor

English variation of French Provencal Alienor, meaning unknown
Eleanor, a stately name that has been in and out of fashion since Queen Eleanor of Aquitaine brought it from France to England in the twelfth century, is hot again. Eleanor's straightforward feminine image, combined with its royal medieval origins, is striking just the right note for parents in search of a girl's name that combines substance and style.

While some think Eleanor is a variation of Helen via Ellen, it actually derives from the Provencal for "other Aenor," used to distinguish the original Eleanor, who was named after her mother Aenor.

Big plus: Eleanor is a serious name, with two nicknames—Ellie and Nell/Nellie—that are seriously endearing. Diane Lane has an Eleanor, and Katie Couric an Elinor, using the variant spelling. (Jane Austen used both versions—Eleanor in *Northanger Abbey* and Elinor in *Sense and Sensibility*.)

A notable namesake is First Lady Eleanor Roosevelt. Two other English queens bore the name: the wives of Henry III and Edward I.

Eleanora and Leonora are pretty, more feminine variations. Ellen and Lenore are shorter forms.

Elena

Spanish variation of Helen, "bright, shining one"

Elena, the pan-European version of Helen, has never been as popular in the U.S. as it is now—ranking at Number 139—due to the overall popularity of 'E' names and to Elena's accessibility as what we might call 'exotic lite.' It is also ranking in other countries as well—it is a Top 25 name right now in Austria, Italy, and Spain.

A worthy namesake is Elena Kagan, Associate Justice of the Supreme Court, the fourth female to hold that position. A fictional bearer is Elena Gilbert, protagonist of *The Vampire Diaries* and Elena Lincoln is a character in *Fifty Shades of Grey*.

Eliana

Hebrew, "my God has answered"

Eliana is a lilting, rhythmic choice, which has begun to catch on here along with many other El-starting names; it is now in the Top 150 and rising. One celebrity who chose it for his daughter is Christian Slater.

A widely multi-cultural choice, Eliana is heard in Israel, Spain, Portugal, Russia, and Italy. The pretty French version is Eliane.

Elise

French variation of Elizabeth, "pledged to God"

Elise is on an upward trend, due in large part to its dash of French flair, and to the love for El- names in general. It is now at its highest ranking ever—151—in the U.S. and is riding a wave in several European countries as well; it's a Top 10 name in Belgium, for example, and well used in Norway and the Netherlands.

Elise was introduced into the English-speaking world in the late nineteenth century. Emily Blunt played a character named Elise in *The Adjustment Bureau*.

Fur Elise is one of Beethoven's most popular piano pieces. Piers Morgan named his daughter Elise.

Eliza

Diminutive of Elizabeth, "pledged to God"

Eliza is one of our favorite names; we love its combination of streamlined modernity and Eliza Doolittle charm and spunk, and offer Eliza as one of our top recommendations.

That said, a lot of other parents like Eliza, too; it has been inching up the popularity lists—plus it's one of the most-searched girls' names on Nameberry.

Eliza could theoretically take the place of Elizabeth, cousin name Isabella, and the last generation's Lisa at the top of the charts, also bearing a similarity to trendy sisters Ella and Lila. Still, it's got a good measure of eighteenth-century backbone and tradition along with its contemporary zip.

Pride and Prejudice's Elizabeth Bennet was often called Eliza; in Harriet Beecher Stowe's *Uncle Tom's Cabin*, Eliza is the intelligent and courageous slave protagonist.

My Fair Lady's spirited Eliza Doolittle is the classic musical character based on the Shaw play *Pygmalion*, who is transformed from cockney flower girl to elegant lady, played on stage by Julie Andrews and on screen by Audrey Hepburn.

Eliza Dushku is a charter member of the Joss Whedon rep company of actors, appearing in *Buffy the Vampire Slayer*, *Angel*, *Dollhouse*, and *Much Ado About Nothing*.

One note: Do not name sisters Eliza and Isabel or Isabella, as they're different forms of mother name Elizabeth.

Elizabella

Combination of Eliza and Bella
Elizabella is a much more obscure smoosh than sisters Isabella and Annabelle, but the mega popularity of Isabella may give this unusual combo name a boost.

Elizabeth

Hebrew, "pledged to God"
Elizabeth, one of the premiere classic girls' names, is just inside the Top 10, even though there are actually fewer babies getting the name these days. Elizabeth has so much going for it—rich history, broad appeal, and timeless style—that no matter how many little girls there are named Lizzie, Eliza, and Beth out there, you can still make Elizabeth your own.

Elizabeth nicknames on the table today include Libby, Bess, Tibby, and even the so-antiquated-it's-cool Betty. Also in play is the fashionable Eliza. There has been only one year throughout all of recorded baby-naming history, since 1880, that Elizabeth slipped one place below the Top 25, and that was in 1945—when Betty was Number 11.

In the Bible, Elizabeth was the mother of John the Baptist, and two of England's most notable queens have been Elizabeth I and II. Another memorable bearer was Elizabeth Taylor—who hated to be called Liz.

The Elisabeth spelling, found in several cultures, is represented by such notables as Elisabeth Kubler-Ross, Elisabeth Shue, Elisabeth Moss, and Elisabeth Hasselbeck. Elisabeth is nicknamed Bethsy in *Buddenbrooks*, Bep in *The Diary of Anne Frank,* and Betsy in *Wolverine*.

Ella

English from German, "all"; shortening of names ending in 'ella'

Following in the path of Emma and Isabella/Bella, Ella has been shooting up the charts since the millennium: it rose from Number 265 in 2000 to a high of Number 12 this past year.

Ella has long been a fave of the glitterati—including the John Travoltas, the Warren Beattys, Ben Stiller, Eric Clapton, Jeff Gordon, Ioan Gruffudd, Alex Rodriguez, and Mark Wahlberg.

Iconic singer Ella Fitzgerald adds a jazzy edge. One other appeal of Ella—it sounds both vintage and modern at the same time. Although it hadn't been used much for a few generations and so sounds fresh, there are an awful lot of little girls named Ella running around—along with those called Ellie and Bella. So while it has much to recommend it, don't say we didn't warn you about *Ella Enchanted*'s popularity.

And that popularity isn't limited to the U.S.: Ella is Number 4 in Sweden and Number 6 in Australia.

Elle

French, "she"

Add the charming heroine of the movie *Legally Blonde* to a supermodel (Elle Macpherson) and to the trend toward all names El-like—Ellie, Ella, Eleanor—and you have one hit name. In 2012, it rose from Number 413 to 383.

Elle Driver is the Darryl Hannah character in *Kill Bill*, Elle Bishop was Kirsten Bell's in *Heroes,* and Elle Fanning (born Mary, sister of Dakota), is a rising young actress.

Ellery

English, "island with elder trees"

In the past few years Ellery has gone from middle-aged male detective to a plausible girls' name, à la Hillary.

Ellie

Diminutive of Eleanor and Ellen, "bright shining one"

Ellie is one of the most popular girls' names in the U.K.—yes, in this nickname form, and this warm and friendly name is also taking off here. In 2011, Ellie entered the Top 100 for the first time.

Ellie has been making many media appearances—she's been seen in the animated film *Up*, on *The West Wing*, and even as a woolly mammoth in the film *Ice Age: The Meltdown*.

One caveat, if you are considering Ellie: Along with all the girls named Ellie and longer forms such as Eleanor and Ella, there are going to be an awful lot of Ellies around in coming years.

Elliot

Anglicization of Elijah or Elias, "the Lord is my God"

Elliot is one more traditional boy's name lured into the girls' camp, this particular raid led by political commentator George Stephanopoulos and his actress wife Ali Wentworth. Variously spelled Eliot, Elliot, Elliott, and Elliotte (used by Marla Sokoloff), its star is definitely on the rise for girls, as well as for boys. Bonus for girls is cute and feminine nickname, Ellie.

Elliot developed in the Middle Ages as a pet form of Elias.

Dr. Elliot Reid was a female character on *Scrubs*.

Ellis

Welsh, "benevolent"

Ellis, a surname used sparingly as a first in the Wallace/Morris period, sounds new now for girls, as an ambisexual alternative to Ella. Ellis Bell was the name chosen by Emily Brontë as her male pseudonym, and Ellis Grey was the mother of Dr. Meredith Grey on *Grey's Anatomy*.

Elodie

French, "marsh flower"; German, "foreign riches"

The lyrical and melodious Elodie, a budding Nameberry favorite, is an overlooked medieval saint's name that could be a more sophisticated tribute to an Aunt Melody.

Élodie (accent over the first E) is a major character in the Émile Zola novel *The Earth*. Princess Elodie is the protagonist of the video game *Long Live The Queen*.

Elodie is currently enjoying popularity in her native France and in England and Wales—in the Top 300 in both.

Eloise

French and English variation of Heloise, probably of German origin, "healthy; wide"
Eloise will be to some forever the imperious little girl making mischief at the Plaza Hotel, while the original version Heloise recalls the beautiful and learned wife of the French philosopher Peter Abelard, admired for her fidelity and piety.

Along with many other names with the El- beginning and featuring the 'l' sound in any place, Eloise is newly chic. Eloise jumped back onto the popularity list at Number 913 in 2009, and then bounded up this year to Number 364, possibly thanks in part to the Eloise Hawking character on the popular TV series *Lost*. Eloise was the name of Jennifer Aniston's character in *Love Happens*. Denise Richards named one of her daughters Eloise. Eloise is currently at Top 100 name in France, Belgium and Australia.

Eloise nicknames might include Ellie, Lolly, or Lola. Eloisa is an Italian alternative, adding some vintage charm.

Elsa

German diminutive of Elisabeth, "pledged to God"
Lost in limbo for decades and decades, Elsa now stands a good chance of following along in the progression from Emma to Ella to Etta, having just about lost her German accent.

Elsa came into English-speaking use in the nineteenth century, boosted by Wagner's operatic bride in *Lohengrin*—the first to walk down the aisle to the famous wedding march. For a while, Elsa took on a leonine image via the lioness in the popular book and movie *Born Free*, but that's all but forgotten. Elsa has lots of varied and interesting human namesakes, including designer Schiaparelli, writer Morante, and *Bride of Frankenstein* Lanchester (born Elizabeth).

Elsie

Diminutive of Elizabeth via its Scottish variation Elspeth, "pledged to God"
Not so long ago, Elsie might have been on a list of Names Least Likely to Succeed—but look at her now! She entered the U.K. Top 100 last year at Number 87, and in the U.S., she's now in the Top 500, having returned to the list in 2005 after a thirty-year hiatus.

Elsie was a popular name at the end of the nineteenth century until its image was damaged in this country by the association with Elsie the Borden cow. But it's rising now on the heels of Ella and Ellie, suddenly sounding fresh and frisky. Singer James Morrison picked it for his baby girl and Ioan Gruffudd has an adorably named little Elsie Marigold. Another youthful bearer is actress Elsie Kate Fisher, the voice of Agnes in *Despicable Me*.

Elspeth

Scottish variation of Elizabeth, "pledged to God"

Elspeth is one of those names that never quite made it out of the British Isles—particularly Scotland, but possesses a winningly childlike charm. Elspeth was used by Sir Walter Scott for several of his female characters.

Elspeth Huxley was a prolific Kenyan-born U.K. writer, best known for the autobiographical *The Flame Trees of Thika*—she was connected by marriage to the illustrous Huxley family.

A close cousin is Elsbeth, as in the recurring character Elsbeth Tascioni on *The Good Wife*. Embeth is a more distant relation.

Eluned

Welsh, "idol, image"

Exotic and mysterious, Eluned's beauty and intelligence were legendary in Welsh legend; she was the handmaiden of the Lady of the Fountain in a Welsh Arthurian romance, who had a magic ring that made the wearer invisible.

The name is also seen as Luned, and is the source of Lynette, in Tennyson's *Gareth and Lynette*.

Embeth

Combination of Emma and Beth

South African-raised actress Embeth Davidtz added this unique smoosh name to the stockpot of names. A perfect solution if you can't decide between Emma and Elizabeth, and much more unusual than Annabeth.

Emerald

Gem name

Emerald is the intriguing color and jewel name of the deep green stone treasured as far back as in ancient Egypt—it's supposed to open one's heart to wisdom and to love and be good for strengthening relationships—which could make for an interesting, unusual name, particularly with the popularity of so many Em-starting names.

Emerald is the birthstone of May, making it extra appropriate for a girl born in that month. Some pleasant associations: the Emerald Isle and the Emerald City.

Esmeralda is the more exotic Spanish version.

Emerson

German, "son of Emery"

The combination of Emily and Emma's popularity—and the fact that *Desperate Housewives* star Teri Hatcher's daughter is named Emerson—have put this formerly strictly male name, embodying the gravitas of Ralph Waldo Emerson, in the limelight for girls.

Shonda Rhimes, creator/producer/writer/director of *Grey's Anatomy*, has a daughter named Emerson Pearl.

Emilia

Latin feminine variation of Emil, "rival"

Emilia, the lovely feminine form of the Roman clan name Aemilius, is rising as an Emily/Amelia alternative, now at Number 268. Its one problem is that it sounds like, and is often seen as, interchangeable with Amelia, which has a different root and meaning.

Emilia also has Shakespearean appeal as the wife of Iago and confidante of Desdemona in *Othello*. In modern pop culture, Emilia is the name of the main character in *The Princess Diaries*.

Emilia is currently enjoying high popularity across some diverse cultures—it's Number 13 in Scotland, Number 16 in Chile, and Number 20 in Austria.

Emily

Feminine variation of Emil, "rival"

Emily may have dropped somewhat in the current standings, but it was the most popular name for over a decade because it appeals as a girls' name on so many levels: Emily is feminine, classic, simple, pretty, and strong. But, at this point, Emily's waaaaaaay overused, though it does have those nice literary namesakes, like Emily Dickinson and Emily Bronte.

Parents who, a decade ago, might have chosen Emily have moved on to Emma, which briefly captured the Number 1 crown, and now are looking at such alternatives as Amelia and Emmeline. But those girls' names, like Emma, may soon feel overused too.

Popularity issues aside, Emily is a wonderful name: simple, musical, classic, feminine, easy to understand and to like. If you have a complicated last name or you want a name that's accessible on every level, Emily may be your girl.

Modern Emilys in the spotlight include a number of the hottest young actresses—Emily Blunt, Emily Mortimer, Emily Deschanel—and even Emma Watson was christened Emily.

Emma

German, "universal"

Emma is the Number 2 name—up from Number 3 last year and the year before—having done handsprings up the popularity charts thanks to a legion of Emma heroines, from Bovary to Goldman to Jane Austen's protagonist. So parents who have turned from Emily to Emma seeking something more distinctive will have to keep looking.

The name was given a big boost when it was given to Rachel and Ross's baby on *Friends* in 2002.

That's not to say that Emma isn't a wonderful name for your baby girl. It's simple but has deep history, is streamlined and modern-feeling yet distinctly feminine. It's hard to find all those qualities combined in one name, which is exactly why so many parents (over seventeen thousand last year) have chosen Emma.

Parents who love Emma but think it's overexposed have been moving to such alternatives as Amelia and Emilia, Amelie, Emmeline, and Ella. But keep in mind that those are poised to move up and take Emma's place near the top of the list.

A very old royal name well used throughout the centuries (Queen Emma married King Ethelred the Unready in 1002), Emma is also historically associated with Lady Hamilton, the mistress of Lord Nelson and muse of painter George Romney.

It's worth noting that Emma, Emily, and the new British Number 1 Amelia all derive from different roots and have different meanings. But they continue to feel like very similar names.

Three of the top young female stars share the name: Emma Watson, Emma Roberts, and Emma (born Emily) Stone.

Emmeline

French form of German Amelina, "work"

Emmeline, also spelled with one 'm,' is an Emma relative and Emily cousin that is destined for greater use in the wake of the mega popularity of those two names. A highly recommended Nameberry fave.

A popular medieval name, Emmeline was introduced to Britain by the Normans. It appeared as a character in *Uncle Tom's Cabin* and is famous in Britain as the name of the illustrious suffragette, Emmeline Pankhurst. Way back in 1980, it was the name of young Brooke Shield's innocent character in *The Blue Lagoon*. More recently, Emmeline Vance was a witch in the *Harry Potter* series.

Christian Bale has a daughter named Emmeline.

Enid

Welsh, "life, spirit"
This Celtic goddess and Arthurian name may sound terminally old-ladyish to many ears—but so did names like Ella and Etta not so long ago. So Enid is yet another forgotten four-letter E-possibility; she's has been M.I.A since 1954.

You might not know it to look at her, but Enid is Welsh, from the word meaning 'life' or 'soul.' Back in the Age of Chivalry, to call a woman 'a second Enid' was the greatest of compliments, as she was a legendary romantic figure, revived in Tennyson's *Idyll of the Kings*. In more modern times, Enid is the title of a Bare Naked Ladies song and a quirky character in the quirky film *Ghost World*.

Esme

French, "esteemed, beloved"
Esmé is a sophisticated, distinctive, and charming J. D. Salinger name, from his classic 1950 story *For Esmé, With Love and Squalor*. Related to the concept of esteem and the French Aimee, which means beloved, it was originally a male name exported from France to Scotland via a member of the royal family.

A current favorite among celebs, including Samantha Morton, Michael J. Fox, and Katey Sagal, Esmé got a lot of publicity via the character Esme Cullen, the vampire matriarch of the Olympic Coven in the *Twilight* Saga.

The final accent indicates the pronunciation of ez-may, though in English you can just spell it Esme.

Esmeralda

Spanish, "emerald"
This Spanish version of the jewel-like Emerald has long been popular with Hispanic parents, and has now climbed to Number 358 on the U.S. list, where it first appeared in 1951.

In the 1831 Victor Hugo novel *Notre-Dame of Paris*, aka *The Hunchback of Notre Dame*, the Gypsy heroine was born Agnes, but called La Esmeralda in reference to the jewel she wears around her neck. The name Esmeralda got increased visibility via the Disney version of the story.

Esperanza

Spanish, "hope, expectation"

Esperanza is a Spanish classic finding its way onto the national popularity list. It came into the spotlight not long ago when jazz singer Esperanza Spalding "stole" the Best New Artist Grammy from favorite Justin Bieber. It's also the name of the main character in the novel *The House on Mango Street* by Sandra Cisneros, about a young Latina growing up in Chicago.

Estella

Latinate form of Estelle, "star"

Estella is a pretty Latin name that's sounding more and more stylish, remembered as the ward of Miss Havisham in Dickens's *Great Expectations*. Though Estella ranked as high as Number 110 in the 1880s, it has been completely off the radar for more than 35 years and so would be well worth considering as an alternative to the popular Stella (now Number 73) or as a namesake for Great Aunt Estelle.

Ali Landry used the Estela spelling for her daughter's name. Estrella is another possibility.

Estelle

French, "star"

Maybe it's because she shares that winning 'elle' sound with Isabel and Bella but Estelle is no longer seen as a muumuu-wearing canasta player of a certain age (think George Costanza's mother on *Seinfeld*) but has become one of the fastest-rising names on Nameberry. Could be in part thanks to the young Royal Couple of Sweden, who chose it for their firstborn daughter, or the single-named British R&B singer.

Latin version Estella, introduced in *Great Expectations*, also has energy and charm, while Estrella is another stylish member of this star-related club. Este and Estee are also in the wind.

After a half-century absence, Estelle has just reappeared on the U.S. Top 1000.

Esther

Persian, "star"

One of the major female figures in the Old Testament, quiet, studious Esther was in the Top 50 a hundred years ago and stayed in the Top 100 until 1935. It is now on the ascent again, appealing to parents—Ewan McGregor is one—seeking an underused biblical name with a strong history and serious image.

In the Bible, Esther, originally named Hadassah, was the captured Jewish wife of the King of Persia who risked her life to save her exiled people from annihilation, a story celebrated by Jews on the holiday of Purim, so that it has traditionally been given to girls around that time.

Judy Garland played two memorable Esthers—in *Meet Me in St. Louis* and *A Star is Born*; Esther Summerson is a main character in Dickens' *Bleak House*, and Esther Greenwood is the autobiographical character's name in Sylvia Plath's *A Bell Jar*. Someone who glamorized the name is champion swimmer-turned-movie-star Esther Williams.

Madonna adopted Esther as her Kaballah name.

Ethel

English, "noble maiden"

Ethel is a name we once declared as "So Far Out They'll Probably Always Be Out," but with the return of other names on that list and with its new starbaby cred via Lily Allen, its soft sound and admirable meaning, we're not so sure.

At the turn of the last century, when Ethel Barrymore was the belle of Broadway, her first name was wildly popular, a Top 10 name for sixteen years and in the Top 100 until 1939. Other well-known bearers have been musical stars Ethel Merman and Ethel Waters and Robert Kennedy's widow. Not so distinguished: Ethel Mertz on *I Love Lucy*.

Ethel fell away from such Old English appellations as Ethelberta, Ethelreda, and Ethelinda. Now THOSE, we think we can safely say, are so far out they'll always be out.

Etta

Diminutive of Henrietta, feminine form of Henry, "estate ruler"

Etta, once a short form of Henrietta, has long been used on its own, and we wonder if it could follow the progression of Emma to Ella to...Etta.

Etta has taken the first step, having recently been picked by a celeb, Carson Daly, who was said to have been inspired by the late great soul singer Etta James, just as previous parents were similarly influenced by Ella Fitzgerald. Etta was born as a shortening of names with that ending—in fact Etta James's birth certificate name was Jamesetta.

Etta was a Top 100 name in the last decades of the 1800s, then slid down until it fell off the list completely in 1966. But with its delicate sound that also has a bit of crackle, and its new starbaby status, we can see this as a likely successor to the currently favored 'E' names. Henrietta "Etta" Bishop was a character on the TV show *Fringe*.

Eudora

Greek, "generous gift"
Eudora is the name of five minor goddesses of Greek mythology and a major goddess (in the person of Pulitzer Prize-winning Eudora Welty) of modern American literature. Eudora is pleasant and euphonious and a possibility for rejuvenation.

In Greek myth, Eudora was one of the Hyades, a set of sisters transformed into the star cluster that bears their name.

In Disney's *The Princess and the Frog*, Eudora was the name of Princess Tiana's mother, who was voiced by Oprah Winfrey, and of Mia Farrow's character in *Zelig*.

Eugenia

Feminine variation of Eugene, "wellborn"
Eugenia, a name scarcely used at all since the 1980s, is another that flourished a century ago and could be due for a revival.

Eugenia has some interesting literary references, including the fascinating Baroness Eugenie Munster in Henry James's *The Europeans* and Eugenia Alabaster, a leading character in A. S. Byatt's *Angels and Insects*, and it was also the birth name of Skeeter in the book and film *The Help*.

The third-century St. Eugenia, an early Roman Christian martyr, is remembered for disguising herself as a man to escape persecution.

Music lovers will be familiar with the name of renowned flute virtuoso Eugenia Zukerman.

Eugenie

Greek, "wellborn"
Eugenie enjoyed a major dusting off when Fergie and Prince Andrew chose it for their daughter, restoring a patina of royal sheen it hadn't had since the time of Napoleon III's

glamorous empress—who spent much of her life in England. It was also borne by Princess Victoria Eugenie of Battenberg, a granddaughter of Queen Victoria, after whom Prince Andrew's younger daughter was named.

Eugenie is the title character of a Balzac novel, *Eugenie Grandet* and also the full name of Scarlet and Rhett's daughter, nicknamed Bonnie Blue because of the color of her eyes, in *Gone with the Wind*.

The elegant Eugenie is pronounced yoo-zhay-nee, versus yoo-jeen-ya for Eugenia.

Eulalia

Greek, "sweet speaking"
Eulalia is a melodious name with a southern drawl, thanks to those lilting double 'l's.

A teenage martyr, Saint Eulalia was born in Spain and is a patron saint of Barcelona, where there is a cathedral in her name. One legend associated with Eulalia is that a dove flew out of her neck when she was killed, thus the association with both sweet speech and peace.

Eulalia is a character in William Faulkner's *Absalom, Absalom*; Marcia Gay Hardin has a daughter named Eulalia Grace.

Eula is the traditional short form, but Lalia or Lally would make more appealing and modern-sounding nicknames. The French version is Eulalie (subject of a Poe poem); in Spanish, it's Olalla.

Eurydice

Greek, "wide justice"
Despite (or because of) her tragic story in Greek myth—Eurydice was poisoned by a snake and condemned to the underworld, where her husband, musician Orpheus, tried and failed to bring her back—she has provided creative inspiration in the arts, namely as the subject of operas by Monteverdi, Haydn, and Gluck, in an eponymous play by Jean Anouilh, and the myth was the inspiration for Tennessee William's drama *Orpheus Descending*. Paintings by Titian, Rubens, and Poussin also focus on Eurydice.

In pop culture, it turns out that in the U.K., TV cult favorite *Absolutely Fabulous*, the outrageous Patsy's full name is Eurydice Colette Clytemnestra Dido Bathsheba Rabelais Patricia Cocteau Stone. Who knew?

Is all this too much for a modern little girl to carry? Quite possibly, though weighty four-syllable Greek myth names like Persephone have recently come under consideration.

Eva

Latin form of Eve, "life"

Eva is a simple, classic name, but be warned: There are suddenly a lot of little girls named Eva (and Ava and Eve) around, perhaps inspired by Eva Longoria—Eva has been a Top 100 name since 2009. Pronunciation can be ee-va, eh-va, or ay-va.

The 1852 publication of *Uncle Tom's Cabin*, the bestselling novel of the nineteenth century, whose tragic figure Little Eva (short for Evangeline) made an enormous impression on the Victorian reading public, propelled the name to popularity.

Some well-known Evas include actresses Evas Marie Saint, Gabor, Green, Longoria, and Mendes, sculptor Eva Hesse, singer Little Eva, and model Eva Herzigová.

The diminutive Evita is still strongly associated with Evita Peron, wife of the Argentine President Juan Peron.

Evangeline

Greek, "bearer of good news"

Evangeline is a romantic old name enjoying a major comeback, thanks to its religious overtones, Eva's popularity, and the hot star of the TV megahit *Lost*, Evangeline Lilly. Evangelica and Evangelina—two variants of Evangeline—are sure to tag along for the ride. This year, Evangeline is just within the Top 300 at Number 292.

Evangeline was introduced to the English-speaking world by Longfellow in his hugely popular eponymous narrative poem, and can also be found in *Uncle Tom's Cabin* (it was Little Eva's full name), as well as two novels by Evelyn Waugh. More recently, there were Evangelines in the films *Nanny McPhee* and Disney's *The Princess and the Frog*.

Eve

Hebrew, "life"

Eve, the oldest name in the Book, is now coming back into style, having the virtues of simplicity and purity, yet with more strength and resonance than other single-syllable names like Ann. British actor Clive Owen chose Eve for his daughter, as did Jessica Capshaw.

While Eve is compromised by its similarity to trendy sisters Ava, Eva, Avery, Evelyn, Evie, ad infinitum, it still has them all beat with its streamlined classic style.

The rapper born Eve Jihan Jeffers goes by the monratum Eve.

The rapper born Eve Jihan Jeffers goes by the mononym Eve.

Fictional Eves have figured prominently in the films *All About Eve*, *Three Faces of Eve*, and *WALL-E*, and on TV in *Angel* and *Xena: Warrior Princess*.

Evelyn

Variation of Avelina, "wished for child"

Evelyn, a soft and feminine name hugely popular a hundred years ago (it was Number 12 in the 1910s), is returning to favor in a big way now. We predict that in the next decade Evelyn will achieve its former heights, joining a legion of contemporary little Evas, Avas, Eves, Evies, and Evelines. In 2009, Evelyn rose fifteen15 places to breach the Top 40—for the first time since 1939!—and in 2011 leaped even further to Number 24. It now sits at the still-high Number 27.

While Evelyn is a lovely name, its problem is its similarity to so many other stylish names these days, so your little Evelyn will seem less distinctive given how many other popular names there are that start with Ev- or Av-, from Eva to Avery, and end with -lyn: Brooklyn, Caitlin, et al.

Originally a masculine name, its most famous bearer is writer Evelyn Waugh. (Trivia note: Evelyn Waugh was married to a woman named Evelyn, and they were known as "He-Evelyn" and "She-Evelyn") Its quiet persona was reversed with the character Evelyn Salt, played by Angelina Jolie.

Ever

Word name

Ever is a name we first heard via the now grown-up Ever Carradine, daughter of Robert. It's a truly unusual and simple name with an evocative meaning. Milla Jovovich and Paul Anderson chose it for their daughter.

Ever has ties to (primarily male) names in the Scandinavian and Hebrew cultures.

The psychic protagonist of Alyson Noel's YA fantasy novel *Evermore* is named Ever Bloom.

Evie

Diminutive of Eve or Eva, "life"

In the land of the nickname name, otherwise known as the U.K., where diminutives like Freddie, Millie, Maisie, Alfie, and Ollie are all the rage, Evie has been in and around the Top 10 for several years now. In the U.S., she entered the popularity ranks in 2007 for the first time since 1941, appreciated for its energy and spunk.

Natalie Portman played an Evie in *V for Vendetta* and Rachel Weiss bore it in *The Mummy*.

Evie, of course, can also be used as a nickname for Eve, Eva, Evelyn, Evangeline, etc.

F

Fable

Word name

Fable, like Story, is a word name with real potential, combining enchanted tale-telling with a moral edge. And sound-wise, it would fit right in with the likes of Abel and Mabel.

Faith

Virtue name

Faith is one of the most straightforward of the virtue names, popularized by the Puritans in the seventeenth century, many parents still choosing it as an indicator of their religious conviction. And Faith is rising in popularity—she's been in the Top 100 for all of the twenty-first century, peaking in 2002 at Number 48. In addition, Faith and Hope was the fourth most popular pairing for twin girls born in 2011.

Nicole Kidman and Keith Urban are the parents of a daughter they called Faith, little sister for Sunday—a sibset suitable for a minister's brood. A prominent adult bearer is country singer Faith Hill.

Farah

Arabic, "happiness"

Farah is a soft and lovely Arabic name, best known here in this original spelling via the last Empress of Iran, Farah Palavi. It's currently a Top 250 name in France and in the Netherlands, which both have large Arabic-speaking populations, and appears in at least two video games.

The variant spelling Farrah had a brief moment of popularity when Farrah Fawcett burst onto the scene in *Charlie's Angels* in 1976: her name shot up to Number 177 the following year, and after many years off the charts, it's back at Number 544 thanks to a Teen Mom named Farrah. Farrah Fawcett claimed that her mother made up the name because she thought it went well with their surname.

Fay

English, "fairy"

Fay, also spelled Faye, who had been napping quietly since the 1930s, has, like cousins May/Mae and Ray/Rae, sat up and started rubbing her eyes, ready for a mini-comeback, especially as a middle name.

The original of the name, Morgan le Fay, was a powerful sorceress in the Arthurian Legends. Two prominent Fay W's are the British novelist Fay Weldon, and actress Fay Wray, most famous for sitting in the hand of King Kong, and there is a character named Fay in Nathanael West's *The Day of the Locust*. Most well-known Faye is actress Dunaway.

Fay was most popular in the U.S. in the early decades of the twentieth century, reaching Number 202 in 1907, while Faye was Number 146 in 1934.

Fay may also be a short form of Faith.

Felicity

Latin, "good fortune, happy"

Felicity is as accessible a virtue name as Hope and Faith, but much more feminine—and dare we say happier. The hit TV show did a lot to soften and modernize the once buttoned-up image of Felicity, and it got further notice as the red-haired Colonial doll, Felicity Merriman, in the American Girl series.

Felicity reached its peak in popularity in 1999, a year after the TV show debuted, but still makes a felicitous choice. A current bearer is actress Felicity Huffman.

Two nicknames for Felicity: Flick and Fee. Other forms include Felicia and Felice.

Fenella

Celtic, "white-shouldered one"

More unusual than Fiona and more user-friendly than Fionnuala, the engaging Scottish Fenella, has been scarcely heard in this country.

Fenella first became known outside of Ireland when Sir Walter Scott used it for the character Finella Christian in his novel *Peveril of the Peak*.

Finola is another underused Anglicization of Fionnuala.

Fernanda

Feminine variation of Ferdinand, "courage"

Fernanda is very popular in the Latino community, ranking at Number 376 on the U.S. list, with a lot more charm than its male counterpart. It's a top name in Chile, now at Number 11. The standard nickname is Nanda, and variations include Ferdinanda and Fernandina.

Oscar-nominated Brazilian actress Fernanda Montenegro was born Arlette, but has said she chose Fernanda because of its "sonority." Fernanda Eberstadt is an American novelist and journalist; Brazil-born Fernanda Rocha is one of The Housewives of Orange County.

Fiona

Scottish, "white, fair"

Fiona entered the American consciousness with the opening of the 1954 Broadway musical *Brigadoon*, but didn't come onto the U.S. popularity list until 1990, and it's only in the last two years that it's entered the Top 300.

Fiona is the best known of a group of related Gaelic names, which is ironic because it's the only one without genuine traditional roots—it was found first in James Macpherson's Ossianic poems and then popularized in the late nineteenth century as a feminine pseudonym for a Scottish male writer. Its recent spike in popularity owes much to singer Fiona Apple and also, possibly, to Princess Fiona in *Shrek*.

In fact, there have been numerous Fionas on the big and small screens, from *The Thorn Birds* to *Josie and the Pussycats* to *Four Weddings and a Funeral* to *Nurse Jackie* to *Shameless*.

Jennie Garth and Chad Lowe have daughters named Fiona. It's also Julia Roberts' middle name.

If you're looking for something more authentic, consider Fionnuala.

Fiorella

Italian, "little flower"

Not only are individual flower names more popular (and exotic) than ever, but so, too, are the more generic names like Florence and Flora. While brother name Fiorello became known via long-term New York Mayor LaGuardia, the lovely Fiorella has never crossed cultures. She could join Arabella as a post-Isabella -ella choice.

And speaking of Isabella, Fiorella is the first of the three middle names of Isabella Rossellini.

Flannery

Irish, "red valor"

Long before the vogue of using Irish surnames for girls, writer Flannery O'Connor gave this one some visibility. It has a warm (flannelly) feel and the currently popular three-syllable ee-ending sound. Mary Flannery O'Connor was an important twentieth century regional writer whose work has been characterized as Southern Gothic, often featuring grotesque characters and concerned with questions of morality.

Fleur

French, "flower"

Fleur is a generic, delicate flower name that immigrated into the English-speaking world when John Galsworthy bestowed it on one of the Forsytes in his celebrated saga. More recently, there was Fleur Delacour, a French witch and the Beauxbatons champion for the Triwizard Tournament in *Harry Potter*.

Fleur is currently Number 12 in Holland, home of the tulip and other fleurs.

As for the literal translation, Flower, don't forget that it was the name of the little skunk in *Bambi*.

Flora

Latin, "flower"

Flora, the name of the Roman goddess of flowers and spring, who enjoyed eternal youth, is one of the gently old-fashioned girls' flower names we think is due for a comeback—alongside cousins Cora and Dora. Also the name of a saint, Flora has long been a favorite in Scotland where it was the name of the young heroine who helped Bonnie Prince Charlie make his way to France. Florence, Fiorella, Fleur, and Flower are translations, but we like Flora best of all.

Flora was a Top 100 name in the 1880s and 1890s but gradually descended until it finally fell off the list in 1972. It is still popular in some European countries—it is Number 29 in Hungary and Number 138 in France.

There have been a number of memorable Floras in literature, including the angelic little girl in Henry James's *Turn of the Screw, Waverly,* and one of the three Good Fairies in Disney's Sleeping Beauty.

Florence

Latin, "flourishing, prosperous"

Florence, which has been neglected for decades, has a lot going for it, both for its floral feel and as a place name connection to the lovely Italian city (after which Florence Nightingale was named—it was her birthplace), and the association to the place seems to be helping Florence stir back to style life, along with cousin Flora.

The hot group Florence + the Machine, headlined by red-haired Florence Welch, has also helped rejuvenate its image.

Florence was most popular in the U.S. at the turn of the last century and in the early decades of the twentieth: it was in the Top 10 from 1886 to 1906 but hasn't been in the Top 1000 since 1981. It is a stylish name in the U.K., now at Number 54.

Florence has a diverse mixture of namesakes and references—a character in Dickens's *Dombey & Sons*, a U.S. First Lady (Harding), one of the Supremes, *The Brady Bunch*'s Henderson, track and field star Florence Griffith Joyner, and several TV characters.

Florence has some particularly lively nicknames—Flo, Flossie, and Florrie.

Frances

Latin, "from France or free man"

Frances, a soft and gentle classic, last popular a hundred years ago, seems to be on the cusp of a possible revival, along with other such neglected quiet and serious names. It's been chosen in recent years by such stylish parents as Kate Spade and Amanda Peet (who nicknamed her daughter the spunky Frankie).

Frances was a favorite of the Tudor aristocracy after being given to Henry VII's granddaughter. Until the seventeenth century, the spellings Frances and Francis were used interchangeably for both sexes. St. Frances (Mother) Cabrini was the first American citizen to be canonized.

Some of the best-known pop culture bearers of the name were known by diminutives—the Franny of J.D. Salinger's *Franny and Zooey*, Francie in *A Tree Grows in Brooklyn*, Frankie in *A Member of the Wedding*, Baby in *Dirty Dancing*, and Gidget in *Gidget*. Traditional nickname Fran feels a bit bland, and Fanny, though possessing some eighteenth-century charm, is still considered rude in Britain if not so much in the U.S.

Frances is the endearing badger in the childhood favorite *Bedtime for Frances* and other *Frances* books.

Among well known bearers are Frances Perkins, Secretary of Labor in the Roosevelt era, actresses McDormand, Dee, Farmer, and Fisher, journalist Fitzgerald, and writers Burney and Hodgson Burnett.

Frances was the abandoned first name of Judy Garland, Dinah Shore, and Dale Evans.

Some attractive foreign versions are the increasingly popular Francesca, Francoise, Franca, Fanya, and Francine.

There has been some speculation that the naming of Pope Francis could have some ancillary effect on the popularity of sister name Frances.

Francesca

Italian variation of Frances, "from France or free man"
Francesca is a lighter and much more feminine choice than the classic Frances, and one that is increasingly popular with upscale parents.

Francesca made an appearance in Dante's *Inferno* and then, centuries later, in the best-selling novel *The Bridges of Madison County*, played on screen by Meryl Streep and co-starring Clint Eastwood, who went on to name his daughter Francesca. Other dads of Francescas include Martin Scorsese, Erik Estrada, Jason Bateman, and (stepdad) Ringo Starr.

Francesca is also having a big renaissance in its country of origin, where it's in the Italian Top 15 at Number 12.

Francine

French diminutive of Francoise, "from France or free man"
With the new Pope Francis, all forms of this ancient and saintly name are up for a fresh look. Along with most other -een and -ine (when pronounced like -een) names for girls, Francine has a dated midcentury *Mad Men* feel. While we prefer the sedate and classic Frances or the exotic Francesca, some parents are finding new appreciation for fancy Francine.

Francine was most popular in her native habitat in the 1940s, while in the U.S. she hit her peak in 1950 at Number 224. A contemporary bearer is writer Francine Prose, and comic actress Fran Drescher was born Francine. There are also Francines in two animated TV series: *Arthur* and *American Dad*.

Frederica

Feminine variation of Frederick, "peaceful ruler"

Frederica is an interesting possibility for the parent unintimidated by its old-fashioned formality and who can appreciate the vintage charm and verve lurking inside its stuffiness.

The name emerged in eighteenth-century Prussia when supporters of King Frederick the Great began to name their daughters in his honor and is currently represented by opera star Frederica von Stade.

Nicknames include the obvious Freddie, plus Rica and Fritzi.

Freya

Norse, "a noble woman"

Freya, the name of the Norse goddess of love, beauty, and fertility, has long been popular in the U.K. but is just beginning to be appreciated here. Freya could make a possible namesake for an ancestral Frieda. There is a Joseph Conrad novel titled *Freya of the Seven Isles*.

Currently, Freya is immensely popular in several English-speaking countries: it's Number 16 in Scotland, 19 in England and Wales, 53 in Northern Ireland, and 61 in Ireland.

A noted bearer was the explorer and writer Freya Stark.

G

Gabriella

Italian feminine variation of Gabriel, "God is my strength"

Gabriella—a strong yet graceful feminine form of Gabriel—is on the rise, given to more than five thousand baby girls last year, with the double 'l' spelling being more popular. Gabriela is the Spanish spelling.

Gabriella has been on the U.S. Top 1000 list since 1984, entering the Top 100 in 2000, while the single 'l' spelling is at 201. It is also riding on a wave of popularity in Canada and Australia.

Gabriella was a major character on *High School Musical*, and real life namesakes include poet Gabriela Mistral and tennis champ Gabriela Sabatini. The French version is Gabrielle.

Gemma

Italian, "precious stone"

Gemma is a jewel of a name, an Italian classic that was very popular in 1980s England but has only recently started to be used here; it entered the list in 2008 and is already at 317.

Coming from a medieval Italian nickname for a precious gem, Gemma was the name of Dante's wife and was borne by a nineteenth-century saint.

Gemma is the name of the character played by Katey Sagal on *Sons of Anarchy*, and there is a bestselling young adult, Victorian fantasy series, written by Libba Bray, called the *Gemma Doyle Trilogy*. There is a bestselling young adult, Victorian fantasy series, written by Libba Bray, called the *Gemma Doyle Trilogy*. Actress Catherine Bell has a daughter called Gemma, as does Kristin Davis.

Bottom line: A stylish cousin of Emma and Jenna.

Geneva

Swiss place name

Unlike its somewhat formal Swiss city namesake, this is a lively and appealing place name that also has a real history as a female name.

Geneva was a relatively popular American name at one time; it reached as high as Number 107 in 1919 and remained in the Top 200 until 1942. Geneva was the middle name of First Lady Mamie Eisenhower and is the name of a leading character on *The Good Wife*.

Genevieve

French, "tribe woman"

Genevieve is a perfect choice for anyone who wants to retain the gen sound but is tired of all the overused Jen names. The medieval saint Genevieve, patroness of Paris, defended the city against Attila the Hun through her rational thinking, courage, and prayer.

Genevieve is both dainty and substantial and can be pronounced either GEN-uh-veev or the French zhahn-vee-EV.

Genevieve is showing signs of a real revival—it is now at its highest ranking since the 1930s.

Georgia

Feminine variation of George, "farmer"

Georgia is so rich, lush, and luscious that it's almost irresistible. Georgia's now a rising star among the feminizations of George, helped by associations with the southern state (named for British King George II) and painter Georgia O'Keeffe, with the Ray Charles song "Georgia on My Mind" or maybe "Sweet Georgia Brown" playing in the background.

This peach of a name is currently enjoying widespread international popularity; it was recently as high as Number 7 in Greece, was 21 in New Zealand, 29 in Australia, and in the Top 70 in England and Wales, Canada, Northern Ireland, and Scotland.

Georgia has been chosen for their daughters by Harry Connick, Jr., Hope Davis, Amy Ryan, Zac Brown, Rebecca Gayheart and Eric Dane, and Felicity Huffman and William H. Macy.

British jazz singer Georgia Brown was born Lillian Klot.

There is also the phonetic spelling Jorja—but we'd recommend sticking with the original.

Georgiana

English feminine variation of George, "farmer"

Long a popular upper-crust form in England, where it's pronounced George-ayna, Georgiana has been neglected here. But with Georgia growing more popular and the general fashion for elaborate feminine names, Georgiana might have room to grow.

Georgiana Cavendish, the Duchess of Devonshire, was a famed beauty and ancestor of Princess Diana who was portrayed by Keira Knightley in the 2008 film *The Duchess*.

Georgiana was a favorite character name for early English novelists: Georgiana was Mr Darcy's younger sister in *Pride and Prejudice*, Georgiana Podsnap appeared in Dickens's *Our Mutual Friend*, and Jane Eyre had a cousin named Georgiana.

Drew Barrymore's great grandmother was Georgiana Drew Barrymore (called Georgie), and Molly Ringwald used it as her daughter Adele's middle name.

Georgiana has been off the U.S. list since 1952 but once was as high as Number 256.

If you want to reduce the syllable count, you can also consider Georgina (a Scottish favorite) or Georgia.

Geraldine

Feminine variation of Gerald, "ruler with the spear"

Though twin brother Gerald is still in baby name limbo, Geraldine is in line to follow the path of Josephine to imminent revival—even though Gerry is not as spunky a nickname as Josie.

Geraldine was at its hottest from the 1910s through the 40s, peaking at Number 38 in 1931. It was invented in the time of Henry VIII by a noble poet who fell in love with a Lady Elizabeth Fitzgerald and, taking off from her surname, referred to her as the "Faire Geraldine."

Geraldine has the distinction of being the name of the first woman to be a major party vice-presidential candidate, Geraldine Ferraro. Other notable bearers include actors Geraldine Fitzgerald, Chaplin and Page, and Spice Girl Geri Halliwell.

Trivia notes: Geraldine is the middle name of Ramona Quimby. And Geraldine was the name of the sassy female character played by Flip Wilson on his popular TV variety show.

Gia

Italian diminutive of Giovanna, "God's gracious gift"

Gia is a cute, if slight, name that calls to mind stylish sisters Mia, Lea, Pia, Tia, and Nia. Gia is a short form of Gianna, which in turn is a diminutive of Giovanna, the feminine form of Giovanni, the Italian equivalent of John—all of them meaning God's gracious gift.

Gia first made a strong impression via Gia Carangi, the ill-fated supermodel whose biopic provided Angelina Jolie's breakout role in 1998. It entered the Top 1000 in 2000, and has been rising ever since.

Gia was chosen by Matt Damon and by Mario Lopez for their daughters and also gained recent fame as the name of the oldest daughter of Real New Jersey Housewife Teresa Giudice.

Giada

Italian, "jade"

Giada is a fresh spin on Jade, which has been quietly and stylishly used in English-speaking countries for several years now. Popular cook Giada De Laurentiis made this a possibility, then semi-subtly self-referenced when she named her daughter Jade.

Giada entered the U.S. pop list in 2007, five years after the debut of DeLaurentiis's Food Network show.

Gianna

Italian diminutive of Giovanna, "the Lord is gracious"

Gianna—a Latin feminization of John—is rapidly gaining favor outside the confines of Italian culture; Gianna is now among the Top 100 in the U.S. at Number 73.

This common Italian classic entered the U.S. list in 1989, breaking into the Top 100 in 2006, along with other such stalwarts. Basketball star Kobe Bryant has a daughter named Gianna.

Also on the U.S. list are Giovanna and Giana—and short-form Gia, which was used by Matt Damon and Mario Lopez.

Gillian

Feminine variation of Julian, "youthful"

Gillian is a name in common usage in Great Britain (where it's often pronounced with a hard 'G'), but until recently had not crossed the Atlantic in significant numbers, except in the short form Jill.

In medieval England, the name Gillian was so common that it was used as a generic name for a girl, just as Jack was for a boy, hence the nursery rhyme Jack and J(G)ill and the expression "every Jack has his Jill." The high profile of actress Gillian (*The X Files*) Anderson did a lot to publicize the name in the U.S.—where it is more often spelled phonetically as Jillian.

Another noteworthy bearer is Australian film director Gillian Armstrong. Gillian Boardman is a key character in Robert Heinlein's *Stranger in a Strange Land.*

Gloria

Latin, "glory"

Gloria is beginning to move beyond its de-glamorized Grandma image, most recently thanks to glamorous Hollywood parents Maggie Gyllenhaal and Peter Sarsgaard, who chose it for their second daughter. Gyllenhaal was quoted as saying they had been inspired by Patti Smith's rendition of the Van Morrison song "Gloria" at a concert and thought, "We'll name our daughter that one day."

George Bernard Shaw was one of the first to use this form of the ancient Latin name Gloriana in his 1898 play *You Never Can Tell.* It was a Top 25 name in the Gloria (born Josephine) Swanson era of the 1920s—reaching as high as Number 20 in 1925-26 and held on in the Top 50 until 1955.

Most prominent current adult bearers: Gloria Steinem and Gloria Estefan. Glorias have also figured prominently in TV sitcoms—as Archie and Edith's only child on *All in the Family* and the sexpot character played by Sofia Vergara on *Modern Family.*

Goldie

Anglicized form of Yiddish Golde or Golda

More Sadie than Sadie, this old canasta player—somewhat modernized and energized by Goldie Hawn—looks like it could be making a comeback. It was recently chosen for their daughter by Ione Skye and Ben Lee, as well as by shoemeister Steve Madden.

Goldie was one of those saucy nickname mainstays from the late 1800s through the 1940s, topping at Number 114 in 1904-05, then sliding off the list completely in 1958.

Goldie Clemens was a major character on the TV show *The New Normal.*

Grace

Virtue name

Grace is now just outside the Top 20, but who would have thought such a simple and pure virtue name as Grace, which originally referred to divine grace, could ever become trendy? Because that's what Grace is, chosen by boldfaced names from Mark Wahlberg to Ed Burns and Christy Turlington and given to more than 7,300 girls in 2012.

Grace is one of the most luminous of names, recalling the cool elegance of Grace Kelly, Princess of Monaco. It existed as Gracia in the Middle Ages, but was not in common use until the Puritans adopted it along with other Christian attribute names in the sixteenth century. Embraced by Americans of the Victorian era, it was the eleventh most popular name in this country in 1875.

Grace is currently even more popular in other countries than it is here—Number 2 in Northern Ireland and 4 in Ireland, 8 in England and Wales, 13 in Australia, 17 in Scotland, and 18 in Canada.

If Grace is too overused for you (there were well over seven thousand little Graces born last year), consider an exotic variation like Engracia or Graziella—or the earthier Gracie. Some parents have even migrated into the boys' camp in search of Grace equivalents such as Gray or Grayson. Choosing nickname Gracie for the birth certificate is an increasingly popular option—she now ranks at Number 158.

Greer

Scottish, contraction of Gregor, "vigilant, a watchman"

This attractive Scottish surname choice has a certain amount of glamour thanks to feisty British-born red-haired forties Academy Award winner Greer Garson, who was born Eileen Evelyn Greer Garson—Greer was her Irish mother's maiden name). Greer was chosen much more recently by Kelsey Grammer for his daughter and by Brooke Shields in the Grier form. As a surname, it's associated with feminist writer/activist Germaine Greer.

Greer makes a good, strong, sophisticated, and distinctive middle-name prospect.

Greta

Diminutive of Margareta, "pearl"

Greta is an Old World name long tied to the exotic, iconic Garbo. Along with other Old Hollywood glamour names, Greta seems to be showing slight signs of a comeback; it was chosen by David Caruso and by Phoebe Cates and Kevin Kline for their daughters.

Greta is currently popular in Germany, Hungary, and especially Italy, where she ranks at Number 16. Dr. Greta Guttman is a character on *Mad Men*, Greta Van Susteren is a familiar face on TV, and Greta Gerwig is an up-and-coming young actress.

Greta returned to the Top 1000 in 1999 after being off for almost twenty years. Her highest point was at Number 318 in 1932 at the peak of Garbo's career, the year she starred in *Grand Hotel* and one year after she was Oscar-nominated for *Anna Christie*.

Greta is a sweet-spot name—sophisticated with a touch of retro glamour. On the other hand, variant Gretel is still out strewing crumbs in the forest with brother Hansel.

Guinevere

Welsh, "white shadow, white wave"

Guinevere was the name of the beautiful but ill-fated queen of Camelot, eclipsed for so many years by its modern Cornish form Jennifer. Today, Guinevere could be a cool possibility for adventurous parents intrigued by this richly evocative and romantic choice.

Guinevere shares the attractive short form Gwyn with Gwyneth. Other cousin ideas: Gwendolen, Genevieve, Jenna, or Gwen.

Gwendolen

Welsh, "white circle"

Gwendolen, an ancient Welsh favorite, retired decades ago in favor of the short form Gwen, but now, as in the case all across the naming board, the nickname has faded and the more distinguished original is up for reappraisal.

Gwendolen means "white circle," probably alluding to an ancient moon goddess, and appears in both Welsh and English legend, once as a fairy with whom King Arthur fell in love and another as the wife of the wizard, Merlin.

Gwendolen is the name of principal characters in George Eliot's novel *Daniel Deronda* and in the Oscar Wilde play, *The Importance of Being Earnest*.

An alternate spelling is Gwendolyn, as in Gwendolyn Brooks, the first African-American woman to win a Pulitzer Prize for poetry. Gwendolyn, always the more popular spelling in the U.S. and the full name of the character Winnie Cooper on *The Wonder Years*, is now at Number 514, having reached as high as 112 in the 1950s.

Singer Gwen Stefani was actually christened Gwen.

Gwyneth

Welsh, "blessed, happy"

Because of Gwyneth Paltrow, this has almost become a one-person name but not in the prohibitive there's-only-one-Oprah sense. Also seen as Gwenyth and Gweneth, this mellifluous appellation is definitely becoming more and more appreciated by American parents—though not enough to land it on this year's Top 1000.

Gwyneth is an Anglicized form of Gwynedd, the name of an ancient Welsh kingdom. Gwyneth Jones is an acclaimed Welsh Wagnerian soprano.

H

Hadley

English, "heather field"

Hadley, most famous as the name of Ernest Hemingway's first wife, is more sophisticated, professional, and modern than cousins Harley, Haley, or Hayden. After debuting on the Top 1000 list in 1998, Hadley has climbed up the popularity list every year, now at Number 130. The recent hit book, *The Paris Wife*, a novel told from the point of view of Hadley Hemingway (born Elizabeth Hadley Richardson), has helped popularize the name, which also appears on the vampire show *True Blood*. Hadley could become this generation's Hailey.

Hannah

Hebrew, "grace"

Hannah is one of the nation's top biblical girls' names—it surpassed Sarah in 1998 and is behind only Abigail and Elizabeth. Hannah is a name with many sources of appeal: Old Testament roots, soft and gentle sound, and a homey yet aristocratic image. The biblical Hannah was the mother of Samuel.

The TV show *Hannah Montana* was a huge TV teen sensation from 2006 to 2011, and in the present, it's the name Lena Dunham chose for her own character in her hit series, *Girls*.

Hannah is also a name that in its varied versions, which include Hana and Hanna, has roots in many cultures, from Hebrew to Arabic and European to Asian. All in all, Hannah is still a wonderful, if very widely, used name.

Harley

English, "the long field"

Once a macho biker name, Harley is now showing its softer side, given to over seven hundred girls last year, which is almost twice the number of boy Harleys. In the U.K., Harley is still much more male—it's currently Number 55 there.

Along with Harper and Hadley, we think it will climb even further. In England, it's associated with Harley Street, home to some of London's most prominent medical specialists.

Harley came over to the girls' side in 1991, long after being the name of the Joker's female assistant in Batman, Harley Quinn, 'born' Harleen Quinsel, and then as a character, Harley Cooper, who was introduced on the soap *The Guiding Light* in 1987—that Harley was named after her father's favorite motorcycle.

Harlow

English surname, "army"
Jean Harlow (born Harlean Carpenter), the original platinum blonde bombshell, was a symbol of 1930s glamour, a factor that first Patricia Arquette and then Nicole Richie and Joel Madden probably had in mind when they gave their daughters the distinctive surname - name Harlow.

Harlow has been rapidly catching on with other parents, moving up over one hundred places this year. It entered the list for the first time in 2009, one year after the arrival of Ms Madden. Harlow would fit right in with contemporaries Arlo and Marlow(e).

Harper

English, "harp player"
Harper is a red-hot name for girls, having jumped an impressive 30 places between 2011 and 2012, a prime example of the trend for using surnames-turned-boys'-names for girls. Harper was rarely heard for either sex before the mid-2000s, entering the girls' list in 2004. (For boys, it was in use until 1906 when it dropped off the scope and didn't reappear until a full century later.)

Harper has been a shooting star in the celebrisphere, chosen first by Ali Wentworth and George Stephanopoulos, followed by Lisa Marie Presley, David Spade, Dave Grohl, Martie Maguire, Tiffani Thiessen, Bill Hader, and Neil Patrick Harris. And since the Beckhams have chosen it for their first daughter, Harper is sure to get even hotter.

It was *To Kill a Mockingbird* author Harper (born Nelle Harper) Lee who brought this family name into the public consciousness as a female first name with offbeat, boyish southern charm, and it's also a name with a musical bent. Harper has recently been used as a female character name on such hot TV shows as *Gossip Girls* and *The Wizards of Waverly Place*.

Harriet

English variation of French Henriette, "estate ruler"

Harriet has long been considered a stylish, upscale name in England but is still waiting to be revived in the U.S.—though some parents seeking a solid, serious, semi-classic are beginning to consider it.

Distinguished namesakes include Harriet Beecher Stowe, author of the influential *Uncle Tom's Cabin*, Harriet Tubman (born Araminta), the famed abolitionist, and in pop culture, Harriet Hilliard Nelson, of *Ozzie & Harriet* TV fame. Many will associate it with the protagonist of the childhood classic *Harriet the Spy*. She has appeared in other books ranging from Jane Austen's *Emma* to *Girl with the Dragon Tattoo*.

Harriet, a Top 100 name at the turn of the last century, hasn't appeared on the list since 1970. On the other hand, it is currently Number 71 in England and Wales.

Cutifying nicknames for Harriet include Hattie, Hetty, and Hatsy. A related idea: Henrietta.

Hattie

Diminutive of Harriet, "estate ruler"

Hattie has a good chance of being one of the next wave of vintage grandma nicknames, supplanting Annie and Jenny, and joining the spunkier Mamie and Mitzi, especially since it was chosen by Tori Spelling and Dean McDermott for their third child.

Hattie was popular at the end of the nineteenth century, in the Top 50 from 1880 to 1900, along with other similar nickname names like Lottie and Letty. It fell off the list in 1969, to return in 2011, the year of Hattie McDermott's birth.

Hattie McDaniel was the first African-American to be awarded an Academy Award for her role in *Gone with the Wind* in 1940. Hattie was the name of the sweet, simple protagonist in Woody Allen's 1999 film *Sweet and Lowdown*; Hattie (born Henriette) Carnegie was a well-known twentieth-century fashion designer.

Haven

English, "a refuge"

Haven is a recently invented safe-harbor name that appeals to an increasing number of parents who don't want to voyage quite as far as Heaven.

Its choice by Jessica Alba for her second daughter has already inspired other baby namers— in 2012 it ranked at Number 432, the highest it's been since entering the list in 1996. Haven Kimmel is the author of the bestselling memoir, *A Girl Named Zippy*, Haven Denney is a medal-winning skater. There was also a supernatural TV series called Haven.

Hayden

English, "heather-grown hill"
A newly successful name for girls, which, like Brayden and Caden, used to be strictly for the boys. Right now it is at Number 109 for boys and 196 for girls, so it's officially ambisexual. Young *Heroes* and now *Nashville* star Hayden Panettiere planted it firmly in the girls' camp.

Hazel

English, "the hazelnut tree"
When Julia Roberts named one of her twins Hazel in 2004, there was a great public outcry against "another one of those nutty celebrity names." But we didn't see why. Now that the old Hazel the Maid cartoon image has faded from view, we're left with a pleasantly hazy, brownish-green-eyed, old-fashioned image of Hazel that more and more parents are choosing to share. Since it reentered the popularity lists in 1998, it has jumped almost 800 points.

In addition to being a celebrity pick, Hazel is a nature name, coming from the hazelnut tree—there was a time when a wand of hazel symbolized protection and authority. Hazel was one of the botanicals that were all the rage at the turn of the twentieth century, when it was in the Top 25, then fell out of favor, off the list completely from 1976 to 1998.

Hazel Motes is the protagonist of Flannery O'Connor's 1952 novel *Wise Blood*, and in *The Hunger Games*, one of the characters is the variant Hazelle.

Helen

Greek, "bright, shining one"
Helen is a name that has connoted beauty since ancient times, the mythological "face that launched a thousand ships," over whom the ten-year Trojan War was fought.

The name Helen has moved in and out of favor over the centuries, often alternating with Ellen. It was a Top 5 name for several decades of the early twentieth century, falling out of the Top 100 in the 1950s. Now, after being unfashionable for decades, we see signs of a comeback for Helen—it's the kind of serious, unadorned classic many parents are returning to. If Helen is too hard-core of an old lady name for you, you might consider one of its many variations that may be tastier for the modern palate: Helena, Eleanor, Elena, Ella, Nell, or Leonora, to mention just a few.

In Greek myth, Helen is the daughter of Leda and Zeus, who came to her mother in the form of a swan.

Helen has legions of eminent namesakes, including author and activist Helen Keller, politician Helen Gahagan Douglas, newspaper reporter Helen Thomas, Cosmo force Helen Gurley Brown, *Bridget Jones* creator Helen Fielding, artist Helen Frankenthaler, and actresses Hayes, Mirren, and Hunt. Beatrix Potter's birth name was Helen.

Helena

Latinate form of Helen, "bright, shining one"

Helena is a more delicate and dainty version of Helen, a favorite of Shakespeare, who used it in both *All's Well That Ends Well* and *A Midsummer Night's Dream*. Historically, Helena was the mother of Constantine the Great (and, supposedly, the daughter of Old King Cole), who became a fourth century saint—Evelyn Waugh wrote his only historical novel, *Helena*, based on her story.

British star Helena Bonham Carter and Danish model Helena Christensen have done much to keep the name alive, and it is also remembered via beauty mogul Helena Rubinstein. Helena is also the title of a song by the group My Chemical Romance.

Helena is a recommended choice for those who find the classic version a bit bland.

HELL-ehn-a is the best modern pronunciation for Helena, but hell-AYN-a or even hell-EEN-a work too.

Henrietta

Feminine variation of Henry, "estate ruler"

Despite a return to such feminizations of male names as Josephine, Clementine, and Theodora, starchy Henrietta has not made it into that group. Still, if you look hard enough, you'll see that Henrietta has the same vintage charm.

The name arrived in England in 1625 via King Charles I's wife, the French princess Henriette Marie, who became known as Henrietta Maria. Her daughter shared her name but was known as Minette.

It has been prominent recently through the bestselling book *The Immortal Life of Henrietta Lacks*, the story of the poor black woman whose cells became one of the most important tools in medical research. Henrietta Szold was a U.S. Zionist leader and founder of the Hadassah Women's Organization.

Henrietta has a number of charming vintage nicknames, including Etta, Hetty, and Hattie.

Hermione

Greek feminine version of Hermes, "messenger god"

Hermione's co-starring role in *Harry Potter* has made this previously ignored, once stodgy name suddenly viable. Hermione could really take off once today's children start having kids of their own.

In ancient Greek myth, Hermione is the daughter of Spartan King Menelaus and his wife Helen; in pre-Potter lit, the name appears in Shakespeare's *The Winter's Tale* and in Walter Scott's novel *The Fortunes of Nigel*.

Hester

Variation of Esther, "star"

The disgraced heroine of *The Scarlet Letter*'s name, after long neglect, just might have a chance at revival, following in the wake of sister name Esther. We've characterized her elsewhere as an eccentric aristocrat, much more accepted in the U.K. than she has been here.

Hester's beyond-Hawthorne literary appearances include as characters in Theodore Dreiser's novel *An American Tragedy*, in Oscar Wilde's play *A Woman of No Importance*, in John Irving's novel *A Prayer for Owen Meaney*, and as Niles and Frasier Crane's mom on *Frasier*.

Hetty is Hester's usual nickname, sometimes used independently. The related Hestia is the name of the Greek goddess of the hearth, home, and chastity.

Hillary

Latin from Greek, "happy, cheerful"

This is the spelling of the name used by Mrs Clinton, whose fame has temporarily taken this name off the table for babies. A pity, really, as it's got so much going for it: the popular, rhythmic three-syllable structure, the fact that it's strong but light, proper but jaunty, with an irresistible meaning—having the same root as hilarious. The Italian Ilaria may be one way to make the name fresh.

Traditionally, Hilary was the form used for males and Hillary for females, but since there are so few boy Hilarys these days, that tradition has fallen by the wayside. A few other modern notables have laid claim to the name: musicians Hilary du Pré and Hilary Hahn and actresses Hilary Swank and Hilary Duff.

Holland

Place name

Holland is one of the coolest geographical names, unadorned and elegant, evocative of fine Rembrandt portraits and fields of pink and yellow tulips.

Holland Taylor is the Emmy award-winning actress most recognized for her work on *Two and a Half Men*; she recently wrote and appeared in a one-woman play on Broadway.

Holly

Nature name

Still just outside the British Top 25, but out of favor here since the 1970s Era of Nickname Names, Holly suddenly seems to be on her way back as a rejuvenated nature name. And she could get a further boost from Baby Holly, daughter of Walter and Skyler on *Breaking Bad*.

Jolly Holly has always been favored for girls born around Christmas, evoking the symbolic shrub with dark green leaves and bright red berries.

A memorable fictional Holly is the enigmatic heroine of Truman Capote's *Breakfast at Tiffany's*, Holly Golightly (almost named Connie—and with the full name Holiday), played indelibly by Audrey Hepburn; a real life one is actress Holly Hunter. Holly Short is a fairy character in Eoin Colfer's *Artemis Fowl* novels; in Galsworthy's *The Forsyte Saga*, Holly and Jolly are siblings.

Honor

Virtue name

Honor is a somewhat more pressured virtue name than Hope or Grace, placing a high standard on any girl carrying it, but it's a goal worth setting. By choosing Honor for her daughter, Jessica Alba brought it very much into the modern world.

Probably the best-known bearer is British actress Honor Blackman, remembered for her roles in *The Avengers* and the James Bond *Goldfinger*.

The more feminine Honora is also pretty and a fresh route to Nora. In another variation, Honoria Blake is a character in the Dickens novel *Bleak House*, Honoria Brady is the hero's cousin in the 1844 novel *The Luck of Barry Lyndon* by W. M. Thackeray, and Honoria Glossop is a character in the "Jeeves" stories by P. G. Wodehouse.

Hope

Virtue name

Can a name as virtuous as Hope be cool and trendy? Strangely enough—yes. But though this optimistic Puritan favorite is experiencing substantial popularity, Hope is too pure and elegant to be corrupted, a lovely classic that deserves all the attention it's getting.

Hope, along with Faith and Charity, is one of the three theological virtues, first used as a Christian name in the seventeenth century by the Puritans. Hope and Faith have often been given to twins.

There have been characters named Hope on four different soap operas. The TV show *Raising Hope* is about, yes, raising a child named Hope—formerly named Princess Beyoncé, and Hope & Faith was a sitcom starring Faith Ford and Kelly Ripa. Brad Garrett has a daughter named Hope.

Hyacinth

Flower name

Though it may not be as sweet and gentle as, say, Violet, the purple-hued Hyacinth still might hold some appeal for the parent seeking a truly exotic flower name.

In Greek mythology Hyacinthus was a Spartan youth accidentally killed by Apollo, from whose blood sprang a beautiful and fragrant flower, and it is also the name of several saints; Hyacinth became exclusively female in the nineteenth century. To the ancients Hyacinth was, in addition to being a bluebell-like blossom, the name of a precious stone.

There is a character named Hyacinth Robinson in Henry James's *The Princess Casamassima* and Hyacinth Bucket is the social climbing character on the British sitcom *Keeping Up Appearances*, with sisters named Daisy, Rose, and Violet.

You might also consider the Spanish version, Jacinta.

I

Ianthe

Greek, "purple flower"

Like Violet, Lavender, and Lilac, Ianthe is a purple flower name. Chosen by the poet Shelley for his daughter, Ianthe has a poetic, romantic, almost ethereal quality. In the ancient myth, she was the daughter of Oceanus, supreme ruler of the sea, and also a Cretan woman so beautiful that, when she died, the gods made purple flowers grow around her grave.

Iantha is also used.

Ianthe was a favorite of the pastoral poets of the seventeenth century and then again in the early nineteenth. She appears in the works of Shelley, Barbara Pym, and Georgette Heyer. Writer Richard Brautigan named his daughter Ianthe.

Ida

German, "industrious one"

Many vowel names stylish a century ago are coming back, and Ida seems like a possible, logical successor to Ada and Ava.

A century ago, Ida was considered "sweet as apple cider," and was Number 10 on the hit parade of names. Its popularity then was inspired by a Tennyson poem, of which the Gilbert and Sullivan operetta, *Princess Ida*, was a "respectful operatic perversion."

Ida hasn't been in the Top 1000 since the 1980s, but we do see it as slated to rise again. It is hugely popular right now in Scandinavia—Number 2 in Denmark, 10 in Norway, and 25 in Sweden, where it's pronounced EE-da.

Ida appears in Greek and Hindu mythology: Mount Ida, on Crete, is considered the birthplace of the god Zeus. The British-born actress-director Ida Lupino has been its most well-known bearer in the U.S.

Imogen

Variation of Innogen, "maiden"

Imogen is a Shakespearean name long fashionable in England, which temporarily lost its way here when spelled and pronounced im-oh-GENE. Pronounced the British way, Imogen is as pretty and classy as it is distinctive. Imogen also gained attention through its link to Grammy-winning musician Imogen Heap.

Imogen originated as a Shakespearean printer's misspelling of the Celtic Innogen, used by him for a charming and impetuous character in one of his last plays, *Cymbeline*.

Though never in the American Top 1000, Imogen has gained a lot of favor in recent years among stylish parents, so you may find more little Imogens in your hip neighborhood than that statistics would suggest. In fact, Imogen recently displaced Charlotte as the breakout Number 1 among girl names on Nameberry for the first half of 2013. In England and Wales, the stylish Imogen is currently Number 42. In *Fried Green Tomatoes*, the character Imogene's nickname was Idgie.

India

Place name from the River Indus

India is one of the first and still one of the loveliest place names: exotic, euphonious, and long stylish in England. India was a character in *Gone with the Wind*, the sister of Ashley Wilkes, and more recently was picked for the daughters of singer Sarah McLachlan, actress Heather Thomas, movie mogul Harvey Weinstein and wife Georgina Chapman, and Avenger Chris Hemsworth.

India Hicks is a high-profile ex-model with ties to the royal family and the mother of a girl called Domino. Singer India.Arie was born India Arie—without the period.

Indigo

Greek, "Indian dye"

Indigo is one of the most appealing and evocative of the new generation of color names. Color names have joined flower and jewel names—in a big way—and Indigo, a deep blue-purple dye from plants native to India, is particularly striking for both girls and boys. Indigo is the name of a character in the Ntozake Shange novel *Sassafrass, Cypress & Indigo* and was used for his daughter by Lou Diamond Phillips.

Some cultural references: The Indigo Girls are a folk duo, "Mood Indigo" is a classic Duke Ellington jazz composition, and there is a 1970s New Age theory that Indigo children possess special, sometimes supernatural abilities.

Inez

Portuguese variation of Agnes, "pure, virginal"

Also spelled Ines, this name of the prudish mother of Don Juan in the Byron poem has an exotic touch of mystery but has also been fully integrated into the American name pool.

Inez Milholland and Inez Hayes Irwin were both important figures in the American suffragist movement. And Inez was the name of the character played by Rachel McAdams in *Midnight in Paris*.

Other spellings variations of Inez: Ines, Ynes, and Ynez; a Russian version is Inessa.

Ingrid

Norse, "Ing's ride"

The luminous Ingrid Bergman's appeal was strong enough to lend universal charisma to this classic Scandinavian name, which has been somewhat neglected in this country. Even today, a child named Ingrid would be assumed to be of Scandinavian ancestry, signaling that the name has never been fully integrated into the English lexicon the way other European choices from the same era, like Danielle or Kathleen, have.

Still popular in its native Scandinavia, where it is a royal name, Ingrid is now Number 5 in Norway; its highest U.S. ranking was Number 383 in 1967.

Its meaning refers to Ing, the Norse god of fertility, peace, and prosperity, and he's looked up to as the ancestor of the Swedish kings.

Ingrid was the name of mother figures in both *Spy Kids* and *White Oleander*. Trivia tidbit: It's Scarlett Johansson's middle name.

Iolanthe

Greek, "violet flower"

Iolanthe is known primarily through the 1882 Gilbert & Sullivan operetta of that name, in which the title character is a fairy. Iolanthe is a softer version of Yolanda, the kind of multi-syllabic classical name once considered too weighty for a modern baby girl, but now within the realm of possibility—this one as a dramatic twist on Violet.

Irene

Greek, "peace"

Serene Irene, the name of the Greek goddess of peace, was hugely popular in ancient Rome and again in the United States a hundred years ago.

One of the most popular names of the Roman Empire and the name of several early saints, this originally Greek appellation (then spelled Eirene) represented a daughter of Zeus who was the goddess of peace. Often pronounced with three syllables, it spread throughout Europe in a range of variations and is a royal name in Greece, Denmark, and the Netherlands.

Much of Irene's popularity in England stemmed from the character Irene Forsyte in Galsworthy's *The Forsyte Saga*, while Americans identified it with the sparkling Irene Dunne of Hollywood's Golden Age. Irene was a Top 20 name from 1915 to 1925, remaining in the Top 100 until 1945. It is currently high up at Number 13 in Spain.

Some other references include the eponymous early smash hit Broadway musical, famed ballroom dancer Irene Castle (portrayed on film by Ginger Rogers), the Hollywood costume designer known simply as Irene, the Uma Thurman character in *Gattaca*, Irene Denholm, a *Harry Potter* student at Hogwarts School, and the lullaby-ready song "Goodnight, Irene."

Trivia tidbit: Carreen, the name of Scarlett O'Hara's younger sister in *Gone with the Wind*, was a smoosh of Caroline Irene.

Iris

Greek, "rainbow"; flower name

Iris is one of the bouquet of turn-of-the-last-century flower names that is gradually beginning to regain its appeal; it is now at the highest point it has been since 1956.

Part of this is due to its celebrity power: Jude Law and Sadie Frost, Renee O'Connor, and Judd Apatow and Leslie Mann all chose Iris for their daughters.

In Greek mythology, Iris was the goddess of the rainbow, a messenger for Zeus and Hera who rode the rainbow as a multicolored bridge from heaven to earth. In ancient times, the Iris was considered a symbol of power and majesty, the three petal segments representing faith, wisdom, and valor. This colorful image led to the naming of the flower and to the colored part of the eye.

A notable modern bearer was the prolific British novelist Iris Murdoch. Frequently seen on screen, characters called Iris have been played by Jodie Foster, Jane Fonda, and Kate Winslet, and Iris Chase is the narrator in the Margaret Atwood novel *The Blind Assassin*.

Isabeau

French variation of Isabel, "pledged to God"

With Isabel getting so popular, parents are searching for new varieties of the name, and Isabeau is one that makes a lovely French twist.

Isabeau of Bavaria was the wife of King Charles VI of France—and it was possibly a nickname for Elisabeth. It is also the name of an opera by Pietro Mascagni, a retelling of the medieval English legend of Lady Godiva, and in the 1985 film *Ladyhawke*, Michelle Pfeiffer plays the heroine, Lady Isabeau d'Anjou, who assumes the form of a hawk during the day.

Isabel

Spanish variation of Elizabeth, "pledged to God"

The charming Isabel is hugely fashionable again, a century after its first wave of success. And it's easy to see why; it's ladylike (à la Isabel Archer in Henry James's *Portrait of a Lady*) and melodic, traditional yet slightly offbeat. Isabel sounds smart as well as pretty.

Two noted cultural namesakes are Chilean author Isabel Allende and painter Isabel Bishop, as well as Cuban-American fashion designer Isabel Toledo.

The Office's Angela Kinsley named her baby girl Isabel, and Annette Bening and Warren Beatty have a teen-aged Isabel.

Isabel is in the Top 90 in several countries—Spain, the Netherlands, Australia, Ireland, and England and Wales. Isabelle is the French version, Isabella the Italian one, and Isobel the Scottish spelling, which has a definite character of her own, the 'o' giving her an extra infusion of strength.

The only downside is, with Isabella ranking at Number 3, there are so many other little Isabels, Isabelles, Isabellas, Belles, and Bellas, that yours would be far from unique.

Nifty nicknames include Izzy, Ibby, Isa and Belle.

Isabella

Spanish and Italian variation of Elizabeth, "pledged to God"

Isabella is a major superstar baby girl name, holding at Number 3 on the charts after being the top name for two years running—due at least in some part to the '*Twilight*' effect and lead character Isabella 'Bella' Swan.

Isabella has incredible cross-cultural appeal, feeling both modern and traditional, and is popular among parents ranging from Anglophile to Hispanic and is more feminine and romantic than Isabel. An amazing success story for a name that wasn't even in the Top 1000 in the 1980s.

Part of the reason Isabella is so successful is that it appeals in a wide variety of ways to a large number of parents. It's feminine but also classic, has a Latinate history yet is comfortable on the international stage. Some parents choose it to get to the short form

Bella, while others prefer to use the irreverent Izzy or Issy, while still others insist on using it in its full four-syllable glory.

Isabella is familiar through various European queens and was used by Shakespeare in *Measure for Measure*.

Variations Isabelle and Isabel are also popular, with the Scottish spelling Isobel another possibility. A little further afield is the smoosh name Isabetta, which was chosen by Amber and Rob Mariano.

Isadora

Greek, "gift of Isis"

Why is Isabella mega popular while Isadora goes virtually ignored? Too close a tie with tragic modern dancer Isadora Duncan (born Angela Isadora), who was done in by her long flowing scarf, perhaps, or with fusty male version Isidore. But we think Isadora is well worth reevaluating as an Isabella alternative. Quirky couple singer Björk and artist Matthew Barney did just that and named their daughter Isadora. Isidora would be an alternative, just as proper but not quite as charming spelling—the one used as the spelling of a fourth-century saint's name.

Another plus is Isadora's connection to Isis, the mythological goddess of fertility and birth.

Isadora Wing was the liberated central character of Erica Jong's 1973 bestseller *Fear of Flying*. There is also Isadora Quagmire in Lemony Snicket's *A Series of Unfortunate Events*—who was named for Isadora Duncan.

And she could share the nickname Izzy with cousin, Isabella.

Isis

Egyptian, "throne"

Isis, the name of the supreme Egyptian goddess of the moon, sky, magic, motherhood, and fertility, is being revived by feminists and others willing to cross into arcane territory. And with the mini-craze for names that start with Is—Isabella, Isla—it's not so surprising that Isis is joining the 'I' crowd.

The ancient Isis, wife of Osiris (who happened to be her brother), was worshiped beyond Egypt into the Greco-Roman world. According to myth, the Nile River floods every year because of Isis's tears of sorrow for the death of Osiris.

Isis first entered the U.S. Top 1000 in 1994 and is now at Number 610, while she's in the Top 75 in the Netherlands.

In popular culture, Isis has been a character on *Stargate* and *Battleship Galactica*, an opera, the title of a Bob Dylan song, and the name of several rock bands.

The Isis is the name given to part of the River Thames.

Isla

Scottish variant of Islay, place name

Isla is the name of a Scottish river, an island (spelled Islay), and the hot young red-haired actress Isla Fisher, wife of Sacha Baron Cohen. Isla is also among the fastest rising names in the U.S. and has been on the Nameberry Top 1000 for girls for the past five years! Surprisingly, it popped up a few times at the turn of the last century. Isla is currently Number 6 in her native Scotland and Number 9 in England and Wales.

Isla Black Hitchens is a *Harry Potter* character.

Is Isla's newborn popularity a plus or a minus? Only you can decide, though the parent who chooses Isla because they've never heard it before and believes they rarely will again is sure to be disappointed.

Isla is part of a trend for simple, old-fashioned girls' names that start and end with a vowel: Ava, Ada, Ella, Emma, Eva, Ida, and Ivy. Some other similar names that are not as trendy as Isla: Islay and Ailsa.

Ismay

Possible variation of Esme, "esteemed, beloved"

The rise of the various Isabel names may give a boost to this variation, which has a sunny, springtime feel.

Although this name has been around since the thirteenth century, its origins remain obscure.

Ismay has appealed to several authors as a character name—Robertson Davies in his *Cornish Trilogy*, Ruth Rendell in *The Water's Lovely*, and Ken Follett in his *World Without End*.

Caveat: Could be confused with Esme.

Isolde

Welsh, "fair lady"; German "ice ruler"

Now that Tristan has been rediscovered, maybe it's time for his fabled lover in the Arthurian romances and Wagnerian opera, a beautiful Irish princess, to be brought back into the light, as well.

This would make an artistic and romantic choice, as the medieval heroine is seen as a symbol of undying—if unhappy—love.

In Marilyn French's novel *The Women's Room*, the character Isolde is nicknamed Iso. Isolde is currently a Top 500 name in the Netherlands.

Variations include Iseult, Isolt, Isoud, Isolda, and Yseult.

Ivy

Plant name

The quirky, offbeat, and energetic botanical name Ivy is enjoying a deserved revival, sure to be propelled even higher by its choice by high-profile recent parents Beyoncé and Jay-Z for baby girl Blue Ivy. Ivy—associated with clinging vines—also has an interesting history: ancient Greeks presented an ivy wreath to newlyweds as a symbol of fidelity. And in the language of flowers, Ivy signifies faithfulness.

At Number 187, Ivy is now the highest it has ever ranked; it's even more popular in Australia, where it's Number 21.

British novelist Ivy Compton-Burnett is a notable namesake and Ivy Baker Priest served as U.S. Secretary of Treasury. Another association is the prestigious Ivy League. Ivy has been a favorite of scriptwriters—she's appeared on everything from *90210* to *Gossip Girl*, *Dollhouse* to *Downton Abbey*, and is the name of a 1970s American Girl doll.

J

Jade

Spanish, "stone of the side"

As cool as the precious green stone said to transmit wisdom, clarity, justice, courage, and modesty, Jade has been rising in popularity since Mick and Bianca Jagger chose it for their daughter in 1971. Super Chef Giada de Laurentiis chose it as the English translation of her own first name.

Jade has been wildly popular in France, where it currently ranks at Number 7; it is also 21 in Belgium.

The Spanish version Jada, influenced by Jada Pinkett Smith, is not far behind Jade at Number 208.

Jamaica

Indian, "Isle with many springs"; Place name

Among the least gimmicky, most appealing, and colorful of all the names found in the atlas, Jamaica almost sings out the exotic rhythms of the West Indies.

Part of the Greater Antilles in the Caribbean, Jamaica is an eminently usable place name. Namesake writer Jamaica Kincaid was born not in Jamaica but on another Caribbean island, Antigua, and her birth name was the more prosaic Elaine Cynthia.

Jamaica's capital city, Kingston, has become a popular name for boys, thanks to its use by Gwen Stefani and Gavin Rossdale.

Jane

English, "God's gracious gift"

No, we don't consider Jane too plain. In fact, for a venerable and short one-syllable name, we think it packs a surprising amount of punch, as compared to the related Jean and Joan.

A very old name, Jane has been around since Tudor times, in this country moving in and out of fashion, once so common that it became generic—as in Jane Doe and G.I. Jane— then spent a considerable time as the back end of such smooshes as Maryjane, Bettyjane, and Sarajane.

In 1935, there were 8,900 baby Janes born in this country, whereas, in 2012 there were just over 900.

We think it's time for a fresh look at Jane—and not just in middle place. Just think of all the awesome Janes of the past, both real and fictive—from Austen to Addams to Eyre to Fonda.

January

Latin, named for Roman god Janus

Thanks to two cultural influences, January has joined March, April, June, and August as a plausible month name.

The first was a character named January Wayne in a bestselling 1973 Jacqueline Susann novel, *Once is Not Enough*, which was later made into a movie. Then, five years later, the mother-to-be of January Jones—future *Mad Men* star—was inspired by that character to give the name to her baby daughter, as did enough other parents in 1978 to bring January to Number 639 on the list.

So if you're looking for a cool namesake for an Aunt Janet or Janice, January might be the perfect wintery choice.

Jasmine

Persian flower name

Jasmine, a delicate and aromatic flower name, burst into popularity after the 1992 release of Disney's *Aladdin*, featuring Princess Jasmine—highly unusual at that time for an animated character. Propagating a garden of spelling variations, Jasmine remained solidly in the Top 50 until 2009, when it started to wilt. It is now at Number 85 and is a Top 50 name in England and Wales and Australia.

Jasmine was first used as a flower name in the West around 1900, during the blossoming of floral-name fashion, but it can be traced back to ancient Persia, where scented oil was made from the plant.

Michael Jordan, Martin Lawrence, and Nigel Barker all have daughters named Jasmine. Variants include Jazmin, Yasmin, Yasmine, and Jessamine.

Jemima

Hebrew, "dove"

Jemima, the name of a strong and beautiful biblical daughter of Job, has long been among the chicest choices of aristocratic Brits. Unfortunately, Jemima is still somewhat linked in this country to the stereotypical smiling Aunt of pancake fame, which we think is a pity. It's time to, once and for all, liberate this excellent name with its admirably peaceful meaning.

Jemima was well used by the Puritans, as was that of her sister, Keziah. Jemima is currently Number 176 in England and Wales.

Some other, more benign, images are Beatrix Potter's Jemima Puddle-Duck and characters in *Chitty, Chitty, Bang Bang, Cats*, and Thackeray's *Vanity Fair*. A real-life namesake is Jemima Kirke, who plays Jessa on *Girls*—and who happens to have a sister named Domino. Jemimah is a variant spelling, as seen in the Antonia Fraser crime series *Jemimah Shore Investigates*.

Jessamine

Variation of Jasmine, Persian flower name

Jessamine, a charming name occasionally heard in England, is just beginning to be appreciated in the U.S. as a possible successor to all the Jess names of the past. It's also spelled Jessamyn, as in Quaker novelist Jessamyn West, author of *Friendly Persuasion*— who started life with Jessamyn as her middle name.

Jessamine began to be used as a first name in Britain around 1900, along with other flower-related names. Yasmin and Yasmine are other Jasmine variations.

This would make a great choice as a namesake honoring a Jessica.

Jocasta

Greek, meaning unknown

Jocasta is a mythological name fashionably used in England but mostly ignored here. She was the mother of Oedipus, King of Thebes, whom he (oops) unwittingly married. If you can ignore that small error in judgment, you'll find an interesting and attractive 'J' name that's neither overused nor terminally dated.

Jocasta is also a moon of Jupiter and a *Cloud Atlas* character, played in the film by Halle Berry.

Jocelyn

German, "member of the Gauts tribe"

Jocelyn has gotten new life and popularity as a result of the current passion for -lyn endings which has brought it new life and popularity. Though it was a male name in medieval times, now Jocelyn couldn't sound more softly feminine. Jocelyn has been in the Top 100 since 2002.

John Galsworthy's 1989 novel *Jocelyn* is part of his *Forsyte Saga*. Singer Joss Stone's birth name was Jocelyn.

Jocelyn would make a pretty namesake name to honor a Grandma Joyce.

Jolie

French, "pretty"

Jolie is as pretty as its literal meaning; nowadays, it is also seen as a surname, via Angelina, though it was originally her middle name.

Although it is French, Jolie is rarely, if ever, used as a name in France. In the U.S., it appeared briefly on the Top 1000 list in the 1970s, then returned in 2000, following Ms Jolie's 1999 Oscar win for *Girl, Interrupted*.

The name Joely, as in actresses Richardson and Fisher, which sounds similar, is unrelated. A nice association is the iconic Picasso painting, *Ma Jolie*.

Josephine

Feminine variation of Joseph, "Jehovah increases"

With its large measure of class and character and a gently offbeat quality, plus an intriguing number of vivacious nicknames, it's no wonder Josephine is a Nameberry favorite and climbing up the national ladder as well, now at Number 160.

There have been many interesting and provocative Josephines in the past to look to: Empress Josephine Bonaparte (born Marie-Josephe-Rose and called Josephine by husband Napoleon) and exotic singer-dancer Josephine Baker (born Freda), to name just a couple.

Some of the Josephines in literature and recent pop culture are known by their nicknames—the admirably headstrong Jo in *Little Women*, Joey Potter (played by Katie Holmes) in *Dawson's Creek*, and Josie of *Josie and the Pussycats*. In *Some Like it Hot*, Josephine was the nom de femme of Tony Curtis.

Josephines have been the subjects of countless songs performed by artists ranging from Fats Domino to Tori Amos to the Black Crowes.

Josie

Diminutive of Josephine, feminine of Joseph, "Jehovah increases"

Josie is jaunty and friendly and among the most winning of all nickname names. She has never NOT been on the Social Security list since records began being kept, and is now at her highest—Number 254—since 1910.

Josie and the Pussycats, revolving around an all-girl pop band, has been a pop culture phenomenon for decades—in comic books in the 1960s, a Saturday morning animated cartoon series in the 70s, and as a live action movie in 2001. In a recent romcom, Drew Barrymore's character mentions that she was named after that Josie.

While Josie is the most stylish short form for Josephine, Jo, Feeny, and even Fifi are other possibilities.

Journey

Word name

One of the new word names, appealing to parents attracted to the idea of a spiritual—or even an actual—voyage. In 2010, Journey jumped 75 places, then another 49 in 2011, and now resides at number 327. The Journee spelling is also being used. Unisex alert: Jenna Jameson used Journey for one of her twin boys, as did the Black Eyed Peas rock musician known as Taboo.

Some might associate it with the San Francisco rock band Journey.

Judith

Hebrew, "woman from Judea"

The biblical Judith, the fourth most popular name in 1940, may be getting ready for a comeback in its full, elegant, if somewhat solemn form. Many, if not most, of those earlier Judiths were called Judy—some after Judy (born Frances) Garland—preferring it over their more formal proper name. Today, Judith, like Deborah, may have shaken off just enough to appeal to parents looking for a traditional, yet under-the-radar biblical name. And Jude would be a likelier nickname these days than the Judge Judyish Judy.

Judith of Bethulia was the singularly beautiful wife of Esau who delivered her people from the invading Assyrians.

Shakespeare named one of his daughters Judith and Dame Judi Dench was, of course, born Judith. Some other namesakes are novelists Judiths Krantz and Rossner and dancer Judith Jamison.

Julia

Feminine form of Julius, "youthful"

An enduring classic, Julia has so much going for it: ancient roots but a modern, fashionable feel, simplicity and sophistication, and connections to both saints and celebs, including actress Julia Roberts and Saint Julia of Corsica. The elegant Julia's one of the least problematic choices a parent could make.

Julia was an ancient Roman imperial name given to females in the house of a Julius, as in Caesar. Julia is also Shakespearean, Dickensian, Orwellian, and Harry Potter-related. The ground-breaking 1960s TV show *Julia* was the first to feature a non-stereotypical African-American woman. Celebrity chef Julia Childs is a notable namesake.

Julia has been in the U.S. Top 150 since Social Security records have been kept. Now at Number 65, it's even more popular internationally—the top name in Poland, Number 3 in Sweden and the Netherlands, 6 in Austria, and in the Top 45 in France, Norway, Canada, Ireland, and Spain.

If you think Julia is too simple, you might want to move to Juliet, Juliette, or Juliana, or even the Italian Giulia. Sixties short form Julie has segued from cute to middle-aged—Jules/Jools is much more current.

Juliet

English form of French Juliette, "youthful"

One of the most romantic names, the lovely and stylish Juliet seems finally to have shaken off her limiting link to Romeo. In Shakespeare's play, it was Juliet who said, "What's in a name?" This year, Juliet sits at number 253, among its highest rankings ever.

French version Juliette, pronounced the same by most English speakers though the French emphasize the last syllable, is also on the rise, but the Juliet spelling is hotter in the U.S.

Juliet Burke was a character on *Lost* and Juliet Sharp on *Gossip Girl*. Juliet Low was the founder of the American Girl Scouts.

Other ideas to consider: the original Julia, still lovely; Juliana; or even Jules.

June

Latin month named for goddess Juno

June, a sweetly old-fashioned month name that was long locked in a time capsule with June (born Ella) Allyson and June Cleaver, may not be exactly busting out all over, but is definitely showing signs of regeneration, especially as a new hipster favorite middle name.

June was a Top 100 name from 1915 to 1941, peaking in 1925 at Number 39. Then, after a quarter-century hiatus, June returned in 2008 and has risen an impressive 434 places since then.

Balthazar Getty has a daughter named June and Amanda Peet used it as her daughter Molly's middle name.

Juni is the Scandinavian version; other related choices are Junia, Juno, Juna, and Djuna.

Juniper

Tree name

Juniper is a fresh-feeling nature name—it's a small evergreen shrub—with lots of energy. A new favorite of fashionable parents, Juniper joins such other tree and shrub names as Hazel, Acacia, and Willow.

Juniper has an interesting variety of associations—it's mentioned in the Old Testament, was used in Renaissance paintings to represent chastity, has berries used to flavor gin, and Jupiter is the Saint of Comedy. A male St. Juniper was a follower of St. Francis of Assisi. *Goodnight, Moon* and *The Runaway Bunny* author Margaret Wise Brown sometimes used the pen name of Juniper Sage. And in the Junie P. Jones kids' books, Junie's full name is Juniper Beatrice. And there have been Junipers is cartoon series (*The Life and Times of Juniper Lee*) and comic strips, as well.

The name got something of a hippieish vibe via the 1969 hit Donovan song, "Jennifer Juniper."

Juniper entered the U.S. Top 1000 for the first time in 2011.

Juno

Latin, "queen of the heavens"

Juno is an ancient name that feels as fresh as if it had been minted—well, not yesterday, but in 2007. Since the release of the popular indie film *Juno*, this lively but strong o-ending Roman goddess name has become more and more prominent as a potential baby name—Coldplay's Will Champion chose Juno for one of his twins (whose brother is the kingly Rex).

Juno was the sister and wife (hmmm) of Jupiter, and the mother of Mars and Vulcan. The patron goddess of Rome and protector of women and marriage, Juno's name is heard in Virgil's *Aeneid*, Shakespeare's *The Tempest*, and Sean O'Casey's 1924 play *Juno and the Paycock*.

Justine

Feminine variation of Justin, "fair, righteous"

Justine is a French name that's never reached the popularity we think it deserves. Like its far-more-common brother Justin, Justine is sleek and sophisticated, but still user-friendly.

Justine has had a very erratic popularity path in this country. It first was noticed in the late 1950s via the eponymous novel that was part of Lawrence Durrell's *Alexandria Quarter*, but reached its highest peak—at Number 175—in the 80s, during the TV run of *Family Ties*, featuring Justine Bateman. Justine is still a Top 60 name in its native France.

K

Kaia

Feminine variation of Kai, Hawaiian, sea

The new Maia, the next Kayla, Kaia has been on the charts since the year 2000 and is now at Number 559. You might see it as a female form of the also-rising Kai, which means sea in Hawaiian and is sometimes used for girls as well, or as a Kardashianization of the ancient goddess name Caia.

Supermodel Cindy Crawford named her daughter Kaia in 2001.

Katherine

Greek, "pure"

Katherine is one of the oldest, most diverse, and all-around best names: it's powerful, feminine, royal, saintly, classic, popular, and adaptable. Katherine also has a profusion of spellings, short forms, and admirable namesakes. The Katherine spelling has been the preferred one in recent years, though Catherine (now associated with the Duchess of Cambridge) has a gentle vintage appeal, while the Katharine spelling relates to actress Kate Hepburn. Sleeker, more modern-feeling Kathryn has in fact been used for centuries and is still popular, if not exactly stylish, and the Irish have favored Kathleen.

Katherine has been used for countless literary figures over the centuries, from the spirited heroine of Shakespeare's *Taming of the Shrew* to the BFF in *Fifty Shades of Grey* to current characters on *Castle* and *The Vampire Diaries*.

Martin Short and Tim Allen have daughters named Katherine.

A profusion of nicknames includes Kate, Katie, Kathy, Kath, Kat, Kitty, Kay, and Kick. Among international variations are Catriona, Catarina, and Katrina. Two literary namesakes are Katherine Anne Porter and Katherine Mansfield.

Kathleen

Anglicized form of Irish Caitlin, "pure"

Kathleen is the early Irish import version that came between Katherine and Kaitlin, and which hasn't been used in so long it's almost beginning to sound fresh again. It was a surprise pick by one of the hip Dixie Chicks, Martie Maguire. But on the popularity list, it's in free fall, plummeting nearly 50 places a year. Kathleen was a Top 10 name from 1948 to 1951 and is the subject of several old sentimental songs, such as "I'll Take You Home Again, Kathleen."

From the eighteenth century, Kathleen Ni Houlihan appears in Irish songs as a symbol of Ireland, representing its struggle for independence.

Kathy Griffin and Kate Walsh were born Kathleen, and it's J.K. Rowling's middle name. JFK's sister Kathleen was known as Kick.

Kay

Diminutive of Katherine, "pure"

Kay, a cigarette-smoking, nightclubbing name of the 1930s, could be ready for a comeback along with cousins May/Mae and Ray/Rae.

Kay has been out of sight since the mid-1980s, but was in the double digits from 1936 to 1945, attached to several glamorous actresses of the period, such as fashion plate Kay Francis, as well as *Eloise* author Kay Thompson.

Kay was also once a unisex name, as in Sir Kay, one of the Knights of the Round Table in Arthurian legend.

Bottom line: Parents in search of a fresh, more cosmopolitan alternative to Kate might consider Kay.

Kerensa

Cornish, "love"

Kerensa, forever exotic, is a romantic Cornish name spelled with an 's' or 'z,' the most modern of the Karen family. Kerensa (or Kerenza) has ties to the Welsh Cerys.

Kerensa is a name favored by novelists who are using a Cornish setting, such as Victoria Holt in *The Legend of the Seventh Virgin.*

The Karenza spelling has a bit more zip.

Keturah

Hebrew, "incense"

Keturah, the Old Testament name of Abraham's second wife, is a possibility for anyone seeking a truly unusual and interesting biblical name—certainly a lot more distinctive than that of Abraham's first wife, Sarah.

Keturah bore Abraham six sons, who were characterized by one historian as "men of courage and of sagacious minds." Through them, Keturah was the ancestor of sixteen tribes. In the eighteenth century, it was believed by some that Keturah was the ancestor of African peoples.

This is a name not readily found in popular culture, though there was a character named Keturah on the TV sci-fi show *Stargate Atlantis*—but he just happened to be male.

Keziah

Hebrew, "cassia tree"

Keziah, also spelled Kezia, is an Old Testament name—she was one of the three daughters of Job, about whom it was said that there were no women in all the land who were so fair as Job's daughters—which was widely used for slaves and is still most common in the African-American community. The lovely, distinctive Keziah—along with others like her biblical sister Jemima—deserves full emancipation. Modern parents are also rediscovering the related, cinnamon-scented Cassia.

Some variations include Kezia, Kazia, Keshia, Kizzie, and Kizzy.

Kiera

Irish feminine form of Kieran, "dark"

Kiera entered the American popularity list in 1988 and has been slowly been making its way up the list, though lagging behind the alternate spelling Keira, largely due to the fame of actress Keira Knightley.

The original Irish spelling is Ciara, the name of an early saint (who was said to have put out fires by the power of her prayer), which was the most popular name in Ireland a couple of decades ago.

Ranking at Number 190, Keira is the more popular spelling, but Kiera is the more authentic—though both have pretty much lost their Irish accents.

Kiki

French nickname

Kiki is one of the Coco-Gigi-Fifi-Lulu bohemian-type French nickname names from the turn of the last century that have endless energy and sparkle. Artist Kiki Smith is its most well-known contemporary representative, and Kiki was the inspiring heroine of Zadie Smith's *On Beauty*.

The notorious artist-actress known as Kiki de Montparnasse (born Alice Ernestine Prin) was most famous as a muse for such Parisian artists as Soutine, Picabia, and Cocteau. English singer Kiki Dee was originally named Pauline Matthews.

Kit

Diminutive of Katherine, "pure"

Kit is a crisp, old-time British-accented unisex nickname that sounds fresh and modern today. Kitty is another so-retro-it's-cool nickname for Katherine. Kit has been used in recent years for several strong-willed movie heroines and may prove a lively alternative to Kate.

Kitty

Diminutive of Katherine, "pure"

This endearing nickname name is one Katherine pet form that predates all the Kathys and Katies, having been fairly common in the eighteenth century. With the current mini-craze for animal-related names, Kitty is sounding cute and cuddly again—she's already jumped back onto the U.K. list, at number 199.

Kitty was one of the Bennet sisters in *Pride and Prejudice* and was a character in Dickens's *Bleak House*; Ginger Rogers won an Oscar for her performance in *Kitty Foyle*, and vintage TV fans might remember the alluring Miss Kitty in *Gunsmoke*. Since then, there have been pop culture Kittys galore, including Calista Flockhart's character on *Brothers and Sisters*, a mom on *That 70's Show*, and Kitty Pryde, one of the X-Men.

Singer Kitty Carlisle was born Catherine, country singer Kitty Wells grew up as Muriel, and Presidential candidate's wife, Kitty Dukakis, was born Katharine.

A historical reference is Kitty Hawk where the Wright brothers performed their aeronautical experiments.

L

Lake

Nature name

This body of water runs deep—the best of a group of new possibilities that includes Bay, Ocean, River, and the more established Brook. It has received attention via the actress Lake Bell. Lake would make a particularly cool and refreshing middle name, as Gisele Bündchen and Tom Brady did for daughter Vivian.

Lake is also a fairly common surname, represented by 1940s blonde femme fatale Veronica (born Constance Ockelman), actress/talk show host Ricki, and Emerson, Lake & Palmer bassist Greg.

Larissa

Russian from Greek, "gull" or "pleasant, sweet"

Larissa is a nymph name that's daintily pretty and a fresh alternative to Melissa or Alyssa. Though this is the more common variation in the Western World, the original is actually Larisa.

And though it may sound like a typical Edwardian/Victorian appellation, Larissa was hardly heard here before 1967, which was two years after the release of the hit film *Doctor Zhivago*, whose heroine was Larissa, called Lara, the inspiration for the haunting "Lara's Theme."

In Greek mythology, Larissa was a nymph who was a daughter of Pegasus and loved by Mercury. In 1991, her name was given to a moon of Neptune, in honor of the nymph.

Today, Larissa is a very attractive yet underused choice that might appeal to parents who like such feminissima names as Melissa and Marissa but are seeking something a bit fresher.

Lark

Bird name

Lark is getting some new and well-deserved attention as a post-Robin and Raven bird name. Although it was first recorded as a name in the 1830s, it has never appeared on the Social Security list.

"The Lark" was used as a nickname for Cosette in *Les Misérables*; Lark Voorhees was a star of *Saved by the Bell*, and Jennifer Connelly and Paul Bettany used Lark as the middle name of their daughter, Agnes.

The expression "happy as a lark" gives this songbird name a cheery image, as well as a 'lark' being a synonym for a merry time.

Larkin is a pretty extension, as is Skylark, which is rich in cultural associations: there's the Percy Bysshe Shelley ode *To a Skylark* and the jazz classic "Skylark" written by Johnny Mercer and Hoagy Carmichael.

Laura

Latin, "laurel"

Laura is a hauntingly evocative perennial, never trendy, never dated, feminine without being fussy, with literary links stretching back to Dante. All of this makes Laura a more solid choice than any of its more decorative enhancements.

Laura has ranked on the popularity list since official U.S. records have been kept: a Top 20 name from 1963 to 1986—reaching Number 10 in 1969—and in the Top 100 until 2001. Laura is currently hot in several countries—she's the fourth most popular name in Denmark and Number 10 in Austria.

The meaning of the name, laurel, implies victory via the laurel wreath worn by Olympic athletes and Roman emperors. It was first made famous by the Laura to whom the Italian Renaissance poet Petrarch dedicated many of his love poems, and was later used by Dickens in *Bleak House*. Well known Lauras include First Lady Bush, *Little House* writer Ingalls Wilder, designer Ashley, and actors Dern and Linney.

Laurel

Latin, "laurel tree"

Laurel takes Laura back to its meaning in nature, resulting in a gentle, underused botanical option. And even more directly than Laura, Laurel relates back to the laurel wreath signifying success and peace in ancient Rome.

Sweet Laurel has been the unlikely name of two DC Comics superheroes—Laurel Kent and Laurel Gand, aka Andromeda.

Laurel received its highest ranking in 1956 when it reached Number 241. Beware though, that it has the likelihood of being mistaken for Laura.

Lavender

Plant and color name

Lavender lags far behind other sweet-smelling purple-hued Violet and Lilac but is starting to get some enthusiastic attention from cutting-edge namers. It does have a history as a name, going back to the eighteenth century, when it was also used for boys. But its recent attention comes from Lavender Brown, a witch character in the *Harry Potter* saga—though Lavender had also been previously featured as a best friend character in Roald Dahl's *Matilda*.

Lavinia

Latin, from ancient place name Lavinium

Lavinia is a charmingly prim and proper Victorian-sounding name, which actually dates back to classical mythology where it was the name of the wife of the Trojan hero Aeneas, who was considered the mother of the Roman people.

Later literary bearers include the protagonist's daughter in Shakespeare's *Titus Andronicus* (which has the line, "She is Lavinia, therefore must be lov'd."), the heroine of G.B. Shaw's *Androcles and the Lion*, and characters in *David Copperfield*, Henry James's *Washington Square*, and the contemporary *The Hunger Games* and *Downton Abbey*—and Lavinia was also used by Thackeray, T. S. Eliot, and by Ursula K. Le Guin for an eponymous novel.

Trivia tidbit: Lavinia was Ava Gardner's middle name.

With its vintage nickname Vinnie, Lavinia might well appeal to parents who favor lavender-tinged names like Amelia, Matilda, and Maude.

Layla

Arabic, "night"

A lovely musical name (remember the old Eric Clapton-Derek & the Dominos song?), Layla's seen a significant surge in popularity, partly through its kinship with hugely successful Kayla and partly because of the stylishness of virtually every name for girls that has a double l: Lila, Leila, Lily, Lillian, and so on.

Layla has rocketed precipitously up the charts to the Top 40 today—it's also in the Top 30 in the U.K., Australia and Scotland. So while the name is beautiful, she'll have plenty of company from other girls with similar names.

The spelling, Laila, is represented by boxer Laila Ali.

Leah

Hebrew, "weary"

For several years now, this serene and gentle biblical name, Leah, has been gaining a considerable following. Many use Leah as a less common alternative to Sarah or Hannah, Rebecca or Rachel.

In the Old Testament, Leah was the patient first wife of Jacob, the mother of one daughter, Dinah, and six sons including Reuben, Simeon, Levi, and Judah, and is considered one of the most important biblical matriarchs.

Leah Clearwater is a female werewolf in Stephenie Meyer's *Twilight* series, Leah Price is a leading character in Barbara Kingsolver's *The Poisonwood Bible*, and actress Leah Remini is a current bearer.

Leah has been in the U.S. Top 50 since 2008 and has been even more popular in countries as diverse as Norway (Number 14) and Ireland (Number 15).

Leatrice

Combination of Leah and Beatrice

Not quite Beatrice or Letitia, Leatrice still has a gently old-fashioned charm of its own, a kind of silent movie star aura—as in one of the top actresses of that era, Leatrice Joy. Largely due to her popularity (and that of her megastar husband John Gilbert), Leatrice was in the Top 1000 from 1922 to 1943, reaching a high of 350 in 1927.

Leila

Arabic, "night"

Leila is the root name for a lush garden of similarly exotic examples, including Laila and Layla. It was popularized by the poet Byron, who used it in his poem *Don Juan* for a ten-year-old Turkish girl, and also appears as a fairy in the Gilbert & Sullivan comic opera *Iolanthe*.

The haunting Leila has been chosen by such celebs as Al Roker and Greta Scacchi and Vincent D'Onofrio. While Leila has managed to appear on the Top 1000 list in the U.S. since its inception in 1880, phonetic form Layla is now much higher on the list. And parents attracted to girls' names with the double 'l' sound will find that most examples—from Leila to Lila to Lily and Lillian—are zooming up the charts, so while classics, they are bordering on trendiness.

Yet another alternative is Lelia, a Latin name used in Roman times.

Lena

English, Scottish, Dutch, German, and Scandinavian diminutive of various names ending in -lena
This pet form of Helena and other ena-ending names, long used as an independent name, is attracting notice again as an option both multicultural and simple. Lena was a Top 100 name from 1880 to 1920.

A past inspiration might be the lovely singer Lena Horne, a contemporary one is the hot creator of and actress in *Girls*, Lena Dunham, and another might be *Game of Thrones* actress Lena Headey.

Lena Grove is a simple but strong character in William Faulkner's *Light in August*.

Leonie

Latin, "lion"
Leonie is a chic French and German form of a name that exists in a range of variations from Leona to Leonia to Leon to Leo to Lionel, all newly fashionable after a couple of generations in style limbo.

Pronunciation can be confusing: The first syllable can be pronounced as lee or lay, the second as on or own, and the accent can be on either the first or the second syllable or be evenly distributed over all three syllables of the name, so that it sounds like the male name Leon with an ee at the end. Take your pick, but know that others might often pick differently.

Aunt Leonie is a major character in Proust's *Remembrance of Things Past*. Leonie Hemsworth is the mother of Liam and Chris, and Leonie is the name picked by Monica Bellucci and Vincent Cassel for their daughter.

Leonora

Italian variation of Eleanor, meaning unknown
Its mellifluous sound makes Leonora—which has a rich history and a tie to the popular Leo names—a keen possibility for revival.

Leonora has the distinction of being three major opera characters, including the heroines of Beethoven's *Fidelio* and Verdi's *Il Trovatore*. It was also the name of two characters played by Elizabeth Taylor—in *Secret Ceremony* and *Reflections in a Golden Eye*.

Leonora Carrington was a notorious British-born surrealist artist and writer who lived most of her life in Mexico.

Related names include Leonore, Lenora, and Lenore, subject of a famous Edgar Allan Poe poem.

Letitia

Latin, "joy, gladness"

Letitia is a delicate, once prim and proper sounding name whose staid image has been unbuttoned by numerous phonetic spellings. The original, often used in Spanish-speaking families, would still make an attractive, delicate choice. After a solid century on the Top 1000 list, Letitia fell off in the early 1980s and has not yet returned.

Letitia has a First Lady heritage, as the wife of President John Tyler. Letitia Baldridge, White House social secretary to Jacqueline Kennedy, was often known as Tish. These days, most parents would prefer the sweet, gold-locket pet forms Letty or Lettie.

Spelled Laetitia, she was the Roman goddess of celebration, happiness, and gaiety. The name appeared in the form Lettice in medieval England.

Lettie

Diminutive of Letitia, "joy, gladness"

Lettie, also spelled Letty, is a nickname name not heard in over a century, giving it the patina of a treasured antique. Lettie's style currency is rising with the trend for old-fashioned, down-to-earth nicknames. Lettie is right in step with Lottie, Hettie, Hattie, Josie, and Maisie.

One of Joan Crawford's early hit roles was in 1932 as the eponymous heroine of the film *Letty Lynton*, in which she wore a dress—dubbed the Letty Lynton dress—that became a national fad.

Lila

Arabic, "night"

Lila is one of the names with a double 'l' sound—Lila, Lola, and Lily—that have recently caught on, particularly among the celebrity set (model Kate Moss and comedian Chris Rock both have little Lilas), and we must admit we love—make that love, love, love!—them all. Sultry and forceful, Lila has a slight Near Eastern tinge. In Hinduism, Lila is a conceptualism of the universe as a playground of the gods.

The only caveat—as a group, the double 'l' names have gotten so stylish so quickly that they're verging on full-blown trendiness and tend to blend into one another. So while there may not be another little girl named Lila in town, between those named Lillian, Lily, Layla and so on, you may feel there's a double-l overload.

Lila has been a recent hot TV character name, seen on such shows as *Damages* and *Dexter*, as well as *Friday Night Lights*, where the name is spelled Lyla—another trendy version.

Trivia tidbit: Diane Sawyer was born Lila Diane.

Lilac

English from Persian, flower and color name
Could Lilac be the next Lila or Lily or Violet? It certainly has a lot going for it—those lilting double 'l's, the fabulous fragrance it exudes, and the fact that it's a color name as well, providing a ready-made nursery theme. In addition, the lilac is symbolic of first love.

Actor Stephen Moyer was ahead of the curve when he named his daughter Lilac in 2002.

Lilia

Russian, "lily"
One of a group of pretty double 'l' names, Lilia is more unusual and distinctive than some others. Truly cross-cultural, the lilting Lilia is heard in the Russian, Spanish, Hebrew, and Hawaiian communities and would be a good choice for a child born to parents of different ethnicities.

Lilia Skala was an Austrian-born Oscar-nominated actress.

Lilith

Sumerian, "of the night"
Lilith has been demonized since medieval times, with Jewish folklore portraying her as Adam's rejected first wife, who was turned into a hideous night demon for refusing to obey him. So, in spite of its gently pleasant sound, Lilith has, for the most part, been rarely heard outside of reruns of *Cheers* and *Frasier*.

But that could be changing, in part due to Lilith Fair, the all-female traveling music festival organized by Canadian singer Sarah McLaughlin, which has raised millions for women's charities.

Yet Lilith's demonic aura has followed her through popular culture in various fantasy novels, including George MacDonald's 1895 *Lilith*, comics such as Neil Gaiman's Sandman series, TV shows like *True Blood*, anime, and numerous video games.

Lillian

Elaborated form of Lily, a flower name

Lillian is having a remarkable revival, now near the Top 20, the highest it's been since the 1920s. It was a Top 10 name in its Lillian Gish-Lillian (born Helen Louise) Russell-Floradora Girl heyday at the turn of the last century.

Now, with its trendy multi-l sounds, Lillian is seen by parents as a more serious and subdued cousin of the mega popular Lily. Lilian is another spelling.

TV actress Mary McCormack and director Baz Luhrmann both have daughters named Lillian.

Lilou

Occitan pet form of French Liliane, "lily"

Lilou is a charming, rarely heard import. Occitan is a language spoken in Provence, in the south of France, in which the suffix "ou" denotes a pet form—thus, making Lilou a short form of Liliane or its Occitan form Liliana or Liliano. Its popularity in France—where it's currently Number 12—can be traced to the 1997 film *The Fifth Element*.

Pronounced lee-loo, this is an enchanting option.

Lily

Flower name

Lily is the most popular of the popular delicate century-old flower names now making a return, thanks to its many irresistible attributes: a cool elegance and a lovely sound, a symbol of purity and innocence, and a role in Christian imagery.

Lily is a favorite of celebrity parents, including Chris O'Donnell, Kate Beckinsale, Greg Kinnear, Fred Savage, and Johnny Depp and Vanessa Paradis (who made it a double bouquet, with Lily-Rose). The more proper Lillian is also rising in popularity, though Lily has long stood on its own.

Lily is an authors' favorite, some notable examples being Lily Bart, the main character of Edith Wharton's *House of Mirth*, Lily Owens in *The Secret Life of Bees*, and both mother and daughter of Harry Potter. Other current bearers are Lily Tomlin, singer Lily Allen, and the Mila Kunis character in *Black Swan*. Two one-time starbaby Lilys are now celebrities on their own: Lily Collins, daughter of Phil, and Lily Rabe, daughter of Jill Clayburgh and David Rabe.

Lily is currently a Top 5 name in England and Wales.

Linnea

Swedish, "twinflower"

Linnea is an attractive Scandinavian name that derives from the renowned eighteenth-century Swedish botanist Carl Linnaeus, who developed the Linnean system of classifying plants and animals.

Linnea is mega popular in Sweden and Norway, ranking in the Top 8—it was the Number 1 name in Norway in a recent year and actually appeared in the U.S. Top 1000 in 1903, reaching as high as 744 in 1945.

There is a charming children's book called *Linnea in Monet's Garden,* in which the protagonist visits the Giverny gardens that inspired the great Impressionist painter.

All in all, Linnea is a lovely, lilting name that could make an interesting namesake for an Aunt Lynn or Linda.

Liv

Norse, "life"

The fame of actress and Aerosmith daughter Liv Tyler helped to infuse life into this short but solid Scandinavian name that was chosen for her daughter by Julianne Moore.

Liv Tyler was given the name after her mother, Bebe Buell, saw an image of Norwegian actress Liv Ullmann on the cover of *TV Guide* shortly before her daughter's birth.

Liv combines the succinct charm of a nickname—people might assume it's short for Olivia—with the solidity of being a classic, stand-alone Scandinavian name with a life-force meaning.

Livia

Latin, "blue"

Though it sounds like a chopped-off variation of Olivia, the distinctively attractive Livia has been an independent name since the days of the ancient Romans when it belonged to Livia Drusilla, the powerful wife of the Emperor Augustus, and is still commonly heard in modern Italy.

Livia was a literary favorite from the sixteenth century, appearing in the plays of John Fletcher and Thomas Middleton and playing a minor role in *Romeo and Juliet*. Anna Livia Plurabelle is the name of a character in James Joyce's *Finnegans Wake*.

Livia entered the U.S. Top 1000 in 2004 and has gradually made her way to Number 739.

Lola

Spanish diminutive of Dolores, "lady of sorrows"

A hot starbaby name—chosen by Kelly Ripa, Chris Rock, Lisa Bonet, Denise Richards and Charlie Sheen, Kate Moss, Carnie Wilson, and Annie Lennox and used as the nickname of Madonna's Lourdes—Lola manages to be sexy without going over the top. Be warned, though: "Whatever Lola wants, Lola gets," to quote a song from the show *Damn Yankees*.

In the past, Lola has been associated with such femmes fatales as the nineteenth-century courtesan/dancer Lola Montez (born Elizabeth Rosanna), the Marlene Dietrich character Lola Lola in *The Blue Angel,* and Jean Harlow's in *Bombshell.* And it's a great Kinks song—L-O-L-A Lola.

Now ranked at Number 231 in the U.S., Lola is enjoying mass popularity internationally: Lola is Number 6 in France, 31 in England/Wales, and 37 in Spain.

London

English place name

The capital of the United Kingdom makes a solid and attractive twenty-first-century choice—with a lot more substance than Paris. This girls' geographic name has had a remarkable ascent: it came onto the popularity list in 1994 and since then, has climbed 888 places, bringing it into the Top 100. It's still in the unisex column though—it's now Number 536 for boys, with one boy starbaby (Saul "Slash" Hudson) and one girl (Neal McDonough).

There was a rich girl character named London Tipton on the Disney TV series *The Suite Life of Zack and Cody,* beginning in 2005.

Lorca

Spanish place and surname

The haunting Lorca is a place name from the Spanish province of Navarre but far more famous as the surname of the eminent Spanish poet and playwright Federico Garcia Lorca—who was the direct inspiration for the name of Leonard Cohen's now grown daughter Lorca.

An undiscovered treasure.

Lorelei

German, "luring rock"

Its double role as the mother and daughter—and even grandmother—on TV's *The Gilmore Girls* modernized, humanized, and popularized a name previously associated with the mythic seductive siren and the gold digger portrayed by Marilyn Monroe in *Gentlemen Prefer Blondes.*

In old German legend, Lorelei was the name of the beautiful Rhine River seductress whose haunting voice led sailors to hazardous rocks that would cause them to be shipwrecked. And this siren image clung to the name for ages.

The popularity of the name has zigzagged in tandem with the more modern cultural references. There was something of an upswing following the Marilyn incarnation of 1953, and again starting in 2004 via *The Gilmore Girls*—who, by the way, used an alternate spelling, Lorelai.

That show also demonstrated that the dated Lori wasn't the only short form of the name: daughter Lorelai was known as Rory, Grandma's seemingly unrelated nickname was Trix.

Loretta

Diminutive of Laura, "laurel"

Though Loretta has long ago lost its Latin flair, fashionable Sarah Jessica Parker's choice of it as the middle name of one of her twin daughters freshens it up a bit. It's one of several such names, like Anita and Rita, that we can envision making a comeback.

It's a name that was once strongly associated with the glamorous, long popular movie and then TV star Loretta Young (born Gretchen), as well as country singer Loretta Lynn—who was named after Loretta Young.

Lorraine

French, "from the province of Lorraine"

Sweet Lorraine might just be old enough to be ripe for reconsideration. This French place name has moved in and out of fashion in the few hundred years it's been used as a girls' first name, somewhat influenced by the alternative name of Joan of Arc—Saint Joan of Lorraine. It was quite popular from the 1920s to the 50s, but has pretty much been in limbo since then.

Some memorable Lorraines are *A Raisin in the Sun* playwright Hansberry, actress Bracco, and original SNL cast member Laraine Newman—the alternate spelling Laraine was popularized by 1940s star Laraine Day. Lorraine is also the name of Jack Nicholson's now grown daughter.

In the movie *Uptown Girls*, Dakota Fanning's Lorraine character was nicknamed Ray—more modern sounding than Lorrie.

Lottie

English diminutive of Charlotte, "free man"

Lottie is a nostalgic great-grandma name that conjures up lockets and lace, and—like Nellie, Josie, Hattie, Tillie, and Milly—has considerable vintage charm. A Top 100 name at the end of the nineteenth century, Lottie fell off the popularity list around 1960 but might well climb back on, most likely as a diminutive for the currently popular Charlotte. It's already an amazing Number 138 in England and Wales.

There are several Charlottes who go by Lottie in kids lit, in particular in *The Little Princess* and the film *The Princess and the Frog*.

Similar feel: Lettie/Letty.

Lotus

Greek, "lotus flower"

Lotus is one of the most exotic and languorous of the flower names, with intriguing significance in both Buddhism and Hinduism, symbolizing purity, grace and spiritual growth—not to mention a familiar yoga position.

In ancient Greece, the lotus was a legendary plant, whose fruit was eaten by the mythical lotus eaters, causing them to go into a state of hypnotic forgetfulness.

Lotus Flower is a Chinese character in the 1931 Pulitzer Prize-winning Pearl S. Buck novel, *The Good Earth*. Rain Pryor, daughter of comedian Richard, named her daughter Lotus Marie.

Lou

Short form of Louise, "renowned warrior"

Lou is usually a short form of Louise, Louisa, or Lucy in English-speaking countries, when Lou is used for girls at all. But in France and Germany, it's a fashionable choice all on its own, sure to gain even more widespread style credibility since Heidi Klum and Seal chose it for their daughter.

At one time Lou was pervasive as a girl's middle name (Mary Lou, Betty Lou), and seems to be making something of a comeback—Louis C.K. has a Mary Lou, and Keri Russell named her daughter Willa Lou.

Louisa

Feminine variation of Louis, "renowned warrior"

Louisa, a quaint vintage name, is an example of the idea that these days, old-style girls' names are more fashionable when they end with an 'a' rather than 'e,' as in Julie/Julia, Diane/Diana. Another plus: the Louisa May Alcott reference. So for the next generation, Louisa may rise again, especially with the growing popularity of other Lou/Lu-starting names, like Lucy and Luna.

Very popular in the eighteenth century, Louisa was finally toppled at the end of the nineteenth by the French form Louise, which was a top name through the first quarter of the twentieth century.

Louisa has many literary associations, including two Dickens novels—*Hard Times* and *Dombey & Sons*, and two by Jane Austen—*Pride and Prejudice* and *Persuasion*.

Louisa is a First Lady name, being the wife of President John Quincy Adams, and one of Meryl Streep's daughters is named Louisa.

Some international variations: Luisa, Lovisa, Ludovica, and Luigia. Nicknames include: Lou, Lu, Lulu, and Ouisa.

Louise

Feminine variation of Louis, "renowned warrior"

Louise has for several decades now been seen as competent, studious, and efficient—desirable if not dramatic qualities. But now along with a raft of other 'L' names, as well as cousin Eloise, Louise is up for re-appreciation—sleek and chic and stylish in Paris and starting to become so in the U.S. as well. Louisa is, perhaps, more in tune with the times, but Louise has more edge.

Louise has been a royal name in several countries, including Denmark, Sweden, France, and England; currently Queen Elizabeth has a granddaughter named Louise via her son Prince Edward. It is now the Number 2 name in Belgium and the 10th most popular name in France.

Among her most notable bearers: iconic film actress Louise Brooks and modern sculptors Louise Bourgeois and Louise Nevelson. Louise is the middle name of both Madonna and Meryl Streep, and Louise was the character played by Susan Sarandon in the feminist road movie *Thelma and Louise*.

And there's also a nature reference—the beautiful Lake Louise in the Canadian Rockies.

Lucia

Latinate feminine variation of Lucius, "light"

A lovely name—the Latinate spelling of Lucy with operatic connections—that used to be given to babies born as daylight was breaking.

A variety of references include Santa Lucia, a fourth-century martyr who was revered in the Middle Ages and the Caribbean island named for her, and the tragic opera *Lucia di Lammermoor* by Gaetano Donizetti.

Lucia is currently the Number 1 name in Spain. It was chosen for their daughters by James Joyce, Mira Sorvino, Giovanni Ribisi, Mel Gibson, and Sasha Alexander and Eduardo Pointi, among others.

Lucienne

French feminine variation of Lucien, "light"

Lucienne is a soft and ultra-sophisticated French-accented option in the Lucy family, one that could provide a fresh alternative to such fatigued Gallic choices as Danielle and Michelle.

So if you're looking for a more elegant take on Lucy, this could be it.

Lucille

French variation of Lucilla, "light"

Lucille is a name that has long been overpowered by its link to Lucille Ball, with an image of tangerine-colored hair, big, round eyes, and a tendency to stage daffy and desperate stunts. But with the newfound craze for double 'l' names like Lily and Lila and the choice of Lucille by hipster parents Maya Rudolph and Paul Thomas Anderson, Lucille may be ready to break free from its old clownish image.

Lucille has a history that far predates the 1950s. It was well used by Christians of the Roman Empire and began to be used in the U.K. and the U.S. is the nineteenth century. Reaching as high as Number 27 on the popularity list of 1919—when there was a vogue for French sounding names like Marguerite and Genevieve—Lucille stayed in the Top 40 from 1906 to 1924. This was followed by an almost thirty-year slump starting in 1977, when it fell off the list completely, only to edge back on in 2003. It has risen steadily every year since, now in the Top 400.

Lucinda

Variation of Lucia, "light"

Lucinda, an elaboration of Lucia created by Cervantes for his 1605 novel *Don Quixote*, is a pleasingly pretty alternative to Lucy. It was subsequently used by Molière in his play *The Doctor in Spite of Himself* (1666). More in tune with the times than Linda, Belinda, and Melinda, it could be used to honor someone with one of those dated names.

Lucinda was a Top 200 name in the late nineteenth century but hasn't been on the charts for more than 25 years—which could make her ripe for revival.

One appealing namesake is country-rock-blues singer Lucinda Williams. Similar in feel: Lucilla and Lucetta.

Lucretia

Feminine form of Lucretius, Roman family name

A pretty and plausible Latin name that's gotten a bad rap through the years via a link to Lucrezia Borgia, who, though long considered a demon poisoner, was actually a patron of learning and the arts.

Lucretia is a U.S. First Lady name, borne by the wife of President James A. Garfield; a worthy namesake is Lucretia Mott, a Quaker abolitionist, and peace and women's rights advocate.

In the *Harry Potter* saga, Lucretia Black Prewett is a pure-blood witch.

Lucy

Feminine variation of Lucius, "light"

In the Top 30 in England, Lucy is slowly but surely catching up here as well because it's so attractive on so many levels: Lucy is both saucy and solid, a saint's name and heroine of several great novels, and is associated with characters as diverse as the bossy Lucy in *Peanuts*, the psychedelic "Lucy in the Sky with Diamonds," and the madcap *I Love Lucy*.

In English-speaking use since medieval times, Lucy Lockit was featured in John Gay's comic opera *The Beggar's Opera*; Lucy Snowe is a main character in Charlotte Brontë's novel *Villette*.

Ludmila

Slavic, "beloved of the people"

This Slavic classic name might begin to make its mark with American parents, what with the growing popularity of the short form Mila. Borne by a tenth-century saint who had been a princess from Bohemia, Ludmila is widely used in Russia, the Ukraine, and Bulgaria.

There have been a number of champion athletes bearing the name, some using the alternate spelling Lyudmila.

This is a name with lots of energizing nicknames, including Lila, Lida, Lula, Luda—and Mila.

Lula

Diminutive of any Lu- name

Lula is one of the livelier nickname names with the fashionable double 'l' sound-- it joins Lulu, Lila, Lily, and Lou among the trendiest names today. Lula might be short for Talullah or for Lucy or Louise, or may stand on its own two adorable feet. Lula was actually a Top 50 name in the late 1880s and continued in the Top 100 for a couple of decades more.

Bryan Adams named his second daughter Lula Rosylea, sister of Mirabella Bunny, and master character namer J. K. Rowling has a Lula in her novel *The Cuckoo's Calling*.

Lulu

Diminutive of Louise or Lucy, "light"

Lulu has a firecracker personality—a singing and dancing extrovert. Interesting that Lulu was a Top 100 name when the Social Security list was born in 1880, but it's been sliding ever since and has not been in the Top 1000 for decades. Modern parents in love with Lulu might well reverse that trend.

Lulu is the now-grown daughter of musicians Edie Brickell and Paul Simon. In the Swinging London 1960s, Lulu was a popular single-named Scottish singer—whose birth name was Marie.

Luna

Latin, "moon"

This strong but shimmery moonstruck name has been growing in popularity, undoubtedly influenced by the *Harry Potter* character, Luna Lovegood. From 2010 to 2012, it quickly jumped 119 places. Luna had an earlier U.S. popularity around the turn of the last century, reaching a high of Number 403.

The name of the Roman goddess of the moon is increasingly popular in Europe—Luna is now Number 22 in Belgium, for example, and also well used in Denmark and the Netherlands.

Luna makes another appearance as the middle name of Harry Potter's daughter and as the *True Blood* teacher/shapeshifter character, Luna Garza.

Constance Marie named her daughter Luna, and Joely Fisher and Ellen Pompeo have used it as a middle name. More recently, Uma Thurman and Arpad Busson have chosen Luna as the nickname they'll use for daughter Rosalind Arusha Arkadina Altalune Florence, and Penelope Cruz and Javier Barden picked it for their little girl.

Lydia

Greek, "woman from Lydia"

Lydia is a very early place name, that of an area of Asia Minor whose inhabitants are credited with the invention of coinage and of having strong musical talent—as well as great wealth.

Although mentioned in the New Testament (Lydia was the first European convert of Saint Paul), it didn't really emerge as a viable first name until the eighteenth century, promoted via the character of Lydia Languish in Sheridan's popular 1775 play, *The Rivals*, and the youngest of the Bennet girls in *Pride and Prejudice*.

Lydia continued to be a literary favorite, found in the novels of George Eliot and D. H. Lawrence. And there's also the iconic Groucho Marx ditty: "Lydia the Tattooed Lady."

Lydia is rising in popularity—it's now in the Top 100—increasingly appreciated for its history and haunting quality. Cute nickname: Liddy or Lydie

Lyra

Greek, "lyre"

Lyra is a constellation name taken from the lyre of Orpheus. It contains the star Vega and thus could make a melodic choice for a parent interested in music, astronomy, or mythology. It has more depth and history than Lyric and is more unusual than Lila.

Lyra was chosen for their daughter by Sophie Dahl and Jamie Cullum. Lyra Belacqua is the heroine of Philip Pullman's *His Dark Materials* series—seen in the movie *The Golden Compass*.

M

Mabel

Diminutive of Amabel, "lovable"

Mabel is a saucy Victorian favorite searching for its place in modern life; if you love offbeat old-fashioned names like Violet or Josephine, only sassier, Mabel is one for you to consider—it could make a comeback à la Sadie. Several celebs have chosen it, including Chad Lowe, Nenah Cherry, Bruce Willis, and Dermot Mulroney.

Last seen on the popularity list (just barely) in 1965, Mabel was a Top 20 name in the 1880s and 1890s. There is a Princess Mabel in The Netherlands today, born a commoner and married to Prince Friso.

Some of Mabel's cultural references include Charlie Chaplin's favorite leading lady Mabel Normand, jazz singer Mabel Mercer, the lead character in Gilbert & Sullivan's *Pirates of Penzance*, and the baby on the sitcom *Mad About You* (in which Mabel was an acronym for Mothers Always Bring Extra Love—a nice thought).

Madeline

Variation of Magdalen, "high tower"

This lovely name with a soft and delicate image is an old-fashioned favorite that returned to favor in the 1990s, combining a classic pedigree with a cute nickname option: Maddy.

Madeline has been found frequently in literature, from the poems of Keats and Tennyson to Dickens's *Nicholas Nickleby* to the charming and much loved children's books of Ludwig Bemelmans, starring the sprightly French schoolgirl.

The name can be found in several spellings, including the French Madeleine and the non-classic Madelyn and Madalyn.

Never off the Social Security list, Madeline entered the Top 100 in 1994, peaking at Number 50 in 1998.

Madrigal

Latin, "song for unaccompanied voices"

Madrigal might be a pretty and highly distinctive choice for a child of a musical family—or for the parent looking for a less conventional path to the nickname Maddie than Madeline or Madison. Definitely more striking than Cadence or even the increasingly popular Aria.

The word madrigal refers both to a medieval short lyrical poem and a form of vocal chamber music that originated in the Italian Renaissance. And on a completely different note, you may have heard it on the TV show *Breaking Bad* as the name of an industrial conglomerate.

Mae

Diminutive of Margaret, "pearl" and Mary, "bitter"

Mae, a sweet and spring-like old-fashioned name, hadn't been on the national charts in forty years, but finally made it back in 2010. Mae is one of the prettiest middle name options (Eric Clapton has an Ella Mae, Greg Kinnear an Audrey Mae, and Ian Ziering a Penna Mae). The May spelling makes it more of a month name, while Mae makes it an antique nickname name. Both can stand on their own—as seen by Kathryn Hahn's choice of Mae as her daughter's first name.

Mae, a top 100 name through 1920, was big in early film history—there were leading actresses named Mae Clarke, Mae Marsh, Mae Busch, and Mae Murray. Towering over them (figuratively) was Mae West, who changed the name from sweet to sexy. This image continued with Madonna's character in *A League of Their Own*, known as "All the way Mae."

Mae Jemison was the first African-American woman to travel to space.

Maeve

Irish, "she who intoxicates"

Maeve is a short and sweet legendary ancient Irish queen's name that is now finding well-deserved favor here—and would make an excellent first or middle name choice, with more character and resonance than Mae/May and more modern charm than Mavis.

Maeve appears in Irish mythology in two forms, one as the powerful Queen of Connacht, the other as the queen of the fairies.

Chris O'Donnell, Lili Taylor, and Kathryn Erbe used Maeve for their daughters. The Irish author Maeve Binchy is a well-known bearer.

Irish spelling Meabh is in the Top 100 in Ireland but not recommended in the U.S. Other Gaelic spellings are Medb and Meadhbh.

Magenta

Color name

Magenta is a vivid Crayola color name that could make a vivid, colorful choice. It was named in 1859 after the Napoleonic Battle of Magenta, a town in Northern Italy.

One of J.K. Rowling's imaginative *Harry Potter* name creations, it was attached to Magenta Comstock, an experimental artist whose portrait eyes would follow the viewer around and out of the room. There are also characters named Magenta in *The Rocky Horror Picture Show* and on the Nickelodeon show *Blue's Clues*, for an artistic puppy who loves to draw.

Magenta is a deep purplish-red color, somewhat similar to Fuchsia—an equally original option.

Magnolia

Flower name

Magnolia, a sweet-smelling Southern belle of a name, made famous via the iconic Edna Ferber novel and musical *Showboat*, is one of the latest wave of botanical names, along with exotic blossoms Azalea and Zinnia.

Magnolia has been chosen for his daughter by Adrian Young of No Doubt—which happens to be a fabulous baby-naming consortium, as well as a great group.

In *Showboat*, the Magnolia character goes by nicknames Noa, Nollie, and Maggie.

Magnolia charted on the popularity list almost every year from 1880 to 1940, topping at Number 420 in 1909.

Magnolia Breeland is a character on the TV show *Hart of Dixie*—who happens to have a sister named Lemon and a father named Brick.

Maisie

Scottish diminutive of Margaret, "pearl"

Maisie, a hundred-year-old favorite, is in perfect tune with today. Spelled Maisy in a popular children's book series, Maisie is rising in tandem with cousin Daisy. While Maisie might be short for Margaret, Mary, or even a name like Melissa or Marissa, it stands perfectly well on its own.

In literature, Maisie is the name of the precocious young title character in the Henry James novel *What Maisie Knew*, and is also the main female character in Rudyard Kipling's *The Light That Failed*. And to bring things up to date, Maisie is a half-blood character in the *Harry Potter* series.

Though she's off the grid in the U.S., Maisie is Number 21 in England and Wales, and Maisy is 99.

Mamie

Diminutive of Mary, "bitter" or Margaret, "pearl"

Mamie is back. Having finally shorn her Mamie Eisenhower bangs, this insouciant and adorable nickname name is perfect if you want a zestier way to honor a beloved Aunt Mary. Meryl Streep's actress daughter, properly named Mary Willa, is called Mamie Gummer. You might think of Mamie as a sister of the stylish Maisie.

Mamie was a Top 100 name from the time records were published through 1912, falling off the list in 1966. There have been Mamie characters on two recent sitcoms: *Hot in Cleveland* and *3rd Rock from the Sun*.

Manon

French diminutive of Marie, "bitter"

Manon is an endearing French pet name for Marie or Marianne; it has the exotic yet straightforward feel that makes it a viable import. *Manon of the Spring* was a gorgeous French film, *Manon Lescaut* a 1731 novel by Abbe Prevost, set in France and Louisiana, that was controversial in its day. It formed the basis of operas by Puccini and Massenet and several films and TV series.

Manon is currently the fourth most popular name in France and Number 9 in Belgium.

British actors Damian Lewis, of *Homeland*, and Helen McCrory have a daughter named Manon.

Mara

Hebrew, "bitter"

Mara is the evocative ancient root of Mary, appearing in the Book of Ruth, in which Naomi, devastated after the birth of her two sons, says, "Call me not Naomi; call me Mara."

Mara is a multicultural name, also a Kiswahili word meaning "a time" and could be conceived as a geographical name, being a river flowing through Kenya and Tanzania.

As a child actress, Mara Wilson played leading roles in *Matilda* and *Mrs Doubtfire*.

It is also spelled Marah.

Margaret

English from Greek, "pearl"

Margaret is a rich, classic name used for queens and saints. Margaret was replaced for decades by less starchy forms like Maggie and Meg, but some stylish parents are reviving Margaret in full, attracted by its strong sound and classic status, as an alternative to Elizabeth or Katherine.

Margaret is also an important family name for many people, having ranked near the top through the first half of the 1900s. An extremely well-used name since medieval times, Margaret is still considered the Scottish national name.

Margaret has been one of the most Christian and royal of female names—attached to the patron saint of women in childbirth and to various queens and princesses in England, Scandinavia, Austria, and the Netherlands, and to the first female prime minister of Great Britain, Margaret Thatcher.

If you're honoring an ancestral Margaret, there are many fresh and new alternatives, from the French Marguerite—very stylish in Paris—to the diminutive Margo (or Margot). In French, Marguerite is another word for daisy, making Daisy another appropriate Margaret short form or honorific, as is Maisie. Other offspring of Margaret include Madge, Marjorie/Margery, Megan, Molly, Polly, Peggy, Greta, and Rita.

Margot

French diminutive of Margaret, "pearl"

Margot, a French pet form of Marguerite, has a lot going for it: spelled with or without the final 't,' it's one of the few girls' names with the dynamic o-ending sound; it's familiar, yet uncommon enough to be distinctive.

Movie buffs will remember Bette Davis's archetypal role as Margo Channing in *All About Eve* (the actress named her own daughter Margot), while balletomanes will associate the name with the great English dancer Margot Fonteyn (born Margaret).

In the film *Margot at the Wedding*, Margot was played by Nicole Kidman; in *The Royal Tenenbaums*, Gwyneth Paltrow was Margot T. Trivia note: Margaux Hemingway was originally Margot, but changed the spelling to honor the wine from the French village of Margaux that was drunk by her parents on the night she was conceived.

Marguerite

French variation of Margaret, "pearl"

Marguerite is a classic French name with a remnant of old-fashioned Gallic charm and is also a variety of daisy. Chic again in Paris, it's definitely ripe for revival here.

Another reason you might want to consider it: Saint Marguerite was an adventurous seventeenth-century nun who set up schools throughout wilderness Quebec. Marguerite has also been a French royal name.

Marguerite was in the Top 100 in this country from 1890 to 1921.

Probably its most famous fictional bearer is Marguerite Gautier, tragic heroine of the Alexandre Dumas novel *La Dame aux Camélias*, known in film as *Camille* and played most notably by Greta Garbo. Marguerite is also the heroine of Gounod's *Faust* and the *Scarlet Pimpernel* novels.

Marguerite Duras wrote many novels, plays, and movies, most notably the bestselling *L'Amant* (*The Lover*) which became a successful film, and she was also the screenwriter of *Hiroshima mon amour*.

Maya Angelou was born Marguerite; it was her younger brother who shortened it.

Maria

Latin variation of Mary, "bitter"

As the most common female name in all Spanish-speaking countries, this saintly Latin variation of Mary is more likely to be an ethnic name, though old-line Wasps still favor it, and it retains a timeless beauty.

This widespread name understandably has produced notable namesakes in almost every field—opera's Maria Callas (born Sophia Cecelia), tennis's Sharapova, education's Montessori, ad infinitum. And she's been celebrated in song as well, from "Ave Maria" to the eponymous song in *West Side Story* to "How Do You Solve a Problem Like Maria?" in *The Sound of Music*.

Mariah

Latin variation of Mary, "bitter";

Thanks to Mariah Carey, everyone now knows this name—and is aware that Mariah's pronounced with a long i—just as Maria was in the Jane Austen era. And though Mariah now sounds modern, it was heard as far back as 1550 in Great Britain.

The song "They Call the Wind Maria" (pronounced Mariah) was introduced in the 1951 Broadway musical *Paint Your Wagon* and was the inspiration for Mariah Carey's name.

Though Mariah reached a peak in the mid-1990s, it is still a popular choice.

Marian

French medieval variation of Marie

Marian's (and sister spelling, Marion's) image has gone through a sea change of late, recalling less middle-aged matron and more Robin Hood's romantic Maid Marian. Some influences: the SJ Parker/M. Broderick twin daughter Marion and the glamorous French actress Marion Cotillard.

Marian was a Top 100 name from 1912 through 1934.

Marian Anderson was a great African-American contralto singer and Marion (born Marian) Ross was the mom on *Happy Days*. And—trivia tidbit—Marion Tweedy was the maiden name of Molly Bloom in James Joyce's *Ulysses*.

At one time, Marian was considered the female form and Marion the male—after all, macho John Wayne was born Marion.

Marigold

Flower name

Marigold, once found almost exclusively in English novels and aristocratic nurseries, is beginning to be talked about and considered here; it does have a sunny, golden feel. The marigold was the symbol of the Virgin Mary.

Marigold appears in several children's book titles, such as *Magic for Marigold, Once Upon a Marigold,* and *Marigold in Godmother's House,* and in the adult *Quartet in Autumn* by Barbara Pym. On the TV show *1600 Penn*, Marigold was the President's young daughter.

Marin

Latin, "of the sea"

Marin is a lovely county north of San Francisco and a lovely baby name on the rise, one which sounds more refreshing than the more familiar Marina.

As a place name, Marin is pronounced with the accent on the second syllable, Ma-RIN, sort of like Marie, though when used as a name, many would say MAR-in, sort of like marry.

Marin is unisex in several European countries (in Croatia it's currently Number 29 for boys); Maren is an alternate, Scandinavian, spelling. In France, a very fashionable alternative for girls is Marine.

Marina

Latin, "of the sea"

This pretty sea-born name was used to dramatic effect by Shakespeare in his play *Pericles* for the virtuous princess who says she is "Call'd Marina, for I was born at sea."

Marina was an epithet of Venus, and there were more than one saint of that name. It was used in Britain from as early as the fourteenth century.

Although it reached as high as Number 219 in 1994, Marina never had the trendy feel of cousins Melissa and Marissa. It's now very popular in Spain—just outside the Top 25.

A prominent current bearer is Marina Abramovic, widely publicized New York-based Serbian performance artist. It was the name chosen for his daughter, Marina Pearl, by Matt LeBlanc.

Maris

Latin, "of the sea"

Maris is an unusual and appealing name that has never appeared in the U.S. Top 1000, overshadowed by its twentieth century elaboration, Marisa/Marissa. It derives from the phrase "Stella Maris," star of the sea, one of the many epithets of the Virgin Mary, and became familiar via the unseen (but unliked) character of sitcom Frasier's ex-sister-in-law.

As a surname, Maris is associated with legendary NY Yankee, Roger Maris.

Marisol

Spanish combined form of Maria and sol, "sun"

Marisol is a Latina favorite, and an excellent candidate for cross-culturization, à la Soledad and Paz.

The striking French-born Venezuelan artist Marisol Escobar—known simply by her first name—is noted for her witty Pop Art figural sculptures.

This is a great idea for a summer baby, combining elements of the sun and the sea.

Marjorie

Scottish variation of Margery, diminutive of Margaret, "pearl"

Scottish Marjorie and her English twin Margery were early twentieth-century favorites that date back to medieval times, when popular among the royals. They were at their height in the 1920s, when they were seen as more lively versions of the old standard. Marjorie was always the preferred spelling—in the Top 25 from 1921 to 1927.

One notable namesake is Marjorie Stinson, a pioneering aviator who was the first female airline pilot. Marjorie Kinnan Rawlings was the author of the moving novel *The Yearling* and Margery Williams's name is on the cover of kiddie favorite, *The Velveteen Rabbit*—plus there's always the old nursery rhyme "See-Saw, Margery Daw."

Nickname Margie was once seen as a prime pert teenager moniker in movies and such vintage TV shows as *My Little Margie*. Marge is strongly associated with Homer Simpson's wife.

Neither Margery nor Marjorie have been around for decades, but their lively three-syllable, ee-sound ending makes it a modern possibility. Trivia tidbit: Marjorie is said to have faded with the advent of the word "margarine."

Marlowe

Variation of Marlow, "driftwood"

Is it Marlo, Marlow, or Marlowe? Suddenly they all seem very much in the air, in tune with rhyming cousins Harlow and Arlo. It all started when Margaret Julia Thomas began being known as Marlo (after being previously nicknamed Margie and Marlow). More recently, Jason Schwartzman used the e-ending version for his young daughter, Marlowe Rivers, as did Sienna Miller for her baby girl Marlowe Ottoline.

While we love the o-sound at the end and think that Marlo or Marlow or Marlowe, however it's spelled, has an attractively lush sound, we do find the trio a bit confusing.

Marlowe is, of course, a popular surname, going back to sixteenth-century poet and playwright Christopher and also exemplified by iconic Raymond Chandler private eye Philip.

Martha

Aramaic, "lady"

The name of our first First Lady still has something of a prim and proper image, academic and efficient. That quiet traditional and tasteful gestalt is exactly what makes Martha appealing to some parents today.

The New Testament Martha, sister of Lazarus and Mary of Bethany, was a solicitous housekeeper who looked after the material welfare of Jesus when he was a guest in her home. For this reason Martha has since been identified with domestic labor and hospitality and is the patron saint of housewives, waiters, and cooks (à la Martha Stewart, who shares her name with her mother).

Martha has been a royal name in Scandinavia, the subject of a Beatles song, "Martha My Dear," and is also associated with the New England island, Martha's Vineyard. Livelier foreign forms that have been used in this country are Marta, Martine, and Martina.

Modern dancer/choreographer Martha Graham would make a notable namesake for a dance aficionado.

Marvel

English word name

Marvel, now a character name in *The Hunger Games* series, was a miracle name of yesterday, on the girls' Social Security list until 1941 and reaching a high of 487 at the turn of the last century, when Marva was also in style.

These days it does have something of a comic book feel, what with Marvel Comics, Captain Marvel, and Mary Marvel, and despite the fact that Marvel is a male character in *The Hunger Games*, we can see some parents reviving this name for their own little marvel of a baby girl.

Mary

Hebrew, "bitter"

Mary, the quintessential New Testament name, was Number 1 for girls for four hundred years. Though still close to the Top 100, at 123, Mary is used now mostly for religious or family reasons. If it's style you're after, Mary's many diminutives and derivatives such as Maire, Mamie, May, Mitzi, Molly, Maura, Marietta, and even Maria are all more fashionable.

Mary was the most popular and enduring female Christian name in the English-speaking world (as were Maria and Marie in Spanish and French) at least until 1950. That was when in the U.S. Mary was finally dethroned by such trendy upstarts as Linda and Karen.

There are six Marys in the Bible, including the Virgin Mary, Mary Magdalene, Mary the sister of Martha and Lazarus, Mary the mother of James and Joseph, and Mary the mother of Mark; and there have been British royal Marys beginning in the sixteenth century. In earliest times, Mary was considered too sacred to be used by ordinary mortals;

it finally began to be employed in England in the twelfth century, and by the sixteenth, had blanketed the female population to the point where dozens of pet forms had to be contrived to distinguish one Mary in the family from the others.

The poet Byron deemed Mary a "magic" name, and the song proclaims it "a grand old name." Mary has always been a good-girl name, as reflected by such mid-century icons of propriety and wholesomeness, Mary Poppins and Mary Tyler Moore. The lovely Lady Mary Crawley of *Downton Abbey* has restored some freshness to the name.

Among the celebs who dropped their birth name of Mary are Meryl Streep, Debbie Reynolds, and Lily Tomlin.

Matilda

German, "battle-mighty"

The comeback of this sweet vintage name has been prompted by a boomlet of starbaby Matildas, beginning with chef Gordon Ramsey's in 2002 and Moon Unit Zappa's two years later, but the renaissance of this name of the charming Roald Dahl heroine was assured when Michelle Williams and the late Heath Ledger chose Matilda for their daughter.

Matilda was introduced to the English-speaking world by the eleventh century Matilda of Flanders, queen of William the Conqueror, then used for his granddaughter, known as Maud. In literature, Matilda appeared in Dickens's *Nicholas Nickleby*. Trivia tidbit: The Matilda in the Australian song "Waltzing Matilda" refers not to a person but to the knapsacks that swing, or waltz, on the backs of itinerant laborers as they walk along.

Currently Number 53 in the U.K. and 18 in Australia, Matilda has a choice of great nicknames: Tillie for the bold, Mattie for the shy, and Tilda for the slightly more eccentric, such as Tilda Swinton, born Katherine Matilda.

Molly Ringwald used the spelling Mathilda for her daughter.

Maude

Variation of Matilda, "battle-mighty"

Maude, also spelled Maud, is a lacy, mauve-tinted name that was wildly popular a hundred years ago, but has been rarely heard in the past fifty. Some stylish parents are starting to choose it again, especially as a middle.

Maud's early popularity was influenced by the Tennyson poem that included the oft-quoted line, "Come into the garden, Maude." Then, in the 1970s, along came the sitcom *Maude*, featuring the vociferous and opinionated character Maude Finlay, putting a very different spin on the name. But enough decades have now passed for the name to have settled back into its soft, sweet pastel image.

The Maud spelling has British royal associations via the daughter of Edward VII, who later became Queen of Norway; Maud Gonne was a famous Irish political activist.

Mauve

French, "violet-colored"

Mauve is an offbeat color name whose soft and sentimental Victorian spirit is conveyed by the name. One of the newer color names, like Blue, Gray and Plum, which are increasingly being used as novel middle names.

Mavis

French, "songbird"

Mavis, another word for the song thrush, is also a relative of the Welsh word for strawberries, mefus. Mavis has something of a British World War II feel, a friend of Beryl and Doris, but it was quite popular in the U.S. a couple of decades earlier, peaking in the Roaring Twenties. With the renewed interest in names ending in 's'—and in bird names— Mavis could make a return, especially with the new interest in Maeve.

Some noted bearers of the name are R&B singer Mavis Staples, a member of the Staple Singers, Canadian writer Mavis Gallant, and the feminist activist Mavis Leno.

Mavis Gary was the name of the Charlize Theron character in the film *Young Adult*. And—trivia tidbit—in her short-running eponymous sitcom, Whoopi Goldberg's character was named Mavis.

Maxine

Feminine form of Max, "greatest"

With the success of all names Max, from Max itself to Maxwell to Maxfield to Maximilian, it's just possible that Maxine could be lured away from her mah-jongg game at the clubhouse and into the nursery. She's already been chosen by hip musician Nick Hexum for his daughter, sister to Echo.

Maxine was a Top 100 name from 1915 to 1930, attached to such celebs at the time as actress Maxine Elliott and one of the singing Andrews Sisters, and now to Congresswoman Maxine Waters and Chinese-born writer Maxine Hong Kingston.

May

Diminutive of Margaret, "pearl" and Mary "bitter"; month name

May is a sweet old-fashioned name that hasn't been on the national charts in several decades, but is definitely sounding fresh and spring-like. Parents are beginning to see it once more as one of the prettiest middle name options.

May started as one of the innumerable pet forms of Mary and Margaret, as well as a springtime month name along with April and June. She's represented in literature by May Bartram in Henry James's *The Beast in the Jungle* and May Welland in Edith Wharton's *The Age of Innocence*.

Actresses Emily Morton and Madeline Stowe named their daughters May, and Eric Clapton and Jodie Sweetin used it in middle place for theirs.

Maya

Variation of Maia, Greek and Roman mythological name

Maya, which has an exotic, almost mystical image, has been steadily climbing in popularity, and is now firmly in the Top 70.

In addition to being the name of a Central American culture, Maya was the legendary Greek mother of Hermes by Zeus, and means "illusion" in Sanskrit and Eastern Pantheism. It can also be spelled Maia.

Famed author Maya Angelou was born Marguerite; Maya was coined by her brother saying "mya sister." Uma Thurman and Ethan Hawke's daughter is Maya Ray; British designer Phoebe Philo also has a Maya, named for Angelou.

To the Romans, Maia/Maya was the incarnation of the earth mother and goddess of spring, after whom they named the month of May.

Melisande

French form of Millicent, "strong, industrious"

This old-time fairy tale name is rarely heard in the modern English-speaking world, but it's so, well, mellifluous, that it would make a lovely choice for a twenty-first century girl—a romanticized tribute to an Aunt Melissa or Melanie.

Pelleas and Melisande is a play by Maeterlinck, the inspiration for the Debussy opera of the same name. In modern times, Melisande became a princess via the Rankin and Bass film *The Flight of Dragons*. And Broadway buffs might remember Melisande as the name the main character Ella Peterson takes in the musical *Bells are Ringing*.

Mercedes

Spanish, "gracious gifts, benefits"

Mercedes is one of the few names attached to luxury living that we can wholeheartedly recommend, it being a legitimate Spanish appellation stemming from one of the epithets given to the Virgin Mary—Santa Maria de las Mercedes, or Our Lady of the Mercies. The car, by the way, was named after the eleven-year-old daughter of the Daimler company's French distributor in 1901.

Always well used in the Spanish-speaking community, Mercedes had a sudden spurt of overall popularity in the 1990s, moving as high as Number 164 in 1991.

Mercedes has been widely used in a variety of art forms—from the opera *Carmen* to Dumas' *The Count of Monte Cristo* to the film *Pan's Labyrinth* to the TV show *Glee*.

Mercy

English, "compassion"

The quality of mercy makes this lovely Puritan virtue name undervalued today. Rarely heard since the late nineteenth century, we see Mercy as one choice destined for a comeback. Right now, it's both stylish and distinctive, a rare and wonderful combination.

Mercy is one of the characters with allegorical names in John Bunyan's *A Pilgrim's Progress*, and Mercy Pecksniff appears in Dickens's novel *Martin Chuzzlewit* with the nickname Merry. Mercy Lewis, in Arthur Miller's play *The Crucible*, was based on a real-life character, a witness at the Salem witch trials. Another historic Mercy is Mercy Warren, Revolutionary period patriot and writer of plays, books, and poetry.

Comic/sidekick Andy Richter, when he named his daughter Mercy, joked, "Just in case Puritanism comes back, we'll be ready with a real Puritan name"; Madonna renamed her Malawi-born daughter Mercy James.

Meredith

Welsh, "great ruler"

Meredith is a soft, gentle-sounding name with subtle Welsh roots, used mainly for girls now, associated with TV personality Meredith Vieira. It's been the name of two TV doctors: Dr. Meredith Grey is the female-surgeon protagonist of *Grey's Anatomy* and Dr. Meredith Fell appears on *The Vampire Diaries*—not to mention red-haired Meredith on *The Office*.

Meredith's highest point of popularity for girls in the U.S. was in the late 1970s and into the 80s, when it ranked as high as Number 140.

Mia

Scandinavian short form of Maria, "bitter"

Mia is an appealingly unfussy multicultural name that has enjoyed a meteoric rise up the charts and is now firmly in the Top 10.

Mia's success is largely attributable to Mia Farrow—born Maria. Her name entered the Top 1000 for the first time in 1964, the very year that Farrow gained wide attention for her role on the nighttime soap *Peyton Place*.

We see Mia as the daughter of Nina, or maybe Maya, and the granddaughter of Mary: a name that has something for nearly everyone. It works for the parent who wants a name that is simple and modern, and for those who seek a name with genuine depth given that it springs from Maria. Mia sidesteps all the curlicues and ruffles attached to names like Isabella and Olivia, yet it's distinctly feminine.

And in some ways, Mia doesn't feel as trendy as its popularity standing might indicate. It's likable yet not really stand out, a compromise choice for a lot of parents. Alternatives include a wide range of rhyming names that are less popular: Leah, Tea, Thea, Gia, Nia, and Pia.

Kate Winslet is the mother of Mia Honey, and Ian Ziering is dad to Mia Loren.

Mia is also an Italian word meaning "mine."

Mignon

French, "delicate, dainty"

Charming French endearment, first used as a name by Goethe, that now makes an appealing choice—though the proper feminine form is Mignonne. Note, though, that this is not actually used as a name in France, where Manon would be the closest choice.

Mignon is the leading character, a young Italian dancer, in Goethe's novel *Wilhelm Meister's Apprenticeship*, upon which an eponymous opera was based. Mignon Eberhart was a popular American mystery writer.

The name is also associated with the flower name Mignonette.

Mila

Diminutive of Milena, "love, warmth, grace"

Mila is an appealing European short-form favorite shared by one-time *That 70s Show* starlet, Ukranian-born Mila Kunis—more recently acclaimed for her work in *Black Swan*. Her full birth name is Milena.

Mila is quickly rising in popularity, jumping nearly 250 places to Number 115 in the past two years alone!

It's also a versatile nickname: former President Bush's daughter, Jenna, recently named her daughter Margaret Laura, after the child's two grandmothers, to be called Mila.

Milena

Czech, "love, warmth, grace"

This popular name in various Slavic countries and in Italy holds considerable Continental appeal. It is the full name of Ukranian-born rising star Mila Kunis, most noted for her award-winning role in the film *Black Swan*. Another actress bearing the name is Milena Govich of *Law & Order*.

Milena, which entered the U.S. Top 1000 this year, is currently Number 20 in Poland. Short form Mila has been on the U.S. list since 2006 and is now ranking at Number 115—and looks to rise even higher.

Millicent

German, "strong in work"

Combining the mild and the innocent, this sweet and feminine name is worthy of a comeback, in the mode of Madeline and Cecilia. Its original, also attractive, form is Melisende.

Millicent has been in use since the Middle Ages and was in the Top 500 in the 1920s.

Millicent Hargrave is a character in Anne Brontë's *The Tenant of Wildfell Hall*, and Millicent Henning is found in Henry James's *The Princess Casamassima*, and she appears not once but twice in *Harry Potter*; she is also Barbie's middle name.

And, of course, Millie/Milly is one of the cutest of the nostalgic nickname names.

Millie

Diminutive of Mildred or Millicent, "strong in work"

Millie is fashionable again in London and Wales where it's Number 35 and especially in Scotland where's it's reached Number 11. It's a possibility here for parents who like the offbeat, frilly, and old-fashioned. Millicent would be the more appealing long form, but many people are using Millie all by its cute self.

Millie was in the Top 1000 here until 1966, peaking at Number 128 way back in 1881; it made a return appearance in 2009 and is beginning to climb. The name got a lot of attention via the 1967 film *Thoroughly Modern Millie*.

Fashionable relative: Milla or Mila. Tillie is another old-school nickname that, like Millie, sounds modern again.

Minerva

Latin, "of the mind, intellect"
Minerva is the long-neglected name of the Roman goddess of wisdom and invention, the arts and martial strength—which might appeal to adventurous feminist parents.

In *Harry Potter*, Minerva McGonagall is a Witch and Deputy Headmistress of Hogwarts, and in the *Artemis Fowl* books, Minerva Paradizo is equally intellectual. There's also a series of kids' mystery books centering around a Minerva Clark.

Nickname Minnie fits right in with the other currently stylish vintage nickname names. Curiously, though, actress Minnie Driver was not born Minerva—but Amelia.

Minnie

Diminutive of Minerva, "of the mind, intellect"
Minnie was wildly popular at the turn of the last century—it was the fifth or sixth most popular name throughout the 1880s—but is completely obscure today. Blame Mickey's girlfriend. Though it's possible that the up-and-coming trend toward old-fashioned nickname names—think Maisie, Mamie, Millie—may give Minnie (all on its own, not as a short form of anything) a new moment in the sun. Minnie Driver (born Amelia) has given it some modern celeb cred.

There have been characters named Minnie in Dickens's *Little Dorrit* and Eugene O'Neill's *Mourning Becomes Electra*. Cab Calloway's "Minnie the Moocher" is a jazz classic.

Minnie can really be short for just about any M name (and some non-M names as well, such as Wilhelmina), including Minerva, Mary, and Margaret.

Minta

English diminutive of Araminta, invented name
Minta is an eighteenth-century short form of a literary beauty still used in England today but yet to be discovered by American baby namers. It has a fresh and dainty feel.

Virtually unheard today, Minta was on the U.S. popularity lists for most years between 1880 and 1901. Minta (born Araminta) Durfee was a popular silent screen actress married to Roscoe 'Fatty' Arbuckle; Minta Doyle was a character in the Virginia Woolf novel *To the Lighthouse*.

Mirabelle

French, "marvelous!"

If you're looking for a fresher -belle name than Isabelle, Mirabelle is lovely, and we also like the extra flourish of Mirabella. And if you want a nature tie, Mirabelle is also the name of a delicate French plum.

Steve Martin chose the name for the heroine of his novel *Shopgirl*—Mirabelle Buttersfield.

Another pretty possibility: Maribel.

Miranda

Latin, "marvelous"

Miranda, a shimmeringly lovely, poetic name that was invented by Shakespeare for the beautiful and admirable young heroine of his play, *The Tempest*, is still a recommended choice, even though its popularity peaked in the 1990s, partially as an antidote to Amanda. But while Amanda now sounds dated, Miranda retains a good measure of its charm.

Miranda made a big impression in *Sex and the City* and *The Devil Wore Prada* and was also a *Harry Potter* character—Miranda Goshawk, author of a Book of Spells. She was a Bond Girl in *Die Another Day*.

Attractive real life Mirandas currently on the scene include actress Cosgrove, singer Lambert, and model Kerr.

Miriam

Variation of Hebrew Maryam, "bitter"

The oldest-known form of Mary, serious, solemn Miriam has been a particular favorite of observant Jewish parents. But we can see it extending beyond that sphere into the next wave of Old Testament names post-Rachel, Rebecca, Sarah, Hannah, and Leah.

In the Old Testament, Miriam appears in Exodus as the older sister of Moses and Aaron, a prophetess who led the triumphal song and dance after the crossing of the Red Sea and deliverance of the Israelites from the Egyptians. Miriam is the Old Testament form of the Hebrew Maryam.

Miriam is an artistic character in Nathaniel Hawthorne's *The Marble Faun*, and in Henry James's *The Tragic Muse*, Miriam Rooth is a talented young half-Jewish actress, Miriam Leviers is a farm girl in D. H. Lawrence's *Sons and Lovers*, and Miriam is the eponymous center of a haunting Truman Capote short story.

One notable namesake is South African singer Miriam Makeba. More relaxed nicknames: Miri and Mimi.

Mitzi

German diminutive of Maria, "bitter"

Mitzi is a spunky German nickname name that might appeal to parents drawn to the genre of peppy vintage chorus girl names that proliferated in 1930s musicals. Lively entertainer Mitzi Gaynor—who was originally named Francesca Marlene de Czanyi von Gerber—made the name notable in mid-century America.

You may be surprised to know that Mitzi was on the Top 1000 list through 1979, as high as Number 420 in 1955.

Molly

Diminutive of Mary, "bitter"

Molly has been used as a stand-alone pet form of Mary since the Middle Ages and has been consistently popular as an independent name in the U.S. over the past several decades, still in the Top 100, and in the Top 40 in most of the English-speaking world.

Likeable and down-to-earth, mild yet saucy, Molly has a distinctly Irish feel as well, with such Gaelic associations as Sweet Molly Malone and the martyred reformers known as the Molly Maguires. In the Jewish culture, Molly Goldberg was an early television personality.

Other references include the Revolutionary War heroine Molly Pitcher and the Molly Bloom character in James Joyce's *Ulysses*, as well as characters in novels by Fielding, Hardy, George Eliot, Dickens, and Thackeray. More recently, "Good Golly, Miss Molly" was a Little Richard hit and Molly Ringwald a celebrity bearer.

Amanda Peet is the mother of a Molly, as are Monica Potter and Veronica Webb.

Morgan

Welsh, "circle; sea"

Morgan has long been a traditional Welsh male name whose most notable female antecedent is Morgan le Fay, King Arthur's half-sister and a famed sorceress in Arthurian legend. In this country, Morgan is now used more for girls than boys, though considerably lower than its Top 25 status in the 1990s.

And although it's been veering south for both sexes, we still find Morgan a sophisticated choice.

Morgan le Fay reappears as a sorceress in Mark Twain's *A Connecticut Yankee in King Arthur's Court*.

Actress Morgan Fairchild—who had an influence on the name's popularity for girls—was born Patsy.

Myrtle

Greek botanical name

Long in our category of so-far-out-it-will-always-be-out names, seen as a gum-cracking 1940s telephone operator, we think maybe it's time to reassess and look at is as a nature name, a plant with pink or white aromatic berries. Ruled by Venus, myrtle is a plant associated with love, peace, fertility, and youth.

Myrtle has lots of literary references as well: in Thomas Hardy's *The Hand of Ethelberta*, Theodore Dreiser's *The Genius*, P. G. Wodehouse's *Meet Mr Mulliner*, and especially *The Great Gatsby*. Fitzgerald's Myrtle Wilson has been played on film by actresses as varied as Shelley Winters, Karen Black, and Isla Fisher.

N

Nadia

Russian, "hope"

Nadia, an exotic but accessible Slavic favorite, which took on added energy and charm when Romanian gymnast Nadia Comaneci won the 1976 Olympics, is currently enjoying a leap in popularity—probably via the character on *Lost* who was known as Nadia, but whose actually name was Noor— along with other Russian 'N' names, Natasha and Natalya.

Octomom Suleman spells her first name Nadya, as in the Queen Nadya character in Noel Coward's play *The Queen was in the Parlour*. And, no, you don't have to explain that Nadia is actually a Russian short form of Nadezhda.

Naomi

Hebrew, "pleasantness"

This long-quiet Old Testament name seems to finally be finding favor with parents seeking a biblical name with a soft, melodic sound and a positive meaning, suddenly sounding fresher than the widely used Sarah, Rachel, and Rebecca. It's now—at Number 81—at an all-time popularity peak after breaking the top 100 for the first time in 2010.

Its biblical reference is the wise mother-in-law of Ruth, and because of this, it is a symbolic name given to girls on Shavuot, when the Old Testament story of Ruth is read in the synagogue.

Beautiful black model Naomi Campbell and blond actress Naomi Watts have helped the modernization. Other namesakes are singer Naomi Judd and feminist writer Naomi Wolf.

The lovely French version is Noemie; in Italian, it's Noemi.

Natalia

Russian, "birthday of the Lord"

More exotic that Natalie, more unusual than Natasha, Natalia has been climbing up the popularity list since 1980; Natalia—also spelled Natalya—is now at Number 119. Heard frequently in Spain, Portugal, and the Slavic countries, this is a distinctive, strong but feminine member of the Natalie/Natasha family, with the appealing short form Talia. Natalia is currently in the Top 10 in Poland, Number 28 in Spain, and 35 in Chile.

Like her cousins, Natalia is a name often given to girls born around Christmas.

Natalie Wood was born Natalia. Other namesakes include renowned Russian-born prima ballerina Natalia Makarova and supermodel Natalia Vodianova.

Natalie

French variation of Natalia, "birthday of the Lord"

Natalie—a Franco-Russian name—became Americanized years ago, and now a new generation is reviving Natalie to join former canasta partners Sophie and Belle. Always well used, it entered the Top 20 in 2004 and is now at Number 17.

Sometimes given to girls born on Christmas, Natalie was Cameron Diaz's character in *Charlie's Angels*, and was attached to first Natalie Wood, then Natalie Cole (named for her father), and now Natalie Portman.

Natalie has been a TV regular ranging from the lovable character on the old *The Facts of Life* to *Monk* to the current *Orange is the New Black*.

She also has musical ties to singers, in addition to Cole—Maines, Imbruglia, and Merchant, and to a not-too-flattering hit song by Bruno Mars.

Nell

Dimunuive of Helen, Eleanor, et al, "bright, shining one"

Nell, once a nickname for Helen, Ellen, or Eleanor, is a sweet old-fashioned charmer that is fashionably used today in its own right. While Nell is perfectly in synch with contemporary vintage name style, it hasn't taken off the way some of its sisters have and so maintains an air of distinction. Use Nell or Nellie as a short for any name from Eleanor to Penelope or just name her Nell.

Nell was the pet name FDR called his wife Eleanor (along with Babs), the famous Little Nell in Dickens' *Old Curiosity Shop* was Elinor, and the infamous mistress of Charles II, Nell Gwynne, was born Eleanor as well.

Nell was the belle of the ball in the Gay Nineties but has been off the charts since 1956. It's currently popular in France though, ranking at Number 144.

Jodie Foster played the title character of the 1994 movie *Nell*, and Helena Bonham Carter and Tim Burton named their daughter Nell, keeping the family tradition of names related to Helen.

Nettie

Diminutive of names ending in -ette or -etta

You may never have known a Nettie personally, but there well might be one hidden in your family history, considering that she was a Top 100 name until 1901 and stayed on the Social Security list until 1962.

Like cousins Hattie and Lottie, Nettie is a charming and nostalgic knitting-and-crocheting-great-grandma name that just might work as a relaxed choice for a contemporary little girl, perhaps to honor an ancestral Annette or Henrietta.

Niamh

Irish Gaelic, "brightness"

Niamh is an ancient Irish name that was originally a term for a goddess; rich in legendary associations. In Irish myth, one who bore it was Niamh of the Golden Hair, daughter of the sea god, who falls in love with Finn's son Oisin/Ossian and takes him to the Land of Promise, where they stay for three hundred years.

Niamh is in the Irish Top 30 and is also well used in England and Scotland. Here, the phonetic Neve would undoubtedly prove simpler, if less intriguing. But if you're worried about pronunciation, just keep in mind Saoirse Ronan and Sinead O'Connor—it never stood in their way.

Niamh is currently Number 21 in Northern Ireland, 30 in Ireland, 39 in Scotland, and 81 in England and Wales.

Niamh Cusack is part of the acting family that also includes Sinéad (wife of Jeremy Irons), Sorcha, and Padraig.

The English version Neve is the name of actress Neve Campbell, for whom it has family connections, and the daughter of Conan O'Brien.

Nicola

Feminine variation of Nicholas, "people of victory"

Nicola, the elegant Latinate feminization of Nicholas, has long been standard issue for English girls but, for some reason, has never voyaged across the Atlantic, which we consider a pity, especially as Nicole's standing has waned.

In Britain, Nicola first appeared around 1940, started rising in the 50s and by the mid-1970s had reached third place on the popularity list, after which it began to be replaced by Nicole.

In his novel *The Well Beloved*, Thomas Hardy spelled it Nichola. Nicola was and still is a unisex name in Italy: one historic bearer Nicola Pisano was a renowned and influential thirteenth-century sculptor, and Nikola Testa was an eminent inventor.

Nicolette

French feminine diminutive of Nicholas, "people of victory"

Nicolette is the ultra-feminine name of an enchanting princess in the medieval French romance, *Aucassin et Nicolette*, a name that got stacks of publicity in the heyday of *Desperate Housewives* and its star Nicolette Sheridan. It was also the name of Chloë Sevigny's character in *Big Love*.

Nicoletta is an Italian variation; the cool nickname Nico modernizes it and makes it less feminissima.

Nina

Russian diminutive of Antonina, "grace"

Nina is as multiethnic as you can get: Nina is a young girl in Spain, a common nickname name in Russia, a Babylonian goddess of the oceans, and an Incan goddess of fire. Here and now, it's a stylish possibility that's been underused. "Weird Al" Yankovic chose this decidedly non-weird name for his daughter.

Currently Number 291, Nina has been a permanent resident on the Social Security list, mainly in the low hundreds. It is now Number 26 in both Austria and Belgium.

In literature, Nina Zarechnaya is one of the principle characters in Chekhov's drama *The Seagull*, as well as appearing in Trollope's *Phineas Finn* and Evelyn Waugh's *Vile Bodies*.

More recent real-life bearers have included jazz singer Nina Simone (born Eunice) and Nina Garcia of *Project Runway* fame.

Natalie Portman was awarded an Oscar for her role as ballerina Nina Sayers in the 2010 *Black Swan*.

Nora

Diminutive of Honora, "honor" or Eleanor, meaning unknown

Nora is a lovely, refined name that conjures up images of Belle Epoch ladies in fur-trimmed coats skating in Central Park, the independent Ibsen heroine of *A Doll's House*, and the female half of the witty Nick and Nora Charles duo, adding up to a most desirable choice.

Nora—long seen as a quintessentially Irish name—is a quietly stylish favorite tiptoeing up the popularity ladder. It is now at Number 107, the highest it has ranked since 1913.

One of Nora's most prominent contemporary namesakes is the late witty writer Nora Ephron.

It is also found spelled Norah, as in Norah Jones.

O

Oceane

French, "ocean"

Oceane (oh-she-ANN) has been one of the chicest names in France for several years and is now rated Number 31.This is a sophisticated name that could easily cross the ocean, and is much more stylish than the English Ocean or Oceana.

This group of names all relate to the ancient Greek god Oceanus, the oldest Titan, son of Uranos and Gaia, god of the open sea.

Octavia

Latin, "eighth"

Octavia began as the Latin, then Victorian name for an eighth child. While there aren't many eighth children anymore, this ancient Roman name has real possibilities as a substitute for the overused Olivia, recommended for its combination of classical and musical overtones. It was chosen for his daughter by Kevin Sorbo.

Octavia has a rich history and literary pedigree. Commonly used in the Roman Imperial family, one first-century (BCE) Octavia was the daughter of Claudius, sister of the Emperor Augustus and the second, pre-Cleopatra, wife of Mark Antony (she appears in Shakespeare's *Antony and Cleopatra*), while another ancient Octavia was the teenage wife of Nero. The British civic reformer Octavia Hill actually was an eighth daughter.

The name came into the spotlight recently via Octavia Spencer, who won a Best Supporting Actress Oscar for her strong performance in *The Help*. And Octavia is part of Cinna's prep team for Katniss Everdeen during the 74th and 75th Hunger Games.

Octavia is also a First Daughter name as the child of President Zachary Taylor.

October

Latin, "eighth"

What is so rare as a month named June? October—and November and December—are a lot rarer. Brisk and substantial, they're so much more memorable and modern than April or May. October got its name via being the eighth month in the old Roman calendar.

October was chosen by innovative author/editor Dave Eggers and wife Vendela Vida for their daughter.

Neil Gaiman wrote a story personifying the month in his collection *Fragile Things,* entitled "October in the Chair."

Some related, more exotic variations are Octavia and Ottavia.

Odessa

Russian place name

Odessa, a Ukrainian port city, was given its name by Russia's Catherine the Great, who was inspired by Homer's *Odyssey*. It would make an original and intriguing choice.

Though rare today, Odessa had more U.S. popularity in the past than you might imagine. It actually ranked in the Top 1000 every year from 1880, the year Social Security records began to be kept, through 1956. Michael Chiklis, one-time *Commish*, has a daughter named Odessa.

Odette

French, "wealthy"

Odette is the good swan in Tchaikovsky's ballet *Swan Lake*, a role for which Natalie Portman won an Oscar—and it would make a particularly soigné, sophisticated yet upbeat choice, unlike some of the more dated other 'ette'-ending names.

Odette de Crecy is the flamboyant wife of Charles Swann in Proust's *À la Recherche du Temps Perdu*.

The name became publicized during World War II via the courageous French Resistance heroine Odette Brailly, who risked her life to supply information to the Allies, was captured by the Germans, and wrote her story, which was retold in an eponymous film.

Actor Mark Ruffalo chose Odette for his daughter.

Variant Odetta is associated with the folksinger, who was one of the first to go by a single name.

Odile, who is Odette's evil *Swan Lake* twin, gives her name a sinuous, sensuous appeal.

Olive

Nature name from Latin, Oliva

Though greatly overshadowed by the trendy Olivia, Olive has a quiet, subtle appeal of its own—and is now enjoying a remarkable comeback. It returned to the Top 1000 in 2007, and has jumped 631 points since then. Cool couple Isla Fisher and Sacha Baron (Borat) Cohen chose it for their daughter, reviving the name to stylishness, and now Drew Barrymore has a baby Olive too, as does country singer Jake Owen.

Olive has positive associations to the olive branch as a symbol of peace and the ancient olive wreath that celebrated success.

Olive was the name of the adorable Abigail Breslin character in the popular movie *Little Miss Sunshine,* and Emma Stone's in the 2010 film *Easy A.* Olive Chancellor is a major character in Henry James's *The Bostonians.* And kids might be familiar with *Olive the Other Reindeer.*

Olive came into fashion at the end of the nineteenth century, along with other botanical names, when it had a run in the Top 100.

Olivia

Latin, "olive tree"

Olivia, a lovely Shakespearean name with an admirable balance of strength and femininity, is, like her fashionable sister names Isabella and Sophia, a mega popular baby girl name. Olivia is currently Number 4 and could be heading towards the very top of the list—so don't say we didn't warn you.

In the U.K., Olivia was the recent number one girls' name in tandem with twin brother Oliver at the top of the charts. It is still the top name in Canada and Number 4 in both Australia and Scotland.

Olivia was first popularized by Shakespeare's *Twelfth Night* as the name of the pampered, wealthy countess. In ancient Greece, the olive was a symbol of Athena as well as a token of peace and fertility, and olive wreaths were awarded to the winners at the Olympic Games.

Olivia has been a popular starbaby name for fifteen years, and has also been a well-used TV character name, such as in Olivia Benson on *Law & Order: SVU* and the current powerful lead Olivia Pope on *Scandal.*

Golden Age star Olivia de Havilland was influential in bringing the name to U.S. attention, followed by Olivia Newton-John, and now we have Olivias Wilde, Munn, and Williams. Bottom line: Parents in search of a distinctive name will have to keep looking. Some related alternatives: Olive, Livia, and Liv.

Olwen

Welsh, "white footprint"

Olwen is a Welsh favorite, the name of a legendary princess in what is believed to have been the earliest Arthurian romance and, in fact, one of the first recorded examples of Welsh prose.

In this tale, *Culhwch and Olwen*, the beautiful giant's daughter Olwen has the magical power to cause white clovers to spring up wherever she walked—an enchanting image.

Olwen is a Bronwen alternative for those with a taste for the more unusual. Those who like Olwen might also want to consider such other Welsh girls' names as Anwen, Rhonwen, and Nolwenn.

24's Xander Berkeley and Sarah Clarke used the Olwyn spelling for their daughter.

Olympia

Greek, "from Mount Olympus"

With its relation to Mount Olympus, home of the Greek gods and to the Olympic Games, this name has an athletic, goddess-like aura, making it the perfect Olivia substitute.

A well-known art reference is the famous 1865 painting of a reclining nude by Édouard Manet titled "Olympia." Contemporary bearers include former Maine Republican Senator Olympia Snowe and actress Olympia Dukakis.

Oona

Irish variation of Una, "lamb"

Oona is a name made famous by Eugene O'Neill's daughter, who became Charlie Chaplin's wife; the double-o beginning gives it a lot of oomph.

In Irish legend, Una/Oona was a daughter of a king of Lochlainn. The name was very popular in Ireland in the Middle Ages and is currently seeing a comeback there—also spelled Oonagh.

Opal

English from Sanskrit, "precious stone"

Opal is on the verge of a re-polishing, following other jewel names like Ruby and Pearl. A Top 100 name during the first two decades of the twentieth century, the opalescent Opal has a good chance of coming back as another O-initial option.

The ancient Greeks believed that opals were formed from the tears of joy wept by Zeus when he defeated the titans and that the opal bestowed prophetic powers; the Romans considered it a symbol of hope and good fortune. It was a favorite gem of Queen Victoria.

Opal Feliss is a character in Theodore Dreiser's seminal 1925 novel *An American Tragedy*.

And keeping with the 'O' theme, Opal is the birthstone of October, making it an appropriate choice for a little girl born in that month.

Ophelia

Greek, "help"

Ophelia is a beautiful name that has long been hampered by the stigma of *Hamlet*'s tragic heroine—for whom Shakespeare seems to have invented the name—but more and more parents are beginning to put that association aside. There is also a gutsy Ophelia in Harriet Beecher Stowe's 1852 *Uncle Tom's Cabin*, which seems to have had some influence on baby namers at the time.

Off the list since 1958, Ophelia once ranked as high as Number 236. Among the actresses who have played modern Ophelias are Jamie Lee Curtis and Blake Lively. The heroine of the film *Pan's Labyrinth* used the Spanish spelling, Ofelia.

Actress Patricia Neal and author Roald Dahl named one of their now-grown daughters Ophelia.

Orchid

Flower name

Orchid is an exotic hothouse bloom that has not been plucked by many modern baby namers—yet. In the language of flowers, orchids symbolize love, beauty, and sophistication.

In a 1926 silent comedy, femme fatale Gloria Swanson played a burlesque chorus girl named Orchid Murphy.

Orla

Irish, "golden princess"

Orla is an Irish name closely associated with the high king Brian Boru, as it was the name of his sister, daughter, and niece. It was very popular in the Middle Ages—the fourth most popular name in twelfth-century Ireland—and has become popular again in Ireland (ranking Number 74) and Scotland (36) today.

In Irish, the name is Orlaith.

There is a student at Hogwarts School named Orla Quirke in the *Harry Potter* books.

An authentic Irish name with a lovely meaning and no pronunciation problems.

Ottilie

Feminine variation of Otto, "prosperous in battle"
Ottilie and its diminutive Ottiline are a pair of names heard among the British upper crust but have rarely been seen here since the 1880s. Though it has German roots via Otto, Ottilie has a distinctively delicate French feel.

Ottilie does have a few cultural references—she is a key character in Goethe's *Elective Affinities*, Robert Louis Stevenson wrote a poem called *To Ottilie*, Franz Kafka had a sister named Ottilie, and it is the name of the protagonist in the John Wyndham sci-fi story *Random Quest*.

Probably the best-known Ottilie is the German journalist, abolitionist, and feminist Ottilie Assing, who had a long involvement with fellow abolitionist Frederic Douglass.

Some attractive Ottilie relatives: Ottoline, Ottilia, and Odile. And Ottilie has the endearing nicknames of Lottie and Tillie.

Ottoline

Diminutive of Ottolie, "prosperous in battle"
Curiously appealing in a hoop-skirted, wasp-waisted way, Ottoline has recently entered the realm of modern possibility, especially since Sienna Miller chose it as the middle name of her daughter Marlowe.

Lady Ottoline Morrell was an influential British aristocrat who was a force in the artistic and literary community of her day, patron of such figures as T. S. Eliot and Aldous Huxley.

The Franco-German Ottolie is an equally intriguing option.

P

Padget

Variation of Page, "page, attendant"

This unusual offshoot of Page is an undiscovered gem with lots of energy and charm. Actress Paget Brewster, star of *Criminal Minds*, presents another spelling possibility. She comes from a family of unique names—her mother is Hathaway, her father Galen.

Padget is more off-the-grid than Bridget, more grown up than Gidget.

Paige

English, "page, attendant"

Paige is more name, and less word than the occupational Page. Paige is also sleek and sophisticated à la Brooke and Blair and has been in or around the Top 100 since 1990, reaching as high as Number 47 in 2003 when there was a very popular television show, *Trading Spaces*, hosted by the energetic Paige Davis.

Paige Matthews was a witch played by Rose McGowan in *Charmed*; Paige McCullers appears on *Pretty Little Liars*. Back in the day, Nicollette Sheridan played a character named Paige Matheson on nighttime soap *Knots Landing*.

Paige Rense was the high-profile, long-time editor of *Architectural Digest* magazine.

Paisley

Scottish place name, "church, cemetery"

For a name related to a Scottish town, a richly patterned Indian fabric, and a country singer named Brad, Paisley has been a remarkable success story. She entered the Top 1000 in 2006 and since then has jumped more than 700 places.

Athlete Jennie Finch named her daughter Paisley Faye, sister to big brothers Ace and Diesel.

There is a character named Paisley in *The Secret Language of Girls.*

Trivia tidbit: Actor Gerard Butler was born in Paisley, Scotland.

Paloma

Spanish, "dove"

Paloma is vibrant and ruby-lipped, à la jewelry designer Paloma Picasso, but also suggests peace, as symbolized by the dove. Paloma is a highly recommended, striking but soft name.

Salma Hayak used Paloma as the middle name of her daughter Valentina, and it was the first name pick of both David Caruso and *Ugly Betty*'s Ana Ortiz.

Pamela

English, "all honey"

Pam was a somewhat pampered prom queen of the 1960s who was never called by her full name, which is a pity because Pamela is so mellifluous and rich in literary history. A Top 25 name from the late 1940s through the late 60s, Pamela has just, sadly, dropped out of the Top 1000.

Pamela was first used by Elizabethan poet Sir Philip Sidney in his sixteenth-century pastoral epic *Arcadia*, but it was Samuel Richardson's enormously popular novel *Pamela, or Virtue Rewarded* two centuries later that really promoted it. Rarely used now, Pamela might almost be ready for a revival, and the appealing Pam (wife of Jim, the male-equivalent name) on *The Office* may help bring it back.

But, no, we won't be recommending the name of Pamela's partner—Linda.

Pandora

Greek, "all gifted"

Pandora has occasionally been used by the British gentry (for girls with brothers who might be called Peregrine) but is rarely heard here, probably because Pandora was the mythological first woman on earth whose curiosity caused her to lift a forbidden box and inadvertently unleash all the evils of the world.

But perhaps she's paid the price long enough—Pandora could conceivably ride the wave of other rediscovered names Dora and Theodora—unless it's too identified with the popular internet radio site.

Pandora is the eponymous title character of an Anne Rice vampire novel and appears in the *Adrian Mole* books.

Patience

Virtue name

Patience is a passive-virtue-turned-engaging name, fresher than Hope, Faith, or even Charity. After slumbering along at the bottom of the Top 1000 for decades, Patience is beginning to climb the list. Its resemblance to the trendy Payton may be one reason for its new-found popularity.

Common in the seventeenth century, Patience is the eponymous heroine of a Gilbert & Sullivan comic operetta. In literature, Patience appears in Shakespeare's *Henry VIII* and in an Anthony Trollope novel.

In the 2004 film *Catwoman*, the non-superhero name of the protagonist, played by Halle Berry, is Patience Phillips—which may have caused the name's bump in popularity two years later.

Patricia

Latin, "noble, patrician"

Patricia still sounds patrician, though its scores of nicknames definitely don't. Wildly popular from the 1940s (Number 4 in 1948) through the 60s, Patricia has been fading ever since—but a comeback in its full form is definitely conceivable—just look at Penelope.

Patricia began not in Ireland, as you may think, but evolved in Scotland, going on to become mega popular in Britain after the christening of Queen Victoria's granddaughter, Princess Patricia of Connaught, known to one and all as "Princess Pat" (though called Patsy by the family).

Several of Patricia's short forms took on lives of their own—first Patsy, which was replaced by Patti/Patty, followed by the more upwardly mobile Tricia, Trisha, Trish, Tisha, and Tish. The one form that hasn't been picked up here but is often heard in England on its own, is the fresher sounding Patia. Patrizia is an attractive Italian version.

Two bestselling contemporary novelists are Patricia Highsmith and Patricia Cornwell.

Trivia tidbits: Pat Nixon was born Thelma, and Patricia is Rooney Mara's birth name.

Paz

Hebrew, "golden"; Spanish, "peace"

Paz, currently represented by actresses Paz Vega and Paz de la Huerta, would make a sparkling middle name choice. It originated as a title of the Virgin Mary—Our Lady of Peace.

Pazia is an attractive elaboration, while Pazit (pronounced Pah-ZEET) and Pazya are Hebrew variations.

Pearl

Latin gem name, "pearl"

Pearl, like Ruby, has begun to be polished up for a new generation of fashionable children after a century of jewelry box storage. The birthstone for the month of June, Pearl could also make a fresher middle name alternative to the overused Rose. Cool couple Maya Rudolph and Paul Thomas Anderson named their daughter Pearl Minnie, followed by Jack Osbourne, and several celebs have put it in the middle spot, as in Busy Philipps's Cricket Pearl, Jake Owen's Olive Pearl and Caleb Followill's Dixie Pearl. After being a Top 25 name in the late nineteenth century, Pearl went into a long slide, but is showing signs of a strong comeback—it reentered the Top 1000 in 2010 and has already risen more than 200 places.

In Nathaniel Hawthorne's *The Scarlet Letter*, Pearl is the illegitimate daughter of Hester Prynne, who gives her the name because she is "her mother's only treasure."

Pearl was also the alter-ego name of Janis Joplin, tied to singer Pearl Bailey, and—hmm—the birth name of western writer Zane Gray.

Interesting variations are Perle and Perla.

Peggy

Diminutive of Margaret, "pearl"

Just when we had written off Peggy as the eternal perky, pug-nosed prom-queen she projected from the 1920s into the 50s, along came *Mad Men*, with intriguing mid-century characters with names like Joan and Betty—and Peggy—causing a bit of a re-think. MM's proto-feminist Peggy Olson was followed by Amy Adams's strong Oscar-nominated Peggy Dodd character in *The Master*.

Peggy has been used independently since the eighteenth century, later combined with other names such as Peggy Sue, made famous by the Buddy Holly song and the film *Peggy Sue Got Married*.

Some notable namesakes who have gone by Peggy include jazz singer Peggy Lee (born Norma), art patron Guggenheim (born Marguerite), skater Fleming, and author/speechwriter Noonan (born Margaret).

It's not likely that Peggy will ever regain the 31st position it held in 1937, but we can see it coming into somewhat wider use.

Penelope

Greek, "weaver"

Penelope's former image of an elderly British gardening lady in a large-brimmed hat has of late been counterbalanced by the dramatic sensuality of Spanish actress Penelope Cruz. Penelope's popularity is on the rise, jumping into the Top 125 this year, and it's sure to climb much further and faster now that it's been chosen by Kourtney Kardashian for her baby daughter. Penelope was also picked for their girls by Tina Fey, by Natalie and Taylor Hanson, of the group Hanson, and by Anna Chlumsky. In 2001, before this rash of celebrity usage, Penelope was down at Number 945.

Penelope has long been associated with the faithful, long-suffering wife of Odysseus in Homer's *Odyssey*. It has several British novelists as namesakes—Penelopes Fitzgerald, Mortimer, Gilliatt, and Lively. And, yes, she's also a *Harry Potter* character: Penelope "Penny" Clearwater is a student at Hogwarts.

Penelope is a strong Nameberry favorite, though, instead of the traditional Penny as a nickname, many Berries suggest Nell or Poppy.

Peridot

Arabic, "a green gemstone"

Peridot is the gem of the month of August, a vibrant green mineral said to be good for helping people put the past behind them, and it's also an interesting, undiscovered jewel name. It was regarded in ancient times as the symbol of the sun.

Peridots figure in the mythologies of several cultures, including the ancient Egyptian and Roman. They are highly valued in Hawaii, where it is believed that they are the tears of the volcano goddess Pele.

If you want a truly original gem name, you might consider this instead of Opal or Ruby.

Persephone

Greek mythology name

Persephone is the esoteric name of the Greek mythological daughter of Zeus by Demeter, the queen of the harvest. After she was kidnapped by Hades to be Queen of the Underworld, it was decreed by Zeus that she would spend six months of the year with her mother, allowing crops to grow, and six in mourning, thus accounting for the seasons.

Despite the mixed message of her mythological past, Persephone has a light and lyrical aura, and pleasant associations with springtime and the harvest—she was also goddess of spring growth. Persephone was seen in the *Matrix* movies, played by Monica Bellucci, and could make an interesting replacement for the overused Stephanie.

Persephone's meaning is in dispute—while some sources give it as the worrisome "bringing death," others indicate that it's associated with dark blue and with speaking. Persephone was called Kore in childhood; in Roman mythology, she is Proserpina.

Persis

Greek, "Persian woman"

Parents seeking a distinctive New Testament name might consider this one. Adopted by some Puritans in the seventeenth century, Persis was used in the William Dean Howells novel *The Rise of Silas Lapham* for the wife of the protagonist.

In Romans 16:12 of the New Testament, Persis is a Roman woman who was an early follower of Christ, mentioned by St. Paul in a letter as "beloved" and having "worked hard in the Lord."

Indian actress Persis Khambatta was Lieutenant Ilia in *Star Trek: The Motion Picture*.

Petal

Floral word name

Petal is the soft and sweet-smelling name of a character in the novel and film, *The Shipping News*. With the rise of such flower names as Poppy and Posy, we believe Petal—down-to-earth yet exotic—has its own appealingly distinctive style.

Celebrity chef Jamie Oliver named his daughter Petal Blossom Rainbow in 2009.

Petra

Feminine variation of Peter, "rock, stone"

An exotic Greek name with something of a Slavic feel, Petra is a relatively recent feminization of Peter, though it relates back to an incredible ancient city in Jordan that was rediscovered in the early nineteenth century.

Currently the second most popular name in Croatia and in the Top 20 in Hungary, Petra actually did rank in the U.S. Top 1000 every year from 1880 to 1951, reaching a high of Number 493 in 1929.

There have been Petras in two European film classics: Ingmar Bergman's *Smiles of a Summer Night* and Rainer Werner Fassbinder's *The Bitter Tears of Petra von Kant*.

The most prominent Petra in recent years is gorgeous supermodel Petra Němcová—who is now an international disaster relief activist.

Peyton

English, "fighting-man's estate"

Peyton is a unisex surname that's not only survived but continues to grow in popularity because of its rich southern-accented softness combined with the pre-*Desperate Housewives* naughtiness of *Peyton Place*. In recent years, more boys have been named Peyton thanks to football star Peyton Manning, but the upcoming film of William Styron's *Lie Down in Darkness* which features heroine Peyton Loftis, may further popularize Peyton as a girls' name. Peyton is now just outside the Top 50 for girls and Number 183 for boys, while the alternate Payton girls' version stands at Number 103.

Phaedra

Greek, "bright"

This name of a tragic figure in Greek mythology, the daughter of King Minos, sister of Ariadne, and wife of Theseus, has a mysterious and intriguing appeal, and would make a dramatic choice.

Phaedra has been a persistent theme in literature, both ancient and modern. There have been plays by Euripides, Racine, Unamuno, and O'Neill, novels, poetry, operas, and film—as recently as the 2011 *Immortals* starring Freida Pinto.

A member of the extreme-naming Geldof family, Peaches Honeyblossom, pulled a gender switch when she named her son Phaedra Bloom Forever.

Philippa

Feminine variation of Philip, "lover of horses"

Philippa is a prime example of a boy's name adapted for girls that was as common as crumpets in Cornwall, but rarely heard stateside, never having appeared in the Top 1000. That was before the advent of royal sister-in-law Philippa Middleton, who goes by the lively nickname Pippa.

Philippa has been fashionable in England since the fourteenth century when King Edward married Philippa of Hainault. There have been several early Saint Philippas, and it was the name of the wife of Geoffrey Chaucer.

Novelist Philippa Gregory authored the bestselling historical novel *The Other Boleyn Girl.*

Philomena

Greek, "lover of strength"

Philomena is an earthy Greek name now used in various Latin countries. While it has felt simply clunky for many years, it's starting—along with such sister names as Wilhelmina and Frederica—to sound so clunky it's cool.

In Greek myth, Philomena was an Athenian princess who was transformed by the gods into a nightingale to save her from the advances of a lecherous king.

Also a saint's name—that of a thirteen-year-old martyr of early Rome—it's commonly seen in Italy and Spain spelled Filomena. Philomena only started appearing in English-speaking countries in the latter half of the nineteenth century, especially in Scotland and Australia.

In the U.S., Philomena ranked in the Top 1000 through 1940, peaking at Number 355 in 1915.

Philomena Guinea is the name of protagonist Esther Greenwood's patron in Sylvia Plath's *The Bell Jar*.

Phoebe

Greek, "radiant, shining one"

A mythological, biblical, Shakepearean, and Salinger name, the warm and captivating Phoebe was given a boost in popularity by one of the Friends.

In classical mythology, Phoebe is the by-name of Artemis, goddess of the moon and of hunting. In the New Testament, she is a church deaconess. Shakespeare used the name (spelled Phebe) for a rustic denizen of the forest in *As You Like It*, Phoebe Pynchon was a cheerful young girl in Hawthorne's *The House of Seven Gables*, while Phoebe is Holden Caulfield's sympathetic, precocious ten-year-old sister in *Catcher in the Rye*.

Bill and Melinda Gates used Phoebe for their daughter.

Phyllida

Variation of Phyllis, "green bough"

Phyllida, a "Masterpiece Theatre"-style appellation, seems far fresher and more unusual than Phyllis.

It's a name used by sixteenth-century poets and writers: Lyly has a character named Phyllida in his 1592 play *Galathea*, and there is a poem of the same period called *Phyllida and Corydon*.

The distinguished Scottish actress Phyllida Law is the mother of actresses Emma and Sophie Thompson; Phyllida Lloyd directed such films as *Mamma Mia!* and *The Iron Lady*.

Pilar

Spanish, "pillar"

The fact that this Spanish classic, which honors the Virgin Mary, does not end in the conventional letter 'a' gives it a special sense of strength, elegance, and style, making it a worthy choice.

The name originated in the legend of the miracle of the Virgin Mary's appearance over a marble pillar. It also is an allusion to her as a pillar of the church.

Pilar is remembered as the valiant heroine of Hemingway's *For Whom the Bell Tolls*.

Piper

English occupational name, "pipe or flute player"

Piper is a bright, musical name that's jumped six hundred places since it entered the list in 1999, one year after the debut of the TV series *Charmed*, which featured a Piper, and it's been chosen by several celebs for their daughters, including Gillian Anderson and Cuba Gooding, Jr.

One of the first Pipers on the scene was Piper Laurie (born Rosetta), after whom actress Piper Perabo was named.

Piper Chapman is a character in the Netflix series *Orange Is the New Black*.

Pippa

Diminutive of Philippa, "lover of horses"

Pippa, a peppy condensation of Philippa that turns it from serious to sprightly, has come into the public eye in a big way via the former Kate Middleton's sister.

Heard far more in the U.K. than the U.S., Pippa has been used on its own since the nineteenth century, popularized by Robert Browning's dramatic poem, *Pippa Passes*. A recent book and film was titled *The Private Lives of Pippa Lee*.

Pippa can and is given as a name in its own right, and may also be short for names other than Philippa: Penelope, for instance, or Patricia, or the more exotic Philippine.

Plum

Fruit name

British-born novelist Plum Sykes has taken this rich, fruity name out of the produce section and put it into the baby name basket. It's more appealing than Apple and more presentable than Peaches. The French equivalent, Prune, is very fashionable there but would not fly with English speakers for obvious reasons.

Plum Sykes was born Victoria, and her nickname derived from the variety of fruit called the Victoria Plum.

Plum makes an appealing middle name choice—Moon Unit Zappa used it as such for her daughter Matilda.

Poet
Word name

A recently entered name on the roster, Poet was used for her daughter by Soleil Moon (Punky Brewster) Frye, who obviously appreciates the advantages of an unusual name. This is a possible middle name choice for verse-loving parents who want to skip specifics like Auden or Poe or Keats or Tennyson and go with the generic.

Possible alternatives: Poetry, Poesie, Sonnet (used by Forest Whitaker)

Polly
Diminutive of Mary, "bitter"

An alternative to the no-longer-fresh Molly, the initial P gives Polly a peppier sound, combining the cozy virtues of an old-timey name with the bounce of a barmaid.

Associated with Tom Sawyer's aunt, "Polly, put the kettle on," parrots, Polly Peachum, Nirvana and Kinks songs, and the movie *Along Came Polly*, as well as characters in Noel Streatfeild's *Ballet Shoes*, C.S. Lewis's *The Chronicles of Narnia*, and now on the Netflix show *Orange Is the New Black*, Polly never achieved the comeback that her cousin did, perhaps because she sounds too Pollyanna-ish.

But we'd love to see some new baby Pollys.

Poppy
Flower name

Poppy, unlike most floral names that are sweet and feminine, has a lot of spunk; Poppy makes an especially good choice for a redhead. Jamie Oliver—the British "Naked Chef"—used Poppy for his daughter Poppy Honey Rosie, as did Anthony Edwards, Jessica Capshaw, and Anna Paquin and Stephen Moyer.

One notable Poppy is Australian *Without a Trace* star Poppy Montgomery (full name Poppy Petal Emma Elizabeth—her mother named all her daughters after flowers: Lily, Daisy, Marigold, and Rosie).

Although she's never made the list in the U.S., Poppy is on a popularity roll in England and Wales, where it's Number 14; she's also at Number 35 in Scotland.

Other Poppy-like names to consider: Pippa, Piper, and Petal.

Portia

Latin, "pig"

Portia is a perfect role-model name, relating to Shakespeare's brilliant and spirited lawyer in *The Merchant of Venice*, and is now also a *Hunger Games* name.

Another Shakespearean Portia was the wife of Brutus in *Julius Caesar*, based on a historical character. In the 1940s, when the name was most used, there was a popular radio soap called *Portia Faces Life*, the heroine being—what else?—a brilliant and spirited lawyer.

Portia is a recommended choice, even though some people might think you named your child for the car. Just don't spell it Porsche, which may sound the same but has a totally different and—despite the posh brand—much more downscale image.

Namesake Portia de Rossi actually started life as Amanda/Mandy.

Posy

English, "a bunch of flowers"

A sweet, nostalgic nosegay kind of name, Posy has long been fashionable in England, a country of gardeners, but this pretty bouquet-of-flowers name is still rarely heard here—though it could be seen as a more unusual possible alternative to Rosy or Josie.

Posy is a little sister name in the *Hunger Games* series. Before that, Posy Fossil was a character in Noel Streatfeild's *Ballet Shoes*.

Posy (or Posey) could also work as a nickname for a range of other names, from Penelope to Sophia—it started as a pet form of Josephine. Other P-beginning flower names you may want to consider along with Posey: Poppy, Petal, and Primrose.

Primrose

Flower name

Still found in quaint British novels, and until recently considered a bit too prim for most American classrooms, some adventurous namers are suddenly beginning to see Primrose as an attractive member of the rose family.

In the H. E. Bates book and 1990s British TV series, *The Darling Buds of May*, there is a character named Primrose Violet Anemone Iris Magnolia Narcissa Larkin—who has twin sisters named Zinnia and Petunia. More current is young Primrose "Prim" Everdeen in The *Hunger Games* trilogy by Suzanne Collins.

Curiously, Primrose was first used as a Scottish surname.

Priscilla

Latin, "ancient"

Despite her somewhat prissy, puritanical air, Priscilla has managed to stay in the Top 500 for every year since records have been kept—it reached as high as 127 in 1940—appreciated for its delicacy and solid history.

A New Testament name, it was Priscilla with whom the apostle Paul stayed while spreading the gospel in Corinth. It was common in the ancient Roman world, and later was a favorite of the seventeenth-century Puritans, including Priscilla Mullins (Alden), remembered for her co-starring role in Longfellow's poem *The Courtship of Miles Standish*. There was also a sympathetic Priscilla in Hawthorne's *The Blithedale Romance*.

The most conspicuous contemporary bearer of the name is Priscilla Presley, and it's what J. R. Tolkien named his only daughter.

And if you find the nickname Prissy too—well—prissy, you could use the British-inflected Cilla.

Prudence

Virtue name

Prudence, like Hope and Faith, is a Puritan virtue name with a quiet charm and sensitivity that is slowly returning to favor, though it hasn't yet registered on the charts.

"The White Album" Beatles song "Dear Prudence" was written for Prudence Farrow, sister of Mia, who was with them in India when studying with the Maharishi Mahesh Yogi, seeking enlightenment.

Prudence Halliwell was one of the three witches on *Charmed*, sister to Piper and Phoebe.

Caveat: a bit of possible "prude"-baiting during adolescence.

Asset: Sweet nickname Pru/Prue.

Q

Quinn

Irish, "descendent of Conn"

One of the first Irish unisex surnames, a strong and attractive choice on the rise for both genders, though there are still more boy Quinns than girls.

Quinn started taking off for girls in the mid-nineties, possibly influenced by the popular show *Dr. Quinn, Medicine Woman*. Since then, there have been female Quinns on the animated MTV show *Daria*, on *Zoey 101*, and—most prominently—on *Glee*, featuring cute blond cheerleader character Quinn Fabray.

Some other, more unusual names with the Q-factor: Quintina, Quintana, Quinta, Quilla—and, on a different note, Queenie.

R

Rae

English diminutive of Rachel, "ewe"

All the old ae/ay middle names are back—Kay, Fay, Mae/May—and Rae is one of the coolest, used by celebrities such as Mark Wahlberg and Daniel Baldwin. Even more popular in the celebrisphere is the jazzy Ray spelling; among those who used it as their daughters' middles are Bruce Willis, Dermot Mulroney, Maggie Gyllenhaal and Peter Sarsgaard, and Uma Thurman and Leelee Sobieski.

But Rae is perfectly capable of standing on her own, as in Rae Dawn Chong; it was in the Top 500 in the first two decades of the twentieth century.

Rafaela

Spanish version of Raphaela, "God has healed"

Spell it Rafaela (Spanish), Raffaela (Italian) or Raphaela (Hebrew/German), this is a euphonious and lovely name with a dark-eyed, long-flowing-haired image, which is, like Gabriella and Isabella, beginning to be drawn into the American mainstream.

Seductive *Girls* star Jemima Kirke named her daughter Rafaella Israel—and her son Memphis.

Rain

Word name

Among a small shower of rain-related names, this pure version can have a cool, refreshing image.

Richard Pryor named his now-grown daughter Rain, and Rain is also one of the nature-named Phoenix family siblings. More recently, *24* actress Marisol Nichols named her daughter Rain India.

Rain also makes a nice nature middle name—Brooke Burke called her daughter Heaven Rain.

If you want to embellish this simple spelling (and alter the meaning), you might also consider Raine, Raina, Rainn, Rayne, Reine, or Reign, the middle name of Willow Smith. Or you could take the Holly Madison route all the way to Rainbow.

Ramona

Feminine variation of Ramon, "wise protector"
Ramona is a Sweet Spot name—neither too trendy nor too eccentric. Kids will associate it with the clever Ramona Quimby character in the series of classic books by Beverly Cleary, also seen on TV. It was chosen by starcouple Maggie Gyllenhaal and Peter Sarsgaard for their little girl, who would be joined by sister Gloria.

Ramona came into prominence in the 1880s via the beautiful half Native American heroine of the bestselling eponymous romance novel by Helen Hunt Jackson, played on screen by Loretta Young and others.

Trivia tidbit: Ramona is the middle name of singer Avril Lavigne.

Ramona was in the Top 1000 through the 1980s, but it reached its peak in 1928 at Number 117.

Ravenna

Italian place name
Ravenna is a lovely, untouristed Italian place name just waiting to be discovered. Renowned for its fantastic Byzantine mosaics, it's a city that has a rich historic and artistic heritage.

Part of the early Roman Republic, Ravenna was where Julius Caesar gathered his forces before crossing the Rubicon. It was the site of Dante's funeral and burial, Ravenna having been mentioned in his *Inferno*. Other poets with a connection: Lord Byron, who lived there, and Oscar Wilde who, wrote a poem called *Ravenna*, as did Hermann Hesse.

Reese

Welsh, "ardor"
The sassy, steel magnolia appeal of Oscar-winning Reese (born Laura Jeanne—Reese is her mother's maiden name) Witherspoon has single-handedly propelled this formerly male name into mass girls' popularity over the past few years. It entered the Top 1000 at Number 886 in the year 2000 and since then has climbed an impressive 760 places! At

the moment, it lags at Number 549 for the blue team—boys just might want to consider the Rhys spelling.

Reese was recently in the Top 10 Unisex names looked at on Nameberry.

Renata

Latin, "reborn"

Widely used across Europe as a common baptismal name symbolizing spiritual rebirth, in this country it has an operatic image via Italian-born divas Renata Tebadi and Renata Scotti.

Renata is back in the U.S. Top 1000 after decades away; she has a larger following in other countries—as Number 34 in Chile.

Writer/critic Renata Adler was a star among the literati. And Renata is a minor vampire character in the *Twilight* series.

Rhiannon

Welsh, "divine queen"

Most of us had never heard this lovely Welsh name with links to the moon until the advent of the 1976 smash hit Fleetwood Mac song of that name, with lyrics by Stevie Nicks. That same year it popped onto the U.S. Top 1000 at Number 593.

After giving his four boys extreme rebel names, director Robert Rodriguez bestowed this sweet name on his first daughter.

According to Celtic legend, Rhiannon's birds sang more sweetly than any others; she herself was known for being forthright and witty.

Rihanna looks similar but is unrelated.

Rhonwen

Welsh, "slender, fair"

The delicate and haunting Welsh Rhonwen is still a rarity in the U.S., where her English version Rowena is better known, but it would be a lovely choice for any parent in search of a name that was both unusual and traditional—classically feminine yet strong.

Though Irish names have long been popular in America, Welsh names are just beginning to be noticed, and we see them as a wave of the future. In medieval Welsh poetry, Rhonwen is called "The Mother of the English Nation," and Rhonwen Baganes was a heroine of Welsh folklore. A soft and gentle name, Rhonwen's meaning—slender and fair—evokes the image of a lovely, light-haired girl. Other appealing -wen choices include Aelwen, Arianwen, Branwen, Bronwen, Gwendolen, Olwen, and Tanwen. Just don't be tempted to change the 'wen' to "wyn," which would transform it into a male name.

Riley

Irish and English, "rye clearing"

Riley—an upbeat, friendly Irish surname name—is red hot for girls (though still going strong for boys). Currently, around five thousand girls are named Riley each year! It's now Number 47 for girls—not to mention Rylee listed at 109, Ryleigh at 184, ad infinitum. Riley is one of the few contemporary androgynous names that did not lose its masculine power when it became popular for girls.

Newsperson Norah O'Donnell has a daughter named Riley Norah.

Roisin

Irish, "little rose"

No, the pronunciation—ro-SHEEN—isn't immediately obvious to the non-Gaelic viewer, but the sound of this shiny Irish version of Rose is pretty enough to make it worth considering. Very popular in its native Ireland, it is now at Number 34 there. Earlier generations Anglicized as Rosaleen, but we say stick to the original.

The name has been associated with a sixteenth-to-seventeenth-century poem called Roisin Dubh (Dark Little Rose), the eponymous heroine of which is usually regarded as a personification of Ireland.

Singer Sinéad O'Connor has a daughter named Róisin.

Romilly

English, "man of Rome"

Originally a male name springing from the Roman twin Romulus, this attractively dainty name was introduced to the English-speaking world by painter Augustus John, who used it for his son. Romilly John became Admiral of the Fleet in England.

A French surname from the twelfth century on, it's more recently and more appropriately been heard as a girls' name; Emma Thompson, for example, used Romilly as her daughter Gaia's middle name.

The logical nickname would be Romy, which is very much in style.

Romy

Diminutive of Rosemary, combination of Rose and Mary; herb name

Austrian actress Romy Schneider seemed to be the singular bearer of this international nickname name until it found new style currency in the past decade.

Like other Ro- names—Roman, Rowan, and Romeo—Romy has gained favor with the celebrity set. Matt Lauer has a daughter named Romy, as do director Sofia Coppola and Phoenix frontman Thomas Mars and others.

Some might remember the 1997 comedy *Romy and Michelle's High School Reunion* with Mira Sorvino as Romy.

Romy hasn't entered the U.S. Top 1000 as yet, but it's Number 71 in the Netherlands and 160 in France.

Rory

Irish, "red king"

Rory is a buoyant, spirited name for a redhead with Celtic roots. The name Rory is getting more popular overall, but for the past few years has been trending decidedly toward the boys' side: at a most recent count, babies named Rory were 69 percent boys, 31 percent girls. Rory (or Rori) might also be a nickname for Aurora. In the TV series *Gilmore Girls*, Rory was the nickname for Lorelai.

Robert Kennedy's youngest daughter, born after his assassination and now a respected documentary filmmaker, is named Rory. Actress Melora Hardin named her daughter Rory Melora.

Rosa

Latinate variation of Rose, flower name

As sweet-smelling as Rose but with a little more substance, Rosa is one of the most classic Spanish and Italian names, which is also favored by upper-class Brits, having an ample measure of vintage charm. Now ranking at Number 614, Rosa has been on the popularity charts for every year that's been counted, especially popular from the 1880s through the beginning of the twentieth century.

The name of a thirteenth-century saint, Rosa has several other notable namesakes. In literature, she was a character in *David Copperfield*. Rosa Parks is a Civil Rights icon, Rosa (born Marie-Rosalie) Bonheur was a noted nineteenth-century French artist, Rosa Ponselle an American operatic soprano, and Rosa Luxemburg a left-wing activist. In the modern world there have been several Rosas in video games, including *Final Fantasy IV*.

Rosalie

French variation of Rosalia, "rose"

Rosalie hit its apex in 1938 and then slid straight downhill until it fell off the U.S. Top 1000 completely in the 1980s, only to spring back to life in 2009 as the name of a character in the *Twilight* series. The beautiful vampire Rosalie Hale has breathed fresh life back into this mid-century name, and the fact that the character is both sympathetic and relatively minor means Rosalie has the chance to thrive again as a baby name without feeling unduly tied to *Twilight*.

For a long time Rosalie's main claim to fame was via the eponymous 1928 Broadway musical, which became a movie ten years later, both of which included a hit song.

Rosalie was used as a character name in literature by Anne Brontë and Oscar Wilde. In the primitive days of TV, Rosalie was the name of the daughter on *The Goldbergs*.

Rosalind

Latin, "pretty rose"

Rosalind has a distinguished literary history—it started as a lyrical name in early pastoral poetry, probably coined by Edmund Spenser. It was further popularized by Shakespeare via one of his most charming heroines, in *As You Like It*—and, along with a bouquet of other Rose names, might be ready for a comeback.

Rosalind was at its height in the 1940s, coinciding with the popularity of the acerbic movie star Rosalind Russell; it was Number 293 in 1943, but fell off the list in 1978.

Uma Thurman gave her young daughter five names, the first of which is Rosalind—though she is being called by her nickname Luna.

Rosamund

German, "horse protection"

This lovely, quintessentially British appellation, also spelled Rosamond, is the name of a legendary twelfth-century beauty. Rare on these shores, it is more than worthy of importation.

There was a time when Rosamund wasn't quite so unusual in the U.S.—she ranked on the Top 1000 from 1881 to 1930, reaching 574 in 1912.

Early on, the name was associated with "fair Rosamond" Clifford, mistress of Henry II, whose story was the basis of the Joseph Addison opera *Rosamund* and the Swinburne play of the same name. Rosamund Vincy is a character in George Eliot's novel *Middlemarch*.

Another, literal, translation of the name's meaning is "rose of the world."

A current bearer is actress and one-time Bond girl Rosamund Pike—who has a son named Solo.

Rose
Flower name

Rose, one of the old-time sweet-smelling flower names, has had a remarkable revival—first of all as a middle name—with parents (e. g. Jennifer Garner and Ben Affleck, Jon Stewart, Eric Clapton, and Ewan McGregor) finding Rose to be the perfect connective, with more color and charm than old standbys like Sue and Ann. At this point in time, though, some parents are finding there are too many roses in the middle spot of the garden.

As a first name, Rose reached its highest point from 1896 to 1921, the early heyday of flower names, when it was in the Top 20, though it had been in use for centuries before. Rosy/Rosie is an irresistibly cheery nickname. There are any number of Rose offshoots, including Rosa, Rosetta, Roseanne, Rosanna, Rosemary, Rosamund, Rosalind, and Rosetta.

Rose and Rosie have long been celebrated in song, and notable Roses range from Rose Kennedy to Rose Byrne, and on-screen Roses have featured in scores of films and TV shows from *Titanic* to *Harry Potter* to *Golden Girls*.

Rosemary
Combination of Rose and Mary; herb name

One of the original smoosh names, this amalgam of two classics projects a sweet, somewhat old-fashioned sensibility; it could come back as an aromatic nature/herb name.

In ancient legend, Rosemary was draped around Aphrodite when she rose from the sea. It was regarded then as beneficial in strengthening the memory and became a symbol for faithful lovers. In *Hamlet*, Ophelia says, "There's Rosemary, that's for remembrance; pray, love, remember."

The name was long associated with George Clooney's aunt, the great pop singer Rosemary; less pleasant associations are with the 1967 movie *Rosemary's Baby*.

A common variation is Rosemarie; many parents are now looking to the stand-alone nickname Romy.

Rosie

Diminutive of Rose, flower name

Rosy-cheeked and cheery, Rosie (also spelled Rosy) has been standing on her own for many decades, back to the days of songs like "Sweet Rosie O'Grady." She's one of the perky nickname names that are filling the popularity lists of other English-speaking countries: she's Number 55 in England and Wales and 65 in Scotland.

A hobbit character in *Lord of the Rings*, Rosie's current representatives include Rosie (born Roseanne) O'Donnell, Rosie Perez (born Rosa), and British-born pregnancy guru Rosie Pope.

Roxy

Diminutive of Roxanne, "dawn"

Roxy, also spelled Roxie, is one of those high-stepping showgal names with plenty of moxie, among the many sassy nickname names on the U.K. popularity list—currently Number 398.

The fictional character Roxie Hart has had a long and interesting life, beginning with the 1926 play *Chicago*, then a silent film, a 1942 hit movie starring Ginger Rogers, and a 1975 Broadway musical with Gwen Verdun as Roxie, plus the 2002 movie *Chicago*, with Renée Zellweger playing the part.

Other Roxys have appeared on *Hannah Montana* and *Sabrina the Teenage Witch*.

Ruby

Gem name

Ruby, vibrant red, sassy, and sultry, has definitely outshone the other revived vintage gem names, with its sparkling résumé of cultural references.

Ruby is an early rock classic—think the Rolling Stones hit "Ruby Tuesday"—and other songs like "Ruby, Don't Take Your Love from Me." She's appeared in such works as *Cold Mountain* and been associated with performers like Ruby Keeler and Ruby Dee. Chosen by Tobey Maguire and a number of other celebs, Ruby makes a cool yet warm choice.

For the past few years, Ruby has been a huge hit across the English-speaking world: right now she's the top name in Australia and Number 7 in England and Wales. Her highest point in the U.S. was from 1900 to 1936 when she was in the Top 50—but she could surpass that number if enthusiasm for her continues to grow.

Rue

English from Greek, "aromatic medicinal plant"; also word name, "regret"

Rue has gone from *Golden Girls* actress to *The Hunger Games* heroine. This botanical name is also a double word name, meaning regret in English and street in French, and has real potential as a middle name.

Actress Rue McClanahan, who played Blanche in *The Golden Girls*, was born Eddi-Rue, named for her parents' middle names Edwin and Rheua-Nell.

Actress Sara Rue made her surname the middle name of daughter Talulah Rue.

The herbal plant Rue was introduced by the Romans and has been prized for its medicinal properties—the ancients believed it guarded against epilepsy and vertigo and improved the sharpness of vision.

Ruth

Hebrew, "compassionate friend"

Ruth, with its air of calm and compassion, was the third most popular name in the 1890s, then gradually faded away, though it's still in use today as some parents tiring of Rachel and Rebecca are giving Ruth a second thought. Some see such Old Testament girls' names as Ruth and Esther rising on the heels of boy equivalents Abel and Moses.

The biblical Ruth was the loyal and devoted daughter-in-law of Naomi who, when electing to leave her people and stay with the older woman, speaks the famous lines, "Whither thou goest, I will go."

Ruth has had numerous notable namesakes, from Supreme Court justice Ginsburg to crime writer Rendell to sexologist Dr. Ruth Westheimer.

S

Sadie

Diminutive of Sarah, "princess"

Sadie started as a nickname for Sarah, but their images couldn't be more disparate. Where Sarah is serious and sweet, Sadie is full of sass and spunk.

Sadie now ranks at Number 124—exactly where she was in her heyday of 1914. She's been chosen for their daughters by Adam Sandler and Christina Applegate, among others.

In popular culture, there's Somerset Maugham's Sadie Thompson, portrayed by Joan Crawford in *Rain*, Sadie Hawkins Day, where the girls get to ask the boys to dance, and songs like the Beatles' "Sexy Sadie."

Saffron

Spice name

Spice and herb names are increasingly appealing to the senses of prospective parents; this one, belonging to a precious spice derived from the crocus has a vaguely orange-scented-incense 1960s feel.

English actress Saffron Burrows is an attractive current representative, and on the cult classic British TV series *Absolutely Fabulous*, Saffron "Saffy" Monsoon was the one sane member of her household. Duran Duran's Simon Le Bon has a grown daughter named Saffron.

Saffron can also be considered a color name via its distinctive yellow hue.

Sage

Herb name; word name, "wise one"

Sage is an evocatively fragrant herbal name that also connotes wisdom, giving it a double advantage. It entered the Top 1000 at about the same time for both genders in the early

1990s, but it has pulled ahead for the girls. At most recent count, Sage was Number 494 for girls, 725 for boys. Toni Collette named her daughter Sage Florence.

The Greeks and Romans wrote that the smoke from burned sage leaves imparted wisdom, and in the tenth century, Arab physicians said that sage brought about immortality, or at the very least, a long and healthy life.

In *The Vampire Diaries*, Sage is a beautiful vampire possessing super strength and speed.

Sally

Diminutive of Sarah, "princess"

Sally is a cheerful, fresh-faced girl-next-door name that was originally a nickname for Sarah but has long been used independently. Sally was popular in the eighteenth century and then again from the 1920s to the 1960s—it was just outside the Top 50 around 1940. Though it hasn't been heard as a baby name for decades, we can see Sally bouncing back, especially after her exposure as young Ms Draper on *Mad Men*.

Sally has a ton of notable references—a few we can single out are astronaut Sally Ride, actress Sally Field, the Sally Bowles character in *Cabaret*, the movie *When Harry Met Sally*, and songs like "Long Tall Sally" and "Mustang Sally."

Salome

Hebrew, "peace"

Salome was a biblical dancer whose unseemly story involving John the Baptist's head on a platter has in the past made parents shy away from her name, but the stigma is definitely fading. Ex-*ER* star Alex Kingston named her daughter Salome Violetta.

Oscar Wilde wrote a play called *Salome* in 1893 and Richard Strauss based an opera on it twelve years later. A similarly seductive vampire, Salome, appeared on *True Blood*.

Samantha

Feminine variation of Samuel, "told by God"

Samantha, a long-popular feminization of Samuel, although still in the Top 30, is finally beginning to fade after years of widespread use, though still a lovely name. The popularity of Samantha was originally inspired by the nose-twitching heroine of TV's *Bewitched*.

Samantha has been in English-speaking use since the eighteenth century, particularly in the American South, and drew attention via Grace Kelly's Tracy Samantha Lord character in *High Society*, featuring the song "I Love You, Samantha," and then was revitalized by the sensual Kim Cattrell character on *Sex and the City*.

Some of today's parents may well go directly to nickname Sam or consider an alternative like Samara.

Saoirse

Irish, "liberty"

Before the young Irish actress Saoirse Ronan made her mark in the films *Atonement* and *The Lovely Bones*, few of us had heard this name, let alone known how to pronounce it. (She says it SIR-sha) But now it is slowly way edging its way into the mainstream, particularly, of course, with parents who have Irish roots.

Saoirse has been a popular name in Ireland since it began to be used in the 1920s revolution as a statement of freedom. It now ranks there at Number 19.

Another related name is Sorcha, pronounced SURK-ha and meaning "radiance"; in the film *Willow*, the character's name is spelled Sorsha—another way to pronounce it.

Sarah

Hebrew, "princess"

Sarah is an Old Testament name—she was the wife of Abraham and mother of Isaac—that is a timeless classic, as perpetually stylish as it is traditional. Sarah is still very widely used, but with such a range of images and variations that any child can make it her own.

According to the Book of Genesis, Sarah was originally called Sarai, but had her name changed by God to the more auspicious Sarah, meaning princess, when she was ninety years old.

Sarah was a Top 10 name from 1978 to 2002, and though it has somewhat slipped in popularity, there were still more than 5,000 little Sarahs born last year. The Sara spelling is another popular option, and diminutives Sadie and Sally are used independently.

A few of her many prominent namesakes are iconic actress Sarah Bernhardt, jazz singer Sarah Vaughan, comedian Sarah Silverman, and actress/fashionista Sarah Jessica Parker.

Sasha

Russian diminutive of Alexander, "defending men"

Sasha, largely male in Russia—and also spelled Sascha and Sacha—is an energetic name that has really taken off for girls here, chosen by Jerry Seinfeld (using the alternate Sascha spelling) and other celebs. The Barack Obamas use it as the nickname for their younger daughter, whose proper name is Natasha. But in line with a trend toward softer-sounding boys' names like Asher and Joshua and, thanks to *Borat* star Sacha Baron Cohen, Sasha also still has life as a boys' name, too—it's popular in France for boys and girls almost equally.

Another notable female bearer is 2006 Olympic silver medalist skater Sasha Cohen; Sasha Alexander, on the TV show *Rizzoli & Isles*, was born Suzana. And Sasha Fierce is the name of Beyoncé's alter ego.

Sasha, now Number 451, was as high as 147 in 1988.

Saskia

Dutch, "Saxon"

From the first time we saw the name Saskia attached to a portrait of Rembrandt's wife (her full name was Saakje van Uylenburgh, but she was always called Saskia), we have found it utterly charming and wondered why it hasn't attracted more fans in this country—she's appreciated by the Brits, who have moved her to Number 392. Saskia is one of those names that's been used in Europe since the Middle Ages but has never crossed the ocean.

One contemporary bearer is actress Saskia Reeves, who was born to a Dutch mother. Pop artist Red Grooms has a grown daughter named Saskia, and more recently, TV's Anne Dudek chose it for her daughter.

Savannah

English word name, "flat tropical grassland"; place name

A place name with a deep Southern accent, the once-obscure Savannah shot to fame, with others of its genre, on the heels of the bestseller *Midnight in the Garden of Good and Evil*, which was set in the mossy Georgia city of Savannah—perhaps as a substitute for the no longer fresh Samantha.

Before that, there were Savannahs in the novel and movie *The Prince of Tides*, in the Terry McMillan hit novel and film *Waiting to Exhale*, played by Whitney Houston, and, even earlier, in a 1982 movie called *Savannah Smiles*.

Savannah has actually been on the popularity list since records started being kept in the 1880s; she's been in the Top 100 since 1993 and is now at a high of Number 42. *Desperate Housewives'* Marcia Cross chose Savannah for her twin daughter, and it's the name of Queen Elizabeth's first great-grandchild. And Savannah Guthrie can be seen every morning on the *Today* show.

Scarlett

Variation on color name

Scarlett Johansson is doing more for this seductively southern name than Scarlett O'Hara ever did. Sylvester Stallone's third 'S' daughter, following Sophia and Sistine, is Scarlet (one 't', as in the color) and The White Stripes' Jack White and Karen Elson also have a Scarlett. The Mick Jaggers were ahead of the curve when they chose Scarlett for the middle name of their daughter Elizabeth in 1984.

In the Margaret Mitchell novel, Scarlett was (Katie) Scarlett O'Hara's grandmother's maiden name. The name entered the Top 1000 in 1940, a year after the movie of *Gone with the Wind* was released. Scarlett moved up nineteen places this year to Number 61.

One of the leading characters on TV's *Nashville* is named Scarlett O'Connor.

Scout

Word name

Scout, a character nickname from *To Kill a Mockingbird* (her real name was Jean Louise), became a real-life possibility when Bruce Willis and Demi Moore used it for their now-grown middle daughter, followed by Tom Berenger a few years later. A unisex choice that is growing in popularity for both genders, it was picked by skater Tai Babilonia for her son and Kerri Walsh for her daughter, Scout Margery.

It makes a virtuous, upstanding choice for a girl—a good scout. And though it hasn't made it onto any popularity lists, it's definitely gone from slightly eccentric to mainstream.

Sela

Hebrew, "rock"

Sela is a biblical place name, the original term for the city of Petra, which is finding new life through actress Sela Ward, star of several TV series, and also the young daughter of singer Lauryn Hill, who spells it Selah. Found on early African-American slave lists, it was sometimes spelled Cela or Cella.

In one of its other incarnations, Selah is a word frequently (71 times!) found in the Book of Psalms, as a musical term that means "interlude." It is the last word in Anita Diamant's novel, *The Red Tent*.

Sela entered the Top 1000 in 2005 and is now at Number 534.

Trivia tidbit: Sela Ward's father and brother are named Granberry.

Selena

Variation of Selene, "moon goddess"

Selena is smooth, shiny, and sensual, a nineteenth-century name that found new life in the Latino community, following the biopic of slain Tejano singer Selena Quintanilla, starring Jennifer Lopez. But you don't have to be Latin to love Selena, which is both distinctive yet in step with stylish modern names such as Seraphina and Celia.

Young Disney channel favorite Selena Gomez, star of *The Wizards of Waverly Place* et al, was named after Selena Quintanilla. Selena Kyle is the nom de real life of Catwoman.

Selena is now Number 304 in the U.S. and 168 in France.

Seraphina

Hebrew, "ardent, fiery"

Seraphina is the Number 2 most-searched name on Nameberry, yet has not quite entered the overall U.S. Top 1000—though we predict it won't be long before it will be solidly among its ranks. The highest-ranking angels, the six-winged seraphim, inspired the lovely name Seraphina, which was brought into the contemporary spotlight when chosen by high-profile parents Jennifer Garner and Ben Affleck for their second daughter, following the influential choice of Violet for their first.

Latinate version Serafina is also getting some attention; the name is enjoying a style revival thanks to the current taste for strong, old-fashioned, yet elaborately feminine names. Seraphina has much in common with top choices Isabella, Sophia, and Olivia, and we predict it could be within the U.S. Top 100 in the next decade.

A variation, Seraphita, is the eponymous heroine of a Balzac novel.

For now, Seraphina remains a beautiful, distinctive choice. Other name ideas if you like Seraphina: Raphaela, Angelica, Serena, and Sabrina.

Seren

Welsh, "star"

Seren is a top girls' name in Wales—and a lovely choice almost unknown elsewhere. Seren, in the Sirona form, was an ancient goddess of the hot springs.

Seren currently ranks as the seventh most popular girls' name in Wales alone (down from Number 3) and is Number 127 in England and Wales combined.

Seren is also a popular Turkish boys' name.

Serena

Latin, "tranquil, serene"

Serena, a name used since Roman times, was given fresh life by tennis star Williams, and then again with the leading character on *Gossip Girl*, Serena van der Woodsen. There have also been Serenas on soap operas and other shows from *Bewitched* to *Law & Order*.

And pre-TV, there was the damsel in Edmund Spenser's *The Faerie Queen* and Serena Merle in Henry James's *The Portrait of a Lady*.

Serena sounds as calm and tranquil as its meaning implies.

Severine

French feminine variation of Latin Severus, "stern"

This long-popular name in France sounds fresh, elegant, and unusual here. Severine is the name of the most recent gorgeous James Bond Girl in the film *Skyfall*. Students of film history will associate the name with the complex character Catherine Deneuve played in the 1967 Bunuel classic, *Belle de Jour*.

Sheba

Diminutive of Bathsheba, "daughter of an oath"

This exotic biblical place name for the region now known as Yemen started to feel fresh again as the name of the heroine of Zoe Heller's *Notes on a Scandal*, played on screen by Cate Blanchett.

Sheba is probably more ready for prime time than the long form mother name, although Bathsheba, which means "seventh daughter," has a rich biblical and literary history.

The Queen of Sheba was a monarch of the ancient kingdom of, yes, Sheba.

Shiloh

Biblical place name; Hebrew, "tranquil"

Cool meets Born Again meets Brad and Angelina, who made Shiloh an instant star when they chose it for their daughter. While Shiloh has risen from obscurity thanks to its celebrity baby use, it hasn't become a star the way brother names Maddox and Pax have. It entered the Top 1000 in 2007, one year after the birth of Ms Jolie-Pitt.

The town of Shiloh is mentioned several times in the Old Testament—it was where Joshua and the Israelites assembled to cast lots for the seven tribes, and for many years, it was where the Ark of the Covenant resided, becoming a place of pilgrimage. Shiloh is also the site in Tennessee of a major, bloody, Civil War battle.

Trivia tidbit: Shiloh is the name Angelina Jolie's parents had picked for their first child before her mother miscarried.

Shoshana

Hebrew, "lily"

This is an exotic and lovely form of Susannah, commonly heard in Israel. Shoshana Shaunbaum—nicknamed Shosh—is the character played by Zosia Mamet on the hit HBO series *Girls*—a fact that could give the name an upward thrust.

And there are other recent references. She's a noble figure in Quentin Tarantino's 2009 film *Inglourious Basterds*, and Shoshannah Stern was a character on the TV show *Weeds*.

Designer Shoshanna Lonstein is the wife of Jerry Seinfeld.

Sidonie

Latin, "from Sidon "

Sidonie is an appealing and chic French favorite that is starting to attract some American fans as a fresher alternative to Sydney. Also spelled Sidony, Sidonie was the birth name of the French novelist Colette.

In the old form Sindony, this was a common name in Tudor period England, the 'n' being dropped in the seventeenth century, leading to Sidony, Sidonie, and Sidney.

Popular in France, Sidonie now ranks at Number 360.

Sienna

Italian place name

The historic Tuscan city is spelled Siena, but the Sienna spelling, used by American-born English actress Miller, is rising even faster. Cable newsperson Campbell Brown chose Sienna for her daughter, as did Kevin James.

The name of the city began to be used for children in the nineteenth century; the Sienna spelling comes from the variety of clay found in the town, which is used to make the paint colors raw and burnt sienna.

Sienna is currently popular throughout the English-speaking world; it's Number 11 in Australia, 36 in England and Wales, and also in the Top 100 in Canada, Northern Ireland, and Scotland.

Simone

French feminine variation of Simon, "the listener"

Simone, the elegant French feminization of Simon, strikes that all-important balance between unusual and familiar, and it's oozing with Gallic sophistication. Dwayne "The Rock" Johnson has a daughter named Simone, and Chris Rock and Kevin Kline and Phoebe Cates used it in middle place for their daughters.

Two French philosophers are notable bearers of the name: feminist icon Simone de Beauvoir, author of the influential *The Second Sex*, and Simone Weil.

The actress who played the lead in the iconic French horror movie *Cat People* is Simone Simon.

Simone is a Top 20 name for boys in Italy, where the feminine version is Simona.

Sinead

Irish variation of Janet, "God's gracious gift"

One of the best known of the Irish girls' names, thanks to singer Sinead O'Connor. Though it's still in the Irish Top 100, it's no longer quite as fashionable in Ireland as Aoife or Aisling. But by now everyone in the Western World knows it's pronounced shin-aid and so would have no trouble fitting in on an American playground.

This name increased in popularity in Ireland via Sinéad de Valera, the wife of President Éamon de Valera, who was born with the name Jane, but later chose to use its Irish form Sinéad. Actress Sinéad Cusack is the wife of Jeremy Irons.

Siobhan

Irish variation of Joan, "the Lord is gracious"

A lovely Irish name whose perplexing spelling has inspired many phonetic variations, but using the original form preserves the integrity of one of the most beautiful Gaelic girls' names.

The name of several early Irish queens, it was introduced to the American public by the distinguished actress Siobhan McKenna. There have been a wide variety of fictional Siobhans, from a Detective Sergeant in the *John Rebus* novels to a vampire in Stephenie Meyers's *Breaking Dawn* to a character in J. K. Rowling's *The Casual Vacancy*.

Skye

Scottish place name

The 'e'-addition takes the name from slightly hippieish nature name to the place name of a picturesque island off the coast of Scotland, and for baby namers, it's by far the more popular spelling.

Skye entered the girls' list in 1987, a year after the introduction of Skye Chandler, a popular character on no less than three soaps—*All My Children*, *One Life to Live*, and *General Hospital*—for decades. More recently, it has lingered in the 400s, while it's Number 45 in its native Scotland and 84 in England and Wales.

A lovely middle name choice.

Sloane

Irish, "raider"

Sloane is a sleek, sophisticated surname name that has gradually morphed over to the girl's side. It entered the Top 1000 (at the very bottom of the baby names list) in 2008, and in three years jumped up over 400 places. Spelled without the final 'e,' Sloan joined Sloane in the Top 1000 for the first time in 2011.

Sloane has been the name of girlfriend characters in *Ferris Bueller's Day Off* and *Entourage*, and is currently the character played by Olivia Munn on *The Newsroom*. Sloane Crosley is a bestselling author, and comedian Rob Corddry named his daughter Sloane Sullivan.

The association with London's Sloane Square and the upscale clique of Sloane Rangers, who have included Princesses Di and Kate, gives it some extra panache.

Snow

English word name

There's definitely a cold front of names moving in, with Summer, Spring, and Autumn giving way to Winter—plus North, January, Frost—and Snow. This name feels brisk, fresh, pure, evocative—and magical. A haunting middle name choice.

Rare as a first name, there have been several notable surnamed Snows—including singers Hank and Phoebe, and scientist/novelist C.P.

Solange

French, "solemn"

This is a soft, soignée French name that has become familiar here via singer Solange Knowles, younger sister of Beyoncé.

It is also the name of a martyred ninth-century saint, a poor shepherdess who came to a tragic end while defending her honor. Among other things, St. Solange is a patron saint of rain.

Solange would make a striking, sophisticated choice. Pronunciation: so-LAHNZH.

Soledad

Spanish, "solitude"

This strong Spanish name that refers to the Virgin Mary (Our Lady of Solitude) has been made accessible by broadcaster Soledad O'Brien—who shows how well it combines with an Anglo surname. Her birth name was Maria de la Soledad Teresa O'Brien.

Ava Gardner portrayed a character named Soledad in the film *The Angel Wore Red.*

Sonnet

Word name

Could there be a more poetic name than Sonnet? Actor Forest Whitaker was inspired to choose it for his daughter.

The word sonnet derives from the Italian *sonetto*, meaning "little song." And although Shakespeare is the most acclaimed master of this fourteen-line form, there have been many other accomplished sonneteers, including Milton, Wordsworth, and Elizabeth Barrett Browning.

Other names beyond Sonnet that can work for the child of a writer or book-lover: Story, Poet, and Fable.

Sophia

Greek, "wisdom"

Sophia, which hit the Number 1 baby names spot in the U.S. in 2011, has a sensuous sound and high-minded meaning. Sophia's been chosen by several celeb parents and reached the top of the charts without losing any—okay, much—of its sophisticated beauty.

Like its sister baby names, Isabella and Olivia, Sophia has gained widespread favor by appealing to a broad range of parents—intellectuals who like it for its meaning and those attracted to its femininity, parents who want a classic name and those looking for a name with Latin roots—the Sofia spelling is also popular. Sophie is the French version of the name, more popular than Sophia in some parts of the world. Legend Sophia Loren was originally Sofia.

The name was first famous via St. Sophia, venerated in the Greek Orthodox Church—St. Sophia was the mother of three daughters named Faith, Hope, and Love. It was first used in England in the seventeenth century and was the name of George I's mother and wife.

Sophia has been an author favorite from the days of early novelists like Henry Fielding (*Tom Jones*) and Jane Austen (*Persuasion*) to the TV scriptwriters of today (*The Walking Dead, Orange is the New Black*).

Sophia's only downside is its huge popularity. Alternative baby names you might want to consider: Sophie, Seraphina, Susannah, or Zofia.

Sophie

French variation of Sophia, "wisdom"

Sophie is Sophia's cuter, more irreverent, near-identical twin. The top choice in Scotland and Northern Ireland and Number 6 in England and Wales, Sophie is much less popular than the Number 1 Sophia in the U.S.

Which do you like better? And do you see them as virtually the same name or very different? While you definitely couldn't name sisters Sophie and Sophia, you may have both on your short list and consider them distinctly separate choices. Sophie is lively and down-to-earth, while Sophia is more sophisticated and buttoned-up.

Sophie was the choice of both Eric Clapton and Luke Perry, as well as of Bette Midler for her now-grown daughter.

Sophie, Duchess of Wessex is the wife of Britain's Prince Edward, and her name is scattered throughout European royal history.

Sophie Zawistowska is the Polish heroine of the iconic William Styron novel *Sophie's Choice*, played in the 1982 film by Meryl Streep—who would play the mother of a Sophie decades later in *Mamma Mia!*

Stella

Latin, "star"

Following on the heels of Ella, Gabriella, Isabella et al, Stella manages to be both celestial and earthy at the same time. Stella is wildly popular among the Malibu set and its star is sure to rise even higher; Stella is firmly in the Top 100, now at Number 62.

The name Stella was coined by Sir Philip Sidney in 1590, was famously bellowed by Marlon Brando in *A Streetcar Named Desire*, and was used for their daughters by Tori Spelling and Dean McDermott, Molly Shannon, Ellen Pompeo, Gena Lee Nolan, Jennifer Grey, and Dave Matthews, among others.

Designer Stella McCartney is a notable bearer, and Stella Adler was an influential acting teacher, with Brando one of her prize pupils.

Story

Word name

An imaginative choice with an uptempo Cory/Rory/Tori sound, perfect for the child of a writer—or anyone with a good story to tell. Story has been finding some appreciation among celebs like Minnie Driver and others as a middle name. This is just one of the literary word names that have recently entered the realm of possibility, such as Fable, Sonnet, and Poem.

Summer

Word name

The temperature is definitely rising for this popular seasonal name, which began being used in the 1970s, and has been heard consistently ever since.

Summers have popped up all over the big and small screens: it was Zooey Deschanel's character in *(500) Days of Summer* and made featured appearances in *Napoleon Dynamite*, *Baywatch*, *The O.C.*, and *The Mentalist*.

Sunny Summer is popular all year round throughout the English-speaking world—it's currently Number 34 in England and Wales.

Susannah

Hebrew, "lily"

Susannah is by far the most stylish form of the classic name now that Susan and Suzanne have retired. Susannah has biblical and musical pedigrees, is impervious to trends, and has an irresistible, flowing rhythm. It can be spelled just as properly with or without the final 'h.'

Susannah is one of the loveliest names that, surprisingly, is not in the Top 1000—and hasn't been since 1978—though we expect that to change as soon as the memory of too many older Susans and Susies and Sues fades.

Susannah and Susanna seem to have traded place over time as the dominant version. How do they differ? The h-less version feels a bit more streamlined and modern, and might refer more directly to an ancestor named Ann or Anna, while Susannah seems more old-school biblical and self-contained.

In the Apocrypha, Susannah is the beautiful and devout wife of Joachim, falsely accused of unfaithfulness by the elders.

William Shakespeare named one of his daughters Susanna.

A European short form that's become popular abroad is Sanna/Sanne. The Hebrew Shoshana has played a prominent role on the TV show *Girls*; Zuzu is an adorable *It's a Wonderful Life* nickname.

Sybil

Greek, "prophetess"

The image of the lovely Lady Sybil, tragic youngest daughter of the Crawley family on *Downton Abbey*, is likely to go a long way towards reviving this almost forgotten name, off the list since 1966 and most popular in the 1920s and 30s.

Sybil is the most common spelling of a name that the ancient Greeks used as the generic word for a prophetess—a woman who claimed to be able to interpret the wishes of the gods through their oracles.

Benjamin Disraeli wrote an influential political novel titled *Sybil*, which increased the popularity of the name in Victorian times. Later, the name was severely undermined by the eponymous book and 1976 movie based on the character of Sybil—played by Sally Field— whose multiple personalities have now been confessed as fake. This is not to mention the harridan wife on the classic British sitcom *Fawlty Towers*. There is also a Sybil in Oscar Wilde's *The Picture of Dorian Gray*, and Sybill Trelawney is a witch and (fittingly) seer in the *Harry Potter* books, a Professor of Divination played on screen by Emma Thompson.

Cybill Shepherd, on the other hand, bears an invented name combining those of her Uncle Cy and Dad Bill.

Sydney

French, from Saint Denis

A couple of decades ago, nerdy boy Sidney morphed into a polished, poised, creative, elegant girl Sydney. Sydney's been on the rise since the 1990s—it was in the Top 25 from 1999 to 2003— and is still very popular.

Katharine Hepburn played a female Sidney in her first movie, *A Bill of Divorcement*, and lately there have been women named Sydney all over the big and small screens, including Annette Bening in *The American President*, and on *Alias*, *Parenthood*, and *Hope & Faith*.

Sylvia

Latin, "from the forest"

The musical, sylvan Sylvia seems poised to join former friends Frances and Beatrice and Dorothy back into the nursery.

Sylvia has consistently been on the popularity list since records started being kept. She was a Top 100 name from 1932 to 1948, reaching a high of Number 48 in 1932.

Spelled Silvia, she was the mother of the twins Remus and Romulus, who were the mythological founders of Rome, and was a character in Shakespeare's *Two Gentlemen of Verona*. The Bard also penned the immortal lines, "Who is Silvia? what is she, that all our swains admire her?"—words echoed in the Edward Albee play *The Goat, or Who is Sylvia?*

Sylvias have also played major roles in Clare Booth Luce's classic play *The Women* and the Fellini film *La Dolce Vita*.

Sylvia Plath was the Tragic Heroine of modern poetry.

Sylvie

French variation of Sylvia, "from the forest"

Although Sylvia seems to be having somewhat of a revival among trendsetting babynamers, we'd still opt for the even gentler and more unusual Sylvie. Jason Bateman chose it as the middle name of his daughter Maple.

In one of Lewis Carroll's lesser-known novels, *Sylvie and Bruno*, Lady Sylvie is the princess of Fairyland—well this is Lewis Carroll, after all.

Sylvie is currently a high-ranking name in the Netherlands.

T

Tabitha

Aramaic, "gazelle"

Though never as popular as the name of her *Bewitched* mother, Samantha, Tabitha has its own quirky, magical charm. The name of a charitable woman who was restored to life by Saint Peter in the Bible, it was a popular Puritan choice. Sarah Jessica Parker and Matthew Broderick chose it for one of their twin daughters, which has brought it back into the spotlight.

One of Beatrix Potter's storybook characters is a cat called Tabitha Twitchet, and indeed, the nickname Tabby is decidedly feline; other old nicknames are Tibby and Tabea.

A contemporary bearer is author Tabitha King, aka Mrs Stephen, and Tabitha Soren was an MTV news reporter. In *The Sisterhood of the Traveling Pants*, one of the quartet of friends is Tabitha Rollins, whose nickname is Tibby.

Tallulah

Irish, "lady of abundance"; Choctaw, "leaping water"

As memories of the outragrous actress Talullah Bankhead have faded, this hauntingly euphonious Choctaw name has re-entered the public domain. A modern hipster favorite, it's been chosen for their daughters by Philip Seymour Hoffman, Patrick Dempsey, Damian Dash, Rachel Roy (spelled Talulah), and Sara Rue, after having been trail-blazed by Demi Moore and Bruce Willis for their now-grown daughter. (Trivia tidbit: Bankhead's namesake was her paternal grandmother who, in turn, was named after the Georgia town of Tallulah Falls.)

When spelled Tallula, as rocker Simon Le Bon did for his daughter, it is also a traditional Irish name that was borne by two saints.

Tamar

Hebrew, "date palm tree"

Tamar is a rich, strong Old Testament name sometimes given to girls born on the holiday of Sukkoth, as palm branches were used to make the roof of the sukkah. In the Bible, there are several Tamars, including a daughter of King David and also Absalom's daughter, who is praised for her "fair countenance."

Tamar is also a river name in ancient Celtic. The River Tamar forms the border between the British counties of Devon and Cornwall, and Tamar is also associated with the Thames.

The Russian form Tamara has long outshone Tamar, but we think Tamar feels fresher. Just don't think about Tammy as a nickname!

Tamsin

English contracted form of Thomasina, "twin"

Tamsin is an offbeat name occasionally heard in Britain and just waiting to be discovered here. U.K. actress Tamsin Greig is a star of the show *Episodes* and Tamsin Olivier is the daughter of Joan Plowright and Sir Laurence Olivier.

Tamsyn is the alternative, medieval Cornish spelling. Other spellings are represented by actresses Tamzin Outhwaite and Tamzin Merchant and by writer Tamasin Day-Lewis, sister of Daniel.

Tamsin is a 1999 fantasy novel by Peter Beagle.

Tansy

Flower name; diminutive of Anthanasia, "immortality"

Tansy is a flower name rarer than Rose, livelier than Lily, and a lot less teasable than Pansy.

Tansy is a perennial herbaceous plant of the aster family that has clusters of small bright yellow blossoms. It was cultivated by the ancients for medicinal purposes, and has found a variety of other uses over the ages, associated with health and immortality.

There have been a couple of eponymous novels titled *Tansy*, and it was the name of a character on *Hart of Dixie*.

Tatiana

Russian, from a Latin family name

Tatiana, long popular in Russia and starting to catch on here, is a delicate, balletic name that carries a touch of the exotic. Fresher than other Russian choices such as Natasha and Sasha, Tatiana is an underused beauty.

The name comes from that of an ancient Sabine king, Titus Tatius, who ruled Rome with Romulus.

Saint Tatiana, a third-century martyr, is venerated in the Eastern Orthodox Church. Grand Duchess Tatiana Romanova was one of the ill-fated daughters of the last Russian Tsar, Nicholas II.

Also translated as Tatyana, the name appears in Alexander Pushkin's verse novel *Eugene Onegin* and the opera based on it, and it was used by Chekhov, as well.

Tatiana Kennedy Schlossberg is the daughter of Caroline Kennedy, and her name is currently chic in France.

Tatum

English, "Tate's homestead"

Tatum is strong, distinctive, energetic, and recommended, especially if your last name is as congenial as O'Neal. While we do also hear Tatum for boys, we still like it best as a girls' name.

Though this surname turned first in the nineteenth century, it didn't become a ranked American girls' name until 1994, two decades after Tatum O'Neal won her Best Supporting Oscar at the age of ten.

Rose McGowan played a Tatum in the movie *Scream*. As a surname, Tatum is now strongly associated with popular actor Channing; in the past, it was jazz pianist Art.

Teagan

Variation of Welsh Tegan, "beautiful"

As Meghan/Megan and Reagan/Regan show signs of wilting, along comes Teagan to take up the slack: definitely one to consider. About 80% of the American babies named Teagan are now girls. A variant spelling is Teaghan.

St. Tegan was a Welsh saint, whose name came into general use in the late twentieth century, partly inspired by a character in *Doctor Who*.

Temple

English word name

The old word name Temple has gained some recent notice as a girls' name via admired autistic writer and inventor Dr. Temple Grandin (born Mary Temple), subject of an acclaimed biopic, in which she was played by Claire Danes.

As a female name, it was seen as the college-girl character of Temple Drake in the William Faulkner novel *Sanctuary* and the 1933 film *The Story of Temple Drake*. And as a surname, it will forever be identified with cute child star Shirley Temple.

Tertia

Latin, "third"

Tertia—which is occasionally used in the U.K., but rarely in the U.S., would make an unconventional but interesting possibility for the third child in a family. Terza and Terzo are lively Italian female and male variations.

This is just one of several Roman numeral names that suddenly sound plausible—like Primo and Prima, Decimus, Quintus, etc.

Tess

English diminutive of Theresa, "to harvest"

With its solid Thomas Hardy background, Tess has a lot more substance, strength, and style than most single-syllable names, with an efficient yet relaxed image.

The iconic literary Tess is the beautiful heroine of Thomas Hardy's *Tess of the D'Urbervilles*, the moral center of the novel. Other Tesses have been portrayed on screen by Katharine Hepburn, Julia Roberts, Shirley Maclaine, Melanie Griffith, Kate Hudson, Jamie Lee Curtis, Cher, Della Reese, and Malin Akerman. Novelist and fashion journalist Plum Sykes named her daughter Tess.

Writer Tess Gerritsen was born Terry but decided to feminize her name when she began writing romance novels.

If you'd like to expand the name, you can consider Tessa—or even Tessie.

Thalassa

Greek, "the sea"

A pretty, rarely used Greek name, Thalassa is the ancient personification of the sea, particularly the Mediterranean, who is sometimes considered the mother of Aphrodite. In 1991, a newly discovered moon of Neptune was dubbed Thalassa.

This name would make a highly original yet accessible and delicate choice.

Thalia

Greek, "to flourish"

Thalia was one of the Three Graces in Greek mythology and also the Muse of comedy and pastoral poetry, making this a Hellenic choice well worthy of consideration.

In the Rick Riordan series *Percy Jackson and the Olympians*, Thalia Grace is the demigod daughter of Zeus. Thalia was also a character on *Everwood*.

The single-named Mexican singer Thalía was born Ariadna Thalia Sodi Miranda.

Now at the lower end of the popularity ladder, Thalia entered the list in 1932 and reached its height of Number 363 in 1993.

Thea

Greek, "goddess"; short form of Dorothea, et al

Thea is the Anglicized spelling of Theia, the Titan of sight and the shining light of the clear blue sky. She is the consort of Hyperion, and mother of Helios, Selene, and Eos. Whether pronounced THEE-a or THAY-a or TAY-a, Thea presents an appealing artistic image, sensitive and serene. Thea has also been used as a short form of the names Dorothea, Althea, Anthea, and Theodora.

Thea is widely heard in Scandinavia: it was the top name in Norway in 2006 and 2007. Although it has never cracked the Top 1000 on the U.S. Social Security list, Thea is beginning to be heard around playgrounds and preschools—but still has a way to go before it catches up with its popular twin, Theo.

Theodora

Feminine variation of Theodore, "gift of God"

Theodora is one of the most revival-worthy of the charmingly old-fashioned Victorian valentine names, softly evocative but still substantial, as is the reversed-syllable Dorothea. It was borne by several saints and by the beautiful ninth wife of the Emperor Justinian, who became the power behind his throne. A later royal was Princess Theodora of Greece and Denmark, the older sister of the present Prince Philip, Duke of Edinburgh.

Keith Richards named his daughter Theodora in 1985; Robbie Williams did the same just last year. In TV's *Grey's Anatomy* Dr. Theodora "Teddy" Altman was a surgeon.

Theodora offers a menu of neat nicknames, from the classic Teddy to Thea to Dora. Some cool international variations as well: Theodosia, Feodora, and Teodora.

Theresa

English form of the Spanish Teresa, "to harvest"

The popular appeal of the strong, intelligent Saint Teresa of Avila, combined with the selfless compassion of the more recent Mother Teresa, have fused to give this second-tier classic a somewhat noble, religious image. Although the origins of the name are uncertain, it has been prevalent particularly in forms Theresa, Teresa, and Therese throughout Europe for centuries.

Mother Teresa was born Anjeze/Agnese Gonxhe; when taking her vows, she chose to be named after Thérčse de Lisieux, the patron saint of missionaries, but because another nun in the convent had already chosen that name, she opted for the Spanish spelling Teresa.

A Top 100 name until the 1960s, reaching Number 32 in 1956, Theresa fell off the list completely in 2011, while the sleeker Teresa still holds at Number 608; it was as high as Number 18 from 1961 to 1963.

Currently, a leading character on *The Mentalist* is Teresa Lisbon.

Short forms Tess, Tessa, Tressa, or Tea are more popular now than the old Terry or Tracy. An interesting variation is Tereza, as in Milan Kundera's *The Unbearable Lightness of Being*.

Thisbe

Mythological name, meaning unknown

Thisbe, the name of a beautiful but tragic lover in mythology, is lively and cute—in a slightly thistly, prickly way. Ovid retold the story of Thisbe and Pyramus, young lovers in ancient Babylon who were kept apart by family rivalry, which was the inspiration for *Romeo and Juliet*. A modern bearer of the name is writer Thisbe Nissen.

In Sarah Dessen's novel, *Along for the Ride*, the baby daughter is named Thisbe, nicknamed Isby.

Tierney

Irish, "descendent of a lord"

An uncommon Irish-accented surname that seems particularly well suited to a girl. Tierney Sutton is a well-known jazz singer. Tierney, in its original Tiarnach form, was the name of several saints. It can also join the ranks of Old Hollywood names, via the haunting actress Gene Tierney. *ER* actress Maura Tierney is a current surname bearer.

Tillie

English diminutive of Matilda, "battle mighty"

A surprise recent hit revival with cutting-edge British, Tribeca, and Malibu parents; Tillie, also spelled Tilly, is cute, frilly, and sassy all at once. Tilly is currently Number 90 on the England-Wales popularity list, joining such other Top 100 nickname names as Milly, Maisie, Kitty, and Lottie.

Writer Tillie Olsen is a feminist favorite. *Tillie's Punctured Romance* is a classic Mack Sennett silent film, starring Charles Chaplin, Mabel Normand and Marie Dressler; *Tillie the Toiler* was an iconic flapper comic strip.

Topaz

Gem name

As a name, Topaz is sophisticated and sultry; as a golden gem, it's said to have healing and energizing properties and also to bring good luck—and being the birthstone for November could make it perfect for a baby born in that month, with that final 'z' giving it some extra sizzle.

The topaz gets its name via French and Latin from Greek; it is probably ultimately of oriental origin.

There is an eponymous novel by Leon Uris—later made into a 1969 Hitchcock movie—in which Topaz was the name not of a person but a spy code name, and in the Dodie Smith novel *I Capture the Castle*, there is a character named Topaz Mortmain.

U

Uma

Sanskrit, "flax"

Uma is a throaty, exotic name for a Hindu goddess...and a Hollywood one. But as popular as Uma Thurman is, other parents have not yet picked up on her name, making it a rarity.

Uma is one of the more than one thousand appellations for the Hindu goddess Sakti—a fact that surely inspired the father of Ms Thurman, a Columbia University professor of Eastern religion. Her middle name, Karuna, is equally exotic.

In Hebrew, Uma means "the nation," and is, therefore, sometimes used for girls born on Israeli Independence Day.

Uma shouldn't be confused with the similarly sounding Una, an ancient Irish name.

Unity

English, word/virtue name

Like Verity and Amity, this inclusive virtue name, used by the colorful British literary Mitford family, is ready to join its more popular peers Hope, Faith, and Grace.

The name was embraced by the Puritans in the seventeenth century but was not as common as others. In literature, it occurs as a servant in Thomas Hardy's *A Pair of Blue Eyes*.

Unity Valkyrie Mitford supposedly inspired the character of Bellatrix Lestrange in J. K. Rowling's *Harry Potter* series. Unity Kincaid is a character In the *Sandman* series by Neil Gaiman.

Ursula

Latin, "little female bear"

A saint's name with a noteworthy literary background, including uses by Shakespeare in Two Gentlemen of Verona and *Much Ado About Nothing*, Ben Johnson, Walter Scott, Longfellow, D. H. Lawrence, and Neil Gaiman. In real life, her two most well-known representatives are writer Ursula K. Le Guin and actress Ursula Andress.

Caveat: Today's kids might associate this name with the campy, corpulent octopus in Disney's *The Little Mermaid*.

Ursula ranked in the Top 1000 through 1983. Time for a comeback?

V

Valencia

Spanish, "brave, strong"; place name

This lovely orange-scented Spanish place name would make an inventive namesake for an Aunt Valerie.

Last on the popularity list in 1994, Valencia reached a high of Number 633 in 1969-70.

The Mediterranean city of Valencia is the third largest in Spain; it was founded as a Roman colony in 138 (BCE), originally called Valentia—and so has a long and storied history.

Valentina

Feminine variation of Valentine, "healthy, strong"

Valentina is a more exotic and artistic ballerina-type successor to Valerie; a pretty, recommended choice. Mexican-born actress Salma Hayek and husband Francois-Henri Pinault named their daughter Valentina Paloma.

Valentina entered the U.S. list in 1994, then shot up from Number 203 in 2009 to Number 165 in 2012. It's even more wildly popular in other countries—Number 4 in Chile and 13 in Austria.

Valentina Tereshkova was the first woman in space, and Valentina Cortese an Oscar-nominated actress.

Vanessa

Literary invention

Vanessa was one of the ultra-feminine three-syllable hits of the 1980s but has proved to have had more staying power than others like Tiffany, Kimberly, and Melissa, due to its classic beauty.

Vanessa was invented by Jonathan Swift for a lover named Esther Vanhomrigh—he combined the first syllable of her last name with the initial syllable of her first and used it in the poem *Cadenus and Vanessa* in 1713.

Vanessa Redgrave is the doyenne of the renowned Redgrave family; Vanessa Hudgens, the young actor and singer on *High School Musical* is a more youthful bearer. On TV, there have been Vanessas on *The Cosby Show*, *Gossip Girl*, and *The Vampire Diaries*.

Velvet

Word name

Velvet is a name that couldn't possibly be softer or more luxuriant. Many people have fond memories of it via the character of Velvet Brown, played by the young Elizabeth Taylor in *National Velvet*, an intrepid young woman willing to masquerade as a boy to race her horse in a dangerous steeplechase.

Velvet actually had a brief sojourn on the Social Security list, from 1961 to 1964. Now, double trending as both a 'V' name and a word name might give Velvet a boost.

Venetia

Italian place name

Venetia, the name of the region encompassing Venice, has a radiant, picturesque authenticity, as do the related Venezia and Venice.

Venetia is the title of a novel by Benjamin Disraeli, centering on the character Venetia Herbert, and Venetia Anastasia Stanley was a famous seventeenth-century beauty.

Verona is another pretty Italian place name possibility.

Venus

Roman mythology name

The name of a heavenly planet and the Roman goddess of beauty and love was an intimidating no-no until tennis champ Venus Williams put an athletic, modern spin on it.

Associated with the Greek Aphrodite, in the Roman pantheon, Venus was considered the mother of the Roman people, and has always been a favorite subject of artists—most well known being the prehistoric sculpture *Venus of Willendorf*, the ancient *Venus de Milo*, and Botticelli's *The Birth of Venus*.

Vera

Russian, "faith"

Vera was the height of exotic fashion in 1910, then was, for a long time, difficult to picture embroidered on a baby blanket. Now, though, some hip parents are beginning to quietly revive it along with other old-fashioned simple names such as Ada and Iris.

Vera was barely known in the English-speaking world until it appeared in the 1860 novel by Ouida, *Moths*, and Vera Rostov is a character in *War and Peace*, published nine years later.

Vern Yip has a young daughter called Vera, and Vera Wang and Vera Famiga have modernized it.

Vera Lynn was an iconic British World War II singer, Vera Miles was a Hitchcock star best known for her role as Lila Crane in *Psycho,* and Vera-Ellen (born with out the hyphen) was a dancing partner of Fred Astaire and Gene Kelly.

In the past two years, Vera has moved up almost two hundred places, and looks to be moving even higher.

Verity

Virtue name

If you love Puritan virtue names and want to move beyond Hope and Faith and Grace, this is a wonderful choice, both for its meaning and its sound. A rare find here, though occasionally heard in England. It was used in Winston Graham's *Poldark* novels, was Madonna's name as James Bond's fencing instructor in *Die Another Day*, and made a brief appearance in *Harry Potter*. Not to mention being a fixture on British and Australian soaps. Verity also appears in one of Agatha Christie's Miss Marple mysteries.

We love the newer sounding three-syllable, y-ending virtue names, and Verity is one of the best.

Veronica

Latin, "true image"

The name Veronica projects a triple-threat image: at once saintly, sensuous, and strong.

Veronica was the name of the compassionate woman who wiped Jesus's face when he was on his way to Calvary and whose cloth was miraculously imprinted with his image; she is now the patron saint of photographers.

Then there was Veronica (born Constance) Lake, the peekaboo blonde of the 1940s, and the sultry, dark-haired rival of Betty in the Archie comics. And, more recently, we've had tough TV teen private eye, *Veronica Mars*.

Veronica is also the name of an herb with small, bright blue flowers.

Veronica was in the Top 100 from 1972 to 1991, but it might not be too soon for a comeback—sans the dated nickname Ronnie.

Vesper

Latin, "evening star"

This Latin word used for evening spiritual services was introduced to baby namers by the Eva Greene character, Vesper Lynd, in the modern James Bond film *Casino Royale* in 2006, based on the Ian Fleming novel, and is just now beginning to provoke interest among namers, with its spiritual reference and soft, whispery sound.

On a more earthly note, the "Vesper Martini" is the famous drink ordered by James Bond in both the book and the movie, Casino Royale.

A name likely to enter the Top 1000.

Victoria

Latin, "victory"

Victoria, the epitome of gentility and refinement, reflects the image of the long-reigning British queen. In the 1990s, Victoria managed to breach the Top 20, but has dropped a bit now to fall just outside the Top 25, a surprisingly high standing for a name that is more of a classic than a fashion favorite these days. One enduring appeal of Victoria is that it's a traditional girls' name with a powerful meaning.

One possible role model is proto-feminist Victoria Woodhull. Ex-Spice Girl Victoria Beckham and Victoria's Secret have given the name a more modern edge, and it also has some *Twilight* cred.

While Vicky (and Vicki, Vickie, and Vikki) and Tory (along with Tori) have traditionally been used as nicknames for Victoria, contemporary parents might want to consider Plum, as in the Victoria plum.

Vienna

Place name

Vienna is one of the most promising of the newly discovered European place names, with a particularly pleasant sound, evoking elegant images of the Blue Danube, of castles and cafes, sweets and sausages and Strauss waltzes—and Sigmund Freud. It could be a possible substitute for the rapidly climbing Sienna.

Joan Crawford plays a strong-willed saloon keeper named Vienna in the classic 1954 western drama *Johnny Guitar*. And there was also a Vienna in the F. Scott Fitzgerald story *The Bowl*.

Trivia tidbit: Vienna's Roman-era name was Vindobono.

Viola

Latin, "violet"

Viola has several positive elements going for it: the rhythm of the musical instrument, the association with the flower, the trending Vi -beginning, and its leading role in Shakespeare's *Twelfth Night*.

In the Bard's gender-bending comedy of identity and disguise, Viola is the appealing, passionate heroine. Later takes on this tale include *Shakespeare in Love*, with Gwyneth Paltrow as Viola de Lesseps, and *She's the Man*, starring Amanda Bynes.

The most distinguished current bearer is Oscar-nominated actress Viola Davis.

Viola was a Top 50 name from 1899 to 1911, falling off the list in 1972, but is still popular in other countries such as Italy, where it is Number 15. And with Violet not sounding quite as fresh as it did, the strong Viola could find herself back in the running.

Violet

Latin, "purple"

Violet is soft and sweet but not shrinking. The Victorian Violet, one of the prettiest of the color and flower names, was chosen by high-profile parents Jennifer Garner and Ben Affleck in 2005, definitely a factor in its current climb to popularity; it is one of the Top 10 most-searched names on Nameberry.

A name that dozed quietly for decades, Violet was popular a hundred years ago, then began its steep descent by 1920, bottoming out in the early 1980s. But it started rising again about a decade ago and climbed even more sharply after the Affleck daughter's name was announced.

Today, Violet is in the Top 100, joining other such popular flower names as Lily, Daisy, and Rose. Viola is the Italian and Scandinavian version, used by Shakespeare in *Twelfth Night*. Violetta is the frillier, more operatic version.

Violet is a particular favorite of both children's book authors and Hollywood celebs—Violet Baudelaire in Lemony Snicket's A Series of Unfortunate Events, Violet Beauregarde in *Charlie and the Chocolate Factory*, and Violet Parr in the animated film *The Incredibles*; other well-known Violet moms and dads include Emily Robison, Christina Milian, Poppy Montgomery, Nathan Followill, Balthazar Getty, and Dave Grohl.

Trivia tidbit: In France, the violet was worn by the followers of Napoleon when he was in exile to show their allegiance to him.

Virginia

Latin, "virginal, pure"

Virginia is a lovely place name starting with the fashionable 'V' initial and having deep historical roots, yet, unlike some other other girls' classics, has been sorely neglected in recent years. For example, last year there were about 9,500 baby Elizabeths and only 502 Virginias born.

The colony/state of Virginia was given its name by Sir Walter Raleigh in honor of Elizabeth I, known as the Virgin Queen, and the first child to be born of English parents in the New World was christened Virginia Dare.

Virginia was in the Top 10 for 25 years, from 1912 to 1937, hitting a high of Number 6 in 1921 when there were 19,000 newborn Virginias in their cradles.

She does have a couple of possible downsides—those teasable virgin associations and the not-quite-ready-for-revival Ginny nickname. But we think they're outweighed by more positive factors and that Virginia is in line for a potential revival.

Virginia has such distinguished namesakes as writer Virginia Woolf, has been the subject of songs by groups ranging from The Rolling Stones to the Foo Fighters, and has appeared as a character in any number of books, movies, and TV shows. Ginger Rogers was born Virginia.

Viva

Latin, "alive, life"

Viva la baby with this life-affirming name! Singer Rufus Wainwright chose it for his baby daughter, perhaps in celebration of a new life entering the world the year after he lost his mother Kate McGarrigle. The baby's middle name is Katherine.

Viva (born Janet Susan Mary Hoffmann) was one of Andy Warhol's single-named superstars.

Other related life-giving names on the rise: cousins Vida and Vita, and Vivian, Aviva, and even Zoe.

Viveca

Swedish variation of German Wibeke, "war castle"

This is one of the most exotic and feminine of the 'V' names, and it's sure to gain more attention as the whole sisterhood of Viv- names rise.

Celebrated Swedish actress Viveca Lindfors, born Elsa Viveca, was one of several notables bearing this pretty, feminine 'V' name in a variety of spellings, including Viveca Paulin, the Swedish-born wife of Will Ferrell and the non-Scandinavian Vivica A. Fox.

Vivian

Latin, "alive, life"

Vivian, once an elderly lady name, is on the rise, along with all forms of names that mean life—from Zoe to Eva to those with the vivid Viv- syllable. It's now at Number 141, its highest ranking since 1950.

The name is famous in legend and literature from Vivian, the enchantress of Merlin in the Arthurian romances, and—spelled Vivien—in Tennyson's *Idylls of the King*. Originally Vivian was the male form, Vivien the female: Vivien Leigh, in fact, changed her name from Vivian.

Vivienne, the elaborated Gallic version, was chosen first by Rosie O'Donnell for her daughter and then catapulted to superstardom when Brad Pitt and Angelina Jolie used it for their twin daughter. This celebrity stamp of approval landed Vivienne on the popularity list at Number 322 last year, up 100 places since 2010. An adult namesake is the British fashion designer Vivienne Westwood.

W

Waverly

English "meadow of quivering aspens"

Waverly, with its literary resonance and lilting three-syllable sound, could well become the next generation's successor to Kimberly.

Spelled Waverley, this is the title of Sir Walter Scott's popular 1814 novel, whose hero is a young English soldier named Edward Waverley (it's believed that Scott named the novel after the model of pen he used to write it). Spelled the more streamlined way, Waverly is the name of the daughter of Buttercup and Wesley in *The Princess Bride* and a memorable character in *The Joy Luck Club*, who was named by her Chinese mother for the San Francisco street on which the family lived.

Waverly Place in Greenwich Village was named for the Scott novel in 1833—dropping the second 'e,' and was the setting of the teen show *The Wizards of Waverly Place*, as well as Don Draper's bachelor pad in *Mad Men*, and as a character on *Friday Night Lights*.

Wilhelmina

German feminine variation of Wilhelm, "resolute protection"

Wilhelmina was long burdened with the Old Dutch cleanser image of thick blond braids and clunky wooden clogs, but that started to be changed somewhat by the dynamic Vanessa Williams character on *Ugly Betty* and, even further by the choice of Wilhelmina by ace baby namers Natalie and Taylor Hanson. For the less adventurous, Willa is, for now, still a more user-friendly female equivalent of William.

Wilhelmina was a lot more commonly heard in the U.S. at one time: it was as high as Number 215 in the 1880s but has been off the list completely since 1955.

Queen Wilhelmina reigned in the Netherlands for most of the early twentieth century, becoming a heroic figure during the two World Wars. The name got an infusion of glamour via Wilhelmina Cooper, the Dutch-born model who established the top Wilhelmina Model Agency in 1967. Wilhelmina "Willie" Scott was the name of the Kate Capshaw character in *Indiana Jones and the Temple of Doom*.

To enliven her image, Wilhelmina has a plethora of nicknames: Mina, Minna, Minnie, Billie, Willa, and Wilma.

Willa

Feminine variation of William, "resolute protection"

Willa has become increasingly fashionable, with its combination of Willa (born Wilella) Cather-like pioneer strength and the graceful beauty of the willow tree. Actress Keri Russell named her newborn daughter Willa Lou, actor Philip Seymour Hoffman used Willa for the youngest of his three children, and David Mamet and Brian De Palma also have daughters named Willa, plus it's the middle name of Meryl Streep's actress daughter Mary (called Mamie).

Willa originated as a short form of Wilhelmina. After a half-century hiatus, it's just reentered the U.S. Top 1000 and is definitely on an upward course.

Willow

English, "willow tree"

An ancient tree that figures in literature from Shakespeare to *Harry Potter* and is believed to possess magical powers, Willow is a lovely name, as graceful as its inspiration, which is growing in popularity along with Willa and Will.

This elegant and charming nature name has been chosen for their daughters by Will and Jada Pinkett Smith, Michelle Monaghan, and Pink. This year, it moved up from Number 200 to Number 171, climbing along with other Will names—Willa, William and Will—having taken off here a year after the character of Willow was introduced on *Buffy the Vampire Slayer* in 1997.

Willow is even more popular in other English-speaking countries: it's Number 43 in Australia and in the Top 100 in the U.K., Canada, and Scotland.

The name has transcended its one-time hippie aura to move into the realm of reappraised and appreciated nature names. The willow is believed by the Romani to possess the ability to heal the sick and rejuvenate the aged.

Pink was quoted as saying her choice was influenced by a willow tree she grew up near, and that it is the most flexible tree that nothing can break—no wind, no elements, it can bend and withstand anything.

Winifred

Welsh, "blessed peacemaking"

One of the few remaining unrestored vintage gems, with a choice of two winning nicknames—the girlish Winnie and the tomboyish Freddie—as well as the slight stretch Freda. Winifred, the name of a legendary Welsh saint, was a Top 200 name into the mid-1920s.

Winifred is one of the Forsytes in *The Forsyte Saga*, Winifred Foster is the heroine of *Tuck Everlasting*, and another appears in Joss Wheden's *Angel*; in *Once Upon a Mattress*, Princess Winnifred (two n's) sings the song "A Girl Named Fred." The Disney folks seem to have been fond of the name—they used it in *Jungle Book*, *Mary Poppins*, and *Hocus Pocus*.

Actress Jacqueline Bisset was born a Winifred.

Winnie

Diminutive of Winifred, "blessed peacemaking"

This pet form of such names as Winifred and Edwina and Gwendolyn has loads of vintage charm, à la Millie and Maisie, with a decidedly winning vibe. And it just got celebrity cred as the baby daughter of Jimmy Fallon.

Winnie had been used regularly on its own in the U.S. through the early 1950s and has a number of varied namesakes. There's the Pooh, of course, and also Winnie Mandela, former wife of South African President Nelson; Winnie Cooper, the charming girlfriend of the young hero on *The Wonder Years*—whose given name was Gwendolyn; Winifred "Winnie" Foster, a main character in the childhood classic *Tuck Everlasting*; and it was also a nickname for Winston Churchill.

Winter

Word name

Fresher, brisker, and, yes, cooler than Summer or Autumn or Spring, Winter is now a full-fledged female choice, especially since Nicole Richie and Joel Madden used it for daughter Harlow's middle name, and Gretchen Mol picked it as her daughter's first, as did media mogul Sean Parker.

Although Winter just entered the U.S. girls' list in 1978, it has been found as a first name as early as the seventeenth century.

Some interesting international words for winter: Aeneva (Cheyenne, Native American), Cole (Chinook, Native American), Hima (Sanskrit), Jara (Hindi), Saradi (Hindi), Vandi (Kashmiri), Zaya (Old Persian), and Zima (Russian, Bulgarian).

Wren

Bird name

Wren, a lilting songbird name, could be the next Robin, and makes a particularly pleasing middle name choice, as does her newly-discovered cousin, Lark.

This petite bird was regarded in Ireland as the "magician of the birds" and the Druids considered it a bird of prophecy, and, thanks to an early fable, it has also been known as King of the Birds.

For architects, there's the link to the great Sir Christopher Wren, the celebrated eighteenth-century designer of London's St. Paul's Cathedral.

Model-turned-designer L'Wren Scott was born Laura—not Lauren.

X

Xanthe

Greek, "golden, yellow"

'X' marks the spot in names these days, usually at the middles or ends of names, but here is one that puts it squarely up front.

This exotic name, which, like all Greek names beginning with 'x' is pronounced as if it were a 'z,' is derived from the Greek word for the color yellow. A Homeric epithet of Demeter, Xanthe, which arose as a name for a blonde, conjures up an image of an exotic, other-worldly being.

Xenia is another alluring 'X' name, this one meaning "hospitality."

Y

Yvaine

Scottish, "evening star"

A mix of Yvonne and Elaine, Yvaine was first noticed in the Neil Gaiman fantasy novel and then movie *Stardust*, in which Claire Danes played the "fallen star" Yvaine. It is now attracting namer attention—just as that other Gaiman-inspired name, Coraline, did. Yvaine has a definite romantic, medieval charm. A small segment of namers are definitely taking notice.

The name probably derives from the Arthurian male name Yvain, one of the Knights of the Round Table.

Z

Zadie

Variation of Sadie, "princess"

When aspiring British writer Sadie Smith decided to change her name to the more distinctive and zippy Zadie at the age of fourteen, this attention-magnet name was born. But though it might sound like a modern initial-switch, Zadie was actually Number 539 in 1881, remaining in the Top 1000 for almost thirty years.

Zahara

Hebrew, "to shine"; Swahili, "flower"

Zahara, a delicate but strong multicultural name, came into the spotlight when Angelina Jolie bestowed it on her Ethiopian-born daughter, and we predict other parents will adopt it, as well. If you want something simpler than Zahara, consider Zara, a royal name in England—but also the name of a Spanish-based clothing store chain.

Zara

Hebrew and Arabic, "princess; flower"; Spanish, "corn"

Zara is an evocative name, often used in early movies and novels for a sultry character from the East—Greta Garbo played one in the 1932 film *As You Desire Me*. Britain's Princess Anne defied royal convention by giving her daughter the exotic Arabic name in 1981, thus bestowing on Zara instant upper-class status.

One of the first uses of Zara was by William Congreve in his 1697 play *The Mourning Bride* as the name of an African queen, and Zara, Priestess of the Golden Flame, was a *Wonder Woman* comic book villain.

Zara can also be spelled Zarah or Zahra, as Chris Rock did for his daughter. The related Zahara is the name of Brad and Angelina's oldest daughter. All forms of Zara connect to the biblical Sarah. Possible downside: the Zara clothing stores now in many malls.

Zara, the heroine of a Gilbert & Sullivan operetta, is currently Number 26 in Australia and 73 in England and Wales; in the U.S. it's climbed over 350 places since it entered the list in 2005.

Zelda

German diminutive of Griselda, "gray fighting maid"

Classified as an early exotic, Zelda has long and often been used as such for characters in books and films. Since 1986, Zelda has been a prime Nintendo name, as in the *Legend of Zelda: Twilight Princess.*

Zelda has been in label limbo for a number of years—off the Top 1000 since 1967—but there could be signs of a comeback with the interest in 'Z' (and 'X') names.

For many, there will always be a strong association to Scott Fitzgerald's tortured wife, herself a writer and a symbol of the 1920s Jazz Age—also the subject of a recent novel. Trivia tidbit: Marilyn Monroe was known to sometimes use the pseudonym Zelda Zonk.

Spelled Zelde, it's a Yiddish name meaning "happiness, good fortune."

Zenobia

Greek, "force of Zeus"

With historical roots as a beautiful and intelligent ancient queen and literary ties to Hawthorne and Edith Wharton novels, this rarity could appeal to adventurous parents seeking the exotically unusual. Tina Fey used it as her daughter Alice's middle name.

Zenobia was the intriguing third-century Queen of Palmyra who, for a time, ruled the eastern Roman Empire, Ethan Frome's wife Zeena was born Zenobia, and Zenobia Moodie was one of the most colorful characters in Nathaniel Hawthorne's *The Blithedale Romance.*

Zenobia reached a high of Number 683 in 1909; by 1925, she was minus 1000.

Zinnia

Flower name

Zinnia is an unusual floral choice with a bit more edge and energy than most and beginning to find its way onto namers' wish lists of botanical possibilities. Named after an eighteenth-century German botanist called Johann Gottfried Zinn, it appears in Roald Dahl's *Matilda* as the young protagonist's mother.

In the language of flowers, Zinnias symbolize remembrance.

Zoe

Greek, "life"

After being on the Most Popular list consistently forever, Zoe has, as of late, been zooming up the popularity lists (rising 450 places in fifteen years), now at Number 30—its highest ever by far. Zoe still makes an ideal fitting in-standing out name, though increasingly leaning toward the fitting-in side of the equation.

The history of the name begins in the third century when the Alexandrian Jews translated Eve, which means "life," to the Greek equivalent Zoe. Zoe was in use as far back as the Roman classical period and was popular with the early Christians, bestowing it with hopes of eternal life, but it didn't migrate to the English-speaking world until the mid-nineteenth century.

Zoe Washbourne was a strong warrior in the sci-fi show *Firefly*, Zoe Hart the leading female character on *Hart of Dixie*, Zoe Barnes a journalist on *House of Cards*, and kids might recognize Zoe from *Sesame Street*.

Zoe is currently hot in Europe—now at Number 11 in France.

Zoe has spawned a number of variant spellings, most successful of which is the phonetic Zoey, which is now ten places ahead of Zoe, at Number 20. Zoey has been embraced by TV scripters—she has been seen on the Nickelodeon show *Zoey 101*, *The West Wing*, and *How I Met Your Mother*. Zoie has also been embraced by enough parents to bring it to Number 571.

Wide-eyed actress Zooey Deschanel was named after Zooey Glass, the male protagonist of the J. D. Salinger novella *Franny and Zooey*.

Zora

Serbo-Croatian, "dawn"

Zora is a meaningful literary heroine name honoring Zora Neale Hurston, an important African-American writer and leader of the Harlem Renaissance.

Spelled Zorah, it is a biblical place name, and is also the name of a character in the Gilbert & Sullivan operetta *Ruddigore*.

Fairly well used from the 1880s until 1940, Zora reached a high of Number 293 in 1885.

Zuleika

Arabic, "fair"

Zuleika is a high-wire act of a name that might appeal to the intrepid baby namer. Like most 'Z'-starting girls' names, it projects an exotic and sensual charm, as exemplified by the character in Max Beerbohm's satirical 1910 novel, *Zuleika Dobson*, a heroine so gorgeous that the entire student body of Oxford University committed collective suicide at the sight of her.

Though not used directly in the Bible, according to medieval legend, Zuleika was the beautiful and passionate wife of Potiphar, a dignitary in the court of the Egyptian Pharoah to whom Joseph was sold; Zuleika and Potiphar were the parents of Ephraim. She was celebrated in several notable poems.

Zuleika comes with a variety of spellings: model Iman named her daughter Zulekha, there was a Miss Universe named Zuleyka Rivera, Zuleikha is the British actress who played Ilana on *Lost*, while Charles Bronson stuck with the original Zuleika for his daughter, who has become a successful model.

THE LIST

Abigail	Amandine	Ariel	Bessie
Abilene	Amaryllis	Artemis	Betty
Abra	Amelia	Arwen	Bianca
Acacia	Amelie	Arya	Billie
Ada	Amethyst	Asia	Birdie
Adair	Amity	Aspen	Blanche
Adela	Amy	Aster	Blue
Adelaide	Anais	Astrid	Blythe
Adele	Anastasia	Athena	Bree
Adeline	Andrea	Aubrey	Bridget
Adriana	Andromeda	Auden	Briony
Africa	Anemone	Audrey	Bronte
Agatha	Angelica	Augusta	Bronwen
Agnes	Angelina	Aura	Brooke
Aida	Anna	Aurelia	Cadence
Ailsa	Annabelle	Aurora	Calista
Aisling	Annalise	Ava	Calla
Alabama	Anne	Avalon	Camellia
Alexa	Anouk	Avery	Cameo
Alexandra	Anthea	Aviva	Cameron
Alexis	Antonia	Azalea	Camilla
Alice	Anya	Aziza	Camille
Alicia	Aphra	Azure	Campbell
Allegra	Apollonia	Bay	Carlotta
Alma	Arabella	Beatrice	Carmen
Althea	Araminta	Beatrix	Carolina
Amabel	Arden	Bella	Caroline
Amalia	Aria	Belle	Carys
Amanda	Arianna	Bernadette	Cassandra

Cassia	Cynthia	Echo	Ethel
Catalina	Dagny	Eden	Etta
Catherine	Dahlia	Edie	Eudora
Cecilia	Daisy	Edith	Eugenia
Cecily	Damaris	Edwina	Eugenie
Celeste	Danica	Eleanor	Eulalia
Celestia	Daphne	Elena	Eurydice
Celestine	Deborah	Eliana	Eva
Celia	Decima	Elise	Evangeline
Charity	Delia	Eliza	Eve
Charlie	Delilah	Elizabella	Evelyn
Charlotte	Delphine	Elizabeth	Ever
Chiara	Demetria	Ella	Evie
Chloe	Desdemona	Elle	Fable
Christina	Destry	Ellery	Faith
Cicely	Devon	Ellie	Farah
Claire	Dharma	Elliot	Fay
Clara	Diana	Ellis	Felicity
Clarissa	Diantha	Elodie	Fenella
Clarity	Dinah	Eloise	Fernanda
Claude	Dixie	Elsa	Fiona
Claudia	Djuna	Elsie	Fiorella
Clea	Doe	Elspeth	Flannery
Clemency	Dolly	Eluned	Fleur
Clementine	Dominica	Embeth	Flora
Cleo	Domino	Emerald	Florence
Clover	Dora	Emerson	Frances
Colette	Dorothea	Emilia	Francesca
Constance	Dorothy	Emily	Francine
Consuelo	Dottie	Emma	Frederica
Cora	Dove	Emmeline	Freya
Coralie	Dree	Enid	Gabriella
Cordelia	Drew	Esme	Gemma
Corisande	Drusilla	Esmeralda	Geneva
Cornelia	Dulcie	Esperanza	Genevieve
Cosette	Dune	Estella	Georgia
Cosima	Easter	Estelle	Georgiana
Cressida	Easton	Esther	Geraldine

Gia	Inez	Kerensa	Lorraine
Giada	Ingrid	Keturah	Lottie
Gianna	Iolanthe	Keziah	Lotus
Gillian	Irene	Kiera	Lou
Gloria	Iris	Kiki	Louisa
Goldie	Isabeau	Kit	Louise
Grace	Isabel	Kitty	Lucia
Greer	Isabella	Lake	Lucienne
Greta	Isadora	Larissa	Lucille
Guinevere	Isis	Lark	Lucinda
Gwendolen	Isla	Laura	Lucretia
Gwyneth	Ismay	Laurel	Lucy
Hadley	Isolde	Lavender	Ludmila
Hannah	Ivy	Lavinia	Lula
Harley	Jade	Layla	Lulu
Harlow	Jamaica	Leah	Luna
Harper	Jane	Leatrice	Lydia
Harriet	January	Leila	Lyra
Hattie	Jasmine	Lena	Mabel
Haven	Jemima	Leonie	Madeline
Hayden	Jessamine	Leonora	Madrigal
Hazel	Jocasta	Letitia	Mae
Helen	Jocelyn	Lettie	Maeve
Helena	Jolie	Lila	Magenta
Henrietta	Josephine	Lilac	Magnolia
Hermione	Josie	Lilia	Maisie
Hester	Journey	Lilith	Mamie
Hillary	Judith	Lillian	Manon
Holland	Julia	Lilou	Mara
Holly	Juliet	Lily	Margaret
Honor	June	Linnea	Margot
Hope	Juniper	Liv	Marguerite
Hyacinth	Juno	Livia	Maria
Ianthe	Justine	Lola	Mariah
Ida	Kaia	London	Marian
Imogen	Katherine	Lorca	Marigold
India	Kathleen	Lorelei	Marin
Indigo	Kay	Loretta	Marina

Maris	Nell	Petal	Rosamund
Marisol	Nettie	Petra	Rose
Marjorie	Niamh	Peyton	Rosemary
Marlowe	Nicola	Phaedra	Rosie
Martha	Nicolette	Philippa	Roxy
Marvel	Nina	Philomena	Ruby
Mary	Nora	Phoebe	Rue
Matilda	Oceane	Phyllida	Ruth
Maude	Octavia	Pilar	Sadie
Mauve	October	Piper	Saffron
Mavis	Odessa	Pippa	Sage
Maxine	Odette	Plum	Sally
May	Olive	Poet	Salome
Maya	Olivia	Polly	Samantha
Melisande	Olwen	Poppy	Saoirse
Mercedes	Olympia	Portia	Sarah
Mercy	Oona	Posy	Sasha
Meredith	Opal	Primrose	Saskia
Mia	Ophelia	Priscilla	Savannah
Mignon	Orchid	Prudence	Scarlett
Mila	Orla	Quinn	Scout
Milena	Ottilie	Rae	Sela
Millicent	Ottoline	Rafaela	Selena
Millie	Padget	Rain	Seraphina
Minerva	Paige	Ramona	Seren
Minnie	Paisley	Ravenna	Serena
Minta	Paloma	Reese	Severine
Mirabelle	Pamela	Renata	Sheba
Miranda	Pandora	Rhiannon	Shiloh
Miriam	Patience	Rhonwen	Shoshana
Mitzi	Patricia	Riley	Sidonie
Molly	Paz	Roisin	Sienna
Morgan	Pearl	Romilly	Simone
Myrtle	Peggy	Romy	Sinead
Nadia	Penelope	Rory	Siobhan
Naomi	Peridot	Rosa	Skye
Natalia	Persephone	Rosalie	Sloane
Natalie	Persis	Rosalind	Snow

Solange	Velvet
Soledad	Venetia
Sonnet	Venus
Sophia	Vera
Sophie	Verity
Stella	Veronica
Story	Vesper
Summer	Victoria
Susannah	Vienna
Sybil	Viola
Sydney	Violet
Sylvia	Virginia
Sylvie	Viva
Tabitha	Viveca
Tallulah	Vivian
Tamar	Waverly
Tamsin	Wilhelmina
Tansy	Willa
Tatiana	Willow
Tatum	Winifred
Teagan	Winnie
Temple	Winter
Tertia	Wren
Tess	Xanthe
Thalassa	Yvaine
Thalia	Zadie
Thea	Zahara
Theodora	Zara
Theresa	Zelda
Tierney	Zenobia
Tillie	Zinnia
Topaz	Zoe
Uma	Zora
Unity	Zuleika
Ursula	
Valencia	
Valentina	
Vanessa	

www.ingramcontent.com/pod-product-compliance
Lightning Source LLC
Chambersburg PA
CBHW061819040426
42447CB00012B/2720